COSSAC

Titles in the series

Studies in Naval History and Sea Power

Christopher M. Bell and James C. Bradford, editors

Studies in Naval History and Sea Power advances our understanding of sea power and its role in global security by publishing significant new scholarship on navies and naval affairs. The series presents specialists in naval history, as well as students of sea power, with works that cover the role of the world's naval powers, from the ancient world to the navies and coast guards of today. The works in Studies in Naval History and Sea Power examine all aspects of navies and conflict at sea, including naval operations, strategy, and tactics, as well as the intersections of sea power and diplomacy, navies and technology, sea services and civilian societies, and the financing and administration of seagoing military forces.

COSSAC

LT. GEN. SIR FREDERICK MORGAN AND
THE GENESIS OF OPERATION OVERLORD

STEPHEN C. KEPHER

NAVAL INSTITUTE PRESS
Annapolis, Maryland

Naval Institute Press
291 Wood Road
Annapolis, MD 21402

Library of Congress Cataloging-in-Publication Data

Names: Kepher, Stephen C., author.
Title: COSSAC : Lt. Gen. Sir Frederick Morgan and the genesis of Operation Overlord /
    Stephen C. Kepher.
Other titles: Lt. Gen. Sir Frederick Morgan and the genesis of Operation Overlord
Description: Annapolis, Maryland : Naval Institute Press, [2020] | Includes bibliographical
    references and index.
Identifiers: LCCN 2019051442 (print) | LCCN 2019051443 (ebook) | ISBN 9781682475089
    (hardback) | ISBN 9781682475218 (ebook)
Subjects: LCSH: Morgan, Frederick, 1894–1967. | Operation Overlord. | Allied Forces.
    Supreme Headquarters. Office of the Chief of Staff—History. | Combined Chiefs of
    Staff (U.S. and Great Britain)—History. | Generals—Great Britain—Biography. |
    Military planning—Great Britain—History—20th century. | Military planning—
    United States—History—20th century.
Classification: LCC D756.5.N6 K465 2020 (print) | LCC D756.5.N6 (ebook) |
    DDC 940.54/21421092—dc23
LC record available at https://lccn.loc.gov/2019051442
LC ebook record available at https://lccn.loc.gov/2019051443

♾ Print editions meet the requirements of ANSI/NISO z39.48–1992
(Permanence of Paper).
Printed in the United States of America.

28 27 26 25 24 23 22 21 20   9 8 7 6 5 4 3 2 1
First printing

CONTENTS

PREFACE

For the English, D-Day might well have stood for Dunkirk Day. The tremendous news that British soldiers were back on French soil seemed suddenly to reveal exactly how much it had rankled when they were beaten off it four years ago. As the great fleets of planes roared toward the coast all day long, the people glancing up at them said, "Now they'll know how our boys felt on the beaches of Dunkirk."

D-Day sneaked up on people so quietly that half the crowds flocking to business on Tuesday morning didn't know it was anything but Tuesday, and then it fooled them by going right on being Tuesday. The principal impression one got on the street was that nobody was smiling. . . . Everybody seemed to be existing wholly in a preoccupied silence of his own. . . . There was no rush to put out flags, no cheers, no outward emotion. . . . Even the pubs didn't draw the usual cronies. . . .

It is in the country districts just back of the sealed south coast that one gets a real and urgent sense of what is happening only a few minutes flying time away. . . . Everything is different now that the second front has opened, every truck on the road, every piece of gear on the railways, every jeep and half-track that is heading toward the front has become a thing of passionate concern. The dry weather, which country folk a week ago were hoping would end, has now become a matter the other way round. Farmers who wanted gray skies for their hay's sake now want blue ones for the sake of their sons, fighting in the skies and on earth across the Channel.[1]

So wrote the correspondent Mollie Panter-Downes in her "Letter from London" for the *New Yorker* magazine on 11 June 1944.

Since then, the OVERLORD D-Day has become *the* D-Day of World War II—recounted, celebrated, and analyzed in countless books, articles, and films.[2] Quite understandably, most of the interest focuses on the story of the battle: Omaha Beach, Pegasus Bridge, the bocage, Sainte-Mère-Église, Falaise, Operation COBRA, and the liberation of Paris.

There is, I submit, another story of great interest: that of the process by which it became possible for the cross-Channel assault to occur—that is, a detailed examination of the arguments, decisions, and context in which they were made that led to a successful reentry into the Continent by a coalition force.

This is a story often told in passing, if at all, as if it were the preliminary to the main event. Relatively few know the story of an ad hoc Allied staff that came to be named COSSAC and of how the outline plan came to be. While changes were made before it became the NEPTUNE/OVERLORD plan of 6 June 1944, it was the plan on which all the political and strategic decisions were based. Its history is essential to a complete appreciation of OVERLORD.

As a result of a decision made by the Combined Chiefs of Staff at the Casablanca Conference in January 1943, forty-nine-year-old British lieutenant general Sir Frederick Morgan, a field artillery officer with twenty years of service with the Indian Army and who had led elements of the 1st Armoured Division in France in 1940, was tasked with examining and evaluating the various studies and proposals that had been written over the prior two years and turning them into something that resembled an outline for a possible assault—or series of assaults—to create a lodgment somewhere in France. The goal was to achieve some understanding of what it might take to reenter the Continent by force. "Against determined opposition" was one term used. There were many in positions of authority who were not convinced it could be accomplished at all.

This examination was necessary because, since the British had been beaten off the Continent, an amphibious assault was the only way back. And getting back was the only way to win the war, or so everyone outside of the Royal Air Force's Bomber Command, and perhaps the U.S. Army Air Force's Eighth Air Force, believed.

Exactly how, exactly when, and with what this assault would take place had not yet been determined. A great debate was starting to rage: should the Allies cross the Channel as soon as forces could be gathered for the assault, or should they wait for the Germans to be worn down and weakened in secondary theaters of operation, thus making success more likely but taking more time? If it were to be an assault across the Channel, there was no agreement as to where the landing should occur. Nor was there a commander in chief, just Morgan, a temporary three-star general designated as chief of staff, who did not have command authority and was not given much guidance from the British Chiefs of Staff one way or the other.

Morgan changed the terms and scope of his assignment, envisioning a design of and approach to a staff that hadn't been attempted before. He created the embryo of what would be the commander's operational staff, resolved arguments, made decisions, created policies, and expanded the work of his staff into areas not previously considered by the Combined Chiefs. There was no template for his concept of a multinational staff that would plan a campaign and then become the core of the operational headquarters for a coalition army (as well as naval forces and tactical air forces) executing that key campaign. Morgan had to invent that as well. He also came up with a name for himself and his staff: COSSAC—Chief of Staff, Supreme Allied Commander.[3]

Along the way he had an hour-long, one-on-one meeting with President Franklin Roosevelt, an extraordinary occurrence for a relatively junior officer of an allied nation. He spent more than a month in Washington, D.C., at the invitation of and as guest of Gen. George Marshall, the U.S. Army's chief of staff. There he was in daily contact at the Pentagon with General Marshall and in frequent contact with the other U.S. chiefs of staff as well as Secretary of War Henry Stimson and high-level officials at the State Department. Marshall also gave Morgan frequent use of the U.S. Army Chief of Staff's private aircraft and its car and driver to tour bases and installations in much of the southeastern United States. Both Marshall and Stimson welcomed Morgan into their homes for private dinners. Throughout his time as COSSAC, Morgan, stationed in

London, routinely met with ministers of state as well as senior military and naval officers from both the United States and Great Britain.

COSSAC, in the short nine months of its existence, created the outline plan that made it possible for the Allied Combined Chiefs of Staff to have discussions at a very practical level, to understand in concrete terms what was meant by choosing either an early cross-Channel assault and drive toward the heart of Germany or using the Mediterranean as a means of exhausting the Germans, hoping that bombing German cities, combined with Russian successes, would fatally weaken Adolf Hitler's forces. This led to a series of decreasingly tentative agreements and a final decision in November 1943 to launch the attack across the Channel. It was because of COSSAC that it was possible to conduct NEPTUNE/OVERLORD on 6 June 1944. The plan and the process should be seen not only in the context of the debates about strategy and timing but also in terms of the competition for resources between theaters of operation and the political and economic considerations that informed both strategic and operational decisions.

Morgan did not create the OVERLORD outline plan on his own, nor was he the innovator behind the solution to every problem. The development of the concept of the cross-Channel assault was iterative, with false starts, blind alleys, and passionate debates that led to a consensus. Not every problem was solved before Dwight Eisenhower was assigned as the Supreme Allied Commander in early December 1943. No one in Morgan's position could have accomplished that, and certainly not with the resources he was told to use in creating the plan or with the deadlines he was given. He had to be both manager and leader, ambassador and advocate. He was speaking on behalf of and guarding the prerogatives of a commander whose name no one knew. For a significant amount of time in 1943, the proposal he championed had not gained the full agreement of the Western Allies' political and military leaders. To succeed, he needed the support of officers senior to him, whom he could not compel to action but only request or persuade. He had to learn to not be bothered by the fact that he was chief of staff to an unnamed commander, writing a plan and taking essential steps to ensure its success, even though it might never happen.

He also insisted that the only way in which this assignment would be successful would be if it were truly an allied staff from the very beginning—British,

American, Canadian, South African, and Australian, and drawn from not only all the military services that were to be involved but also the diplomats and politicians whose advice and expertise would be needed. The staff was not created all at once; it was constantly evolving, adding components as new requirements emerged and taking on modifications as circumstances changed. At the end of the process, it finally got a commander, having been built more from the bottom up than one would usually find to be the case. One would expect that a commander would be assigned the mission. He or she would then recruit staff or use existing staff to plan and then conduct the operation. COSSAC developed the other way around. Morgan started with an empty office, recruited staff, formulated a plan, and then, at the last minute, received the commander.

In his task, Morgan had the support of Maj. Gen. Ray Barker, USA, who was his deputy. The two, who met for the first time in the spring of 1943, worked together as if they had known each other for years. This was at a time when coalition staffs were rare, at best.[4] With the North African landings (Operation TORCH) that had just occurred, there was now Eisenhower's headquarters, with both British and American staff, and some inferences could be drawn from the way it operated. Morgan and Barker, however, were creating a different role for themselves and their team of planners. There was no history or experience to draw on to help them shape the structure and purpose of the staff. They made it up as they went along. The success they achieved together in a short period of time was remarkable. The story is, fundamentally, about the individuals who worked eighteen to twenty hours a day, six and a half days a week, for months on end to make it possible.[5] It is a story that has its beginnings at the Casablanca conference in January of 1943 and that ends with the arrival of Eisenhower and Montgomery in January of 1944.

In writing this story I have used place names in English as they existed in 1943; hence, for example, Dutch East Indies (Indonesia). In direct quotes, the spelling and punctuation is as the original author wrote; thus, the reader will encounter both English and American versions of words (for example, theatre and theater) as well as occasional peculiarities of spelling (lodgment and lodgement). I have also used both the British and American names for things, so the reader will discover British armoured divisions as well as American armored divisions. If the quote is a translation from the original (as in Hitler's Directive 40), the translation is as provided by the source material.

The British Chiefs of Staff (Gen. Alan Brooke, Air Marshal Sir Charles Portal, and Adm. Dudley Pound[6]) are most often referred to as the Chiefs of Staff (COS), while the American chiefs of staff, Gen. George Marshall, Adm. Ernest King, and Gen. Henry Arnold, are the Joint Chiefs of Staff (JCS). The Combined Chiefs of Staff (CCS) was the organization made up of the British and American Chiefs, plus their various staffs and planners. The British Joint Service Mission was located in Washington, D.C., and its personnel served as permanent representatives of the British Chiefs on a daily basis. Headed by Field Marshal John Dill, they made important contributions to the functioning of the alliance.

Other headquarters that figure prominently in the story are the British Combined Operations Headquarters, or COHQ. (The American name for combined operations is amphibious operations.) ETOUSA stands for European Theater of Operations, United States Army.

COSSAC as a term is used both in the singular to refer to Morgan and in the plural to refer to the staff who were creating the outline plan. This was also the practice in 1943. I have chosen to make one exception to the conventions for the naming of army corps. Typically they are identified by using Roman numerals, for example V Corps, for Fifth Corps. Morgan, in his memoirs, referred to his command of I Corps as 1st Corps or 1st British Corps. I have decided to honor his choice here.

A more complete glossary is provided at the end of the book.

ACKNOWLEDGMENTS

As a first-time author there are many people to whom I am grateful for their encouragement, patience, advice, and consideration.

The librarians and staff at the National Archives UK, the Liddell Hart Centre for Military Archives, Kings' College London, and the Imperial War Museum London, all in London; the Eisenhower Library, Abilene Kansas; the U.S. Army Heritage and Education Center at Carlisle Barracks, Pennsylvania; and the Harley Library at the University of Southampton have all been both professional and generous with their support and guidance.

Maj. Miguel Lopez, USAF, an instructor at the Air Force Academy, was kind enough to respond to my request to present a paper at the 2017 Society for Military History Annual Meeting and to include me in the panel he was forming. Jay Lockenour, from Temple University, chaired the session, providing helpful feedback on my presentation, which was an early version of one of the chapters.

I wish to thank the sponsors and organizers of the Normandy 75 conference (*Global War Studies* journal, Brécourt Academic, and the University of Portsmouth, UK) for accepting my two proposals for presentations at the conference, held in July 2019, both of which were based on material from this book.

Glenn Griffith, my acquisitions editor at the Naval Institute Press, has been amazingly supportive during the process and deserves special recognition for encouraging a first-time author to submit a proposal and having the courage to accept it. Everyone at NIP has been great to work with.

A most special acknowledgment must go to Evan Mawdsley, Emeritus Professor of History at the University of Glasgow, one of the general editors of the *Cambridge History of the Second World War*, friend, mentor, and supervisor for my master's degree, for taking the time to thoughtfully read the manuscript and being generous with his comments and observations. I also want to thank him for his ongoing encouragement and friendship (as well as for leading a wonderful Sunday outing to the site of the Hollywood Hotel, also known as HMS Warren, in Largs, Scotland).

It approaches the impossible to express or explain the thanks I need to give my wife. It was she who first said, "Why don't you just write the . . . book." She has hosted General Morgan and General Barker at our dinner table for more than a decade. She has asked insightful and important questions, requiring me to clarify and refine many of my thoughts and approaches to telling the story. She has read the manuscript not just searching for sentence fragments or typographical errors but as an editor. Just before we learned that my proposal was accepted, we made the decision to move to France. As a consequence, she took on disproportionate responsibility for an international move with grace and skill that was amazing but not surprising. For all that and for so much more, I am most grateful. This book is dedicated to her.

It is a commonplace but nonetheless true that while many people have been helpful in the writing of the book, any errors that may be found are solely my responsibility.

PROLOGUE

Winston Churchill wrote that "the history of all coalitions is a tale of reciprocal complaints of allies."[1] The Western Allies of World War II unquestionably fit that description, yet they were also one of the most successful coalitions in modern history. Mid-twentieth-century war was a complex mix of traditional military and naval strategy, combined with new and emerging technologies that promised both new ways to bring the fight to the enemy and potentially dramatic results.

World War II was also a conflict that demanded industrial planning and resource allocation by all the combatants on a scale beyond even that required by World War I (1914–18). Domestic and international politics were also key considerations and influences. The world's premier power—the British Empire—was joined by two emerging superpowers, the United States and the Soviet Union, both of which would eclipse Britain before the end of the 1940s.

This complex global war required the Western Allies to engage in unprecedented levels of coordination regarding almost every aspect of planning and fighting against the Germans and the Japanese, most obviously in the realm of strategy. Tough decisions had to be made between competing strategies for winning the war: what allocation of resources, for what purpose, against which enemy, how, when, where, and by whom.

Consequently, the British and Americans established mechanisms to facilitate planning and communication, starting with the Combined Chiefs of Staff (CCS). Composed of the service heads of the U.S. and UK armed forces, along with supporting staffs, the CCS evolved into an effective means of waging the war against the Axis. Britain had broad experience of coalition warfare—both good and bad—during the 150 years or so leading up to the alliance with the United States and Soviet Union: against Napoleon, in the Crimea, and in World War I. The United States, by comparison, had little experience, except as an Associated Power for the last year of World War I. In the beginning, the difference was obvious.

Meetings between British and American military planners began before U.S. entry into the war, starting in January 1941 in Washington, D.C. At these meetings, planners agreed to an exchange of military missions (of both naval and army officers), and in May 1941 the U.S. Army Special Observer Group was formed in London, joining Adm. Robert Lee Ghormley, USN, who had been the special naval observer since the fall of 1940. In Washington, there was the British Joint Service Mission, which represented the British Chiefs of Staff. "With the establishment of these 'nucleus missions' the exchange of views between the British and American staffs became continuous, and the problems of coalition warfare came to be a familiar part of the work of American planners."[2]

After U.S. entry into the war, nine interallied conferences were held between December 1941 and July 1945, to debate and reach agreement on what the strategy of the Western Allies should be. It was at these conferences that the discussions over priorities and allocation of resources played out. It is rare for allies to devote so much time to the coordination of effort over so long a period. Given that Great Britain and the United States were essentially equals with different strategic priorities, it isn't surprising that there were serious differences of opinion over complex issues that took time to resolve while circumstances and context kept changing.

The change in circumstances became clear over the course of 1943, as was reflected in the narrative of the five conferences held during that year. The story of COSSAC is intertwined with that narrative. How the Allies got there and what happened next is where we begin.

— **1** —

"A COMMON BOND OF DANGER"

Just weeks after the American entry into World War II, British and American political and military leaders met for the first time as coalition partners, in Washington, D.C. The meetings set out in broad terms how the British, who wrote most of the meeting documents, thought the war should be fought. At this meeting, code-named ARCADIA (22 December 1941 to 14 January 1942), a memorandum of understanding was agreed to that became, to a large degree, one of the sources of ongoing debate and mistrust between the Allies. This was because circumstances overtook many of the assumptions on which the understanding was based and because there was as yet only the embryo of a U.S. strategic planning structure and no American strategic plan.[1]

The memo, titled "W.W.-1," affirmed the agreements reached the year before at the so-called ABC (American-British conversations) meetings that Germany was "the prime enemy and her defeat is the key to our victory.... In our considered opinion, therefore, it should be a cardinal principle of American-British strategy that only the minimum of force necessary for the safeguarding of vital interests in other theatres should be diverted from operations against Germany."[2]

"A Common Bond of Danger" is a phrase used by Maurice Matloff, *Strategic Planning for Coalition Warfare, 1943–1944*, in *U.S. Army and World War II* (Washington, D.C.: Center of Military History, 1959), 18.

"W.W.-1" went on to list the essential strategic concepts, including "closing and tightening the ring around Germany" and "wearing down and undermining German resistance by air bombardment, blockade, subversive activities and propaganda."[3] This ring would be strengthened by "sustaining the Russian front, by arming and supporting Turkey, by increasing our strength in the Middle East, and by gaining possession of the whole North African coast."[4]

The evaluation of the opportunities for offensive actions was straightforward: "It does not seem likely that in 1942 any large-scale land offensive against Germany except on the Russian front will be possible. . . . In 1943 the way may be clear for a return to the Continent, via the Scandinavian Peninsula, across the Mediterranean, from Turkey into the Balkans, or by simultaneous landings in several of the occupied countries of Northwestern Europe."[5] The only option not mentioned was one massive cross-Channel assault.

The memorandum was, by necessity, sweepingly general and vague. How, when, and by what path the fight was to be taken to Germany had yet to be determined. In short, while the concept of offensive action existed at ARCADIA, the ways and means and any particular strategy did not. Identifying Germany as the "prime enemy" was simply the lowest common denominator.

While there was no disagreement that Allied resources needed to be concentrated against Germany, just what constituted "the minimum of force necessary" for the Pacific and the strategic value of increasing Allied strength in the Mediterranean quickly became the subjects of serious debate that remained unresolved until the end of 1943. Indeed, for the American military and the American public, the crisis of early 1942 was in the Pacific.

Two long-lasting agreements did come out of the ARCADIA conference; first, agreement with the proposal by the U.S. Army's chief of staff, Gen. George Marshall, to unify command at the strategic level—each theater of operations would have one supreme commander, either British or American, who would direct all forces of all nations in that theater. While occasionally honored in the breach, notably for OVERLORD, this was at least a concept that was embraced; and, second, agreement to create the U.S. Joint Chiefs of Staff and the Anglo-American Combined Chiefs of Staff (CCS), bringing together the military and naval service heads from both countries. Formed to direct the theater commanders, the chiefs, reporting directly to the president and prime minister, were responsible for reaching agreement on the general strategic direction of the war and on the actions necessary to achieve the agreed strategic goals. The nine high-level interallied conferences held between 1943 and 1945 were attempts to achieve those agreements.[6] Beyond that, Americans and British were in constant contact with each other, often through the offices of the British Joint Service Mission in Washington, D.C., where the American Joint Chiefs could talk to their counterparts "in real time." The Joint Staff Mission represented the British Chiefs of Staff (COS) and was headed by Field Marshal John Dill, former chief of the Imperial General Staff. He quickly gained the trust and respect of the Americans. His great ability to find common ground between the Americans and British at times of profound disagreement has been overlooked by some historians. Of equal importance were the various joint and combined staffs that would be formed to support and inform the decisions reached by the CCS.

Just over six weeks after the end of the ARCADIA conference, at the end of February 1942, the new director of the War Plans Division of the U.S. Army, Brig. Gen. Dwight Eisenhower, submitted a memo to General Marshall that outlined what would become a fundamentally different central idea in the American approach to strategy. Rejecting the British peripheral approach spelled out at ARCADIA, Eisenhower agreed that keeping Russia in the war was one of three key objectives for the Allies, but the best way to do that was for the United States to develop, "in conjunction with the British, a definite plan for operations in Northwest Europe. It should be sufficiently extensive in scale as to engage from the middle of May [1942] onward, an increasing portion of the German Air Force, and by late summer an increasing amount of his ground forces."[7]

By the end of March 1942, Eisenhower and what was now the Operations Division of the Army's Chief of Staff office had prepared an outline of "Operations in Western Europe" that Marshall would present to the British chiefs in April. There were three components: BOLERO, the concentration of troops and supplies in Britain in preparation for an invasion; ROUNDUP, the invasion, anticipated for the spring of 1943; and SLEDGEHAMMER, conceived as an emergency operation for 1942, to be conducted if the situation in Russia became desperate, with the hope that it would temporarily divert some German forces from the East, even at the sacrifice of the Allied troops involved.

There was no disagreement about BOLERO. From the British perspective, having a buildup of American forces in Great Britain would be beneficial in any conceivable set of circumstances, either offensively or defensively.

SLEDGEHAMMER was rejected by the British in relatively short order. The Americans would have been able to provide and support perhaps two and a half divisions and some air assets. The rest of this sacrificial force would be British and Canadian, and they had by this time little interest in intentional operations of this type. Indeed, SLEDGEHAMMER resembled many proposed cross-Channel operations that suffered from the same flaws, most notably Operation IMPERATOR.

In response to a paper submitted by the British Joint Planning Staff in March 1942 that pointed out that the Russian situation was critical and a major diversion in the West might be required, the British COS proposed IMPERATOR as a response to an anticipated Russian cri de coeur. They suggested sending a reinforced infantry division across the Channel as a raid-in-force, to stay for about a week, hoping to draw German air force units into battle under favorable conditions.

This prompted a scathing reply from Churchill:

1. . . . Certainly it would not help Russia if we launched such an enterprise, no doubt with world publicity, and came out a few days later with heavy losses. We should have thrown away valuable lives and material, and made ourselves and our capacity for making war ridiculous throughout the world. The Russians would not be grateful for this worsening of the general position. The French patriots who would rise to our aid and their families would be subjected to pitiless Hun revenge. . . . It would be cited as another example of sentimental politics dominating the calm determination and common sense of professional advisors.

2. In order to achieve this result, we have to do the two most difficult operations of war—first landing from the sea on a small front against a highly prepared enemy, and second, evacuating by sea two or three days later the residue of the force landed.

... When our remnants returned to Britain a la Dunkirk, [the result] would be that everyone, friend and foe, would dilate on the difficulties of landing on a hostile shore. A whole set of inhibitions would grow up on our side prejudicial to effective action in 1943.

I would ask the Chiefs of Staff to consider the following two principles:

(a) No substantial landing in France unless we are going to stay, and

(b) No substantial landing in France unless the Germans are demoralized by another failure against Russia.[8]

SLEDGEHAMMER, while championed by the Americans who wanted to go on the offensive in Europe in 1942, was never realistic in terms of tactics, troops, supplies, or shipping. It did, however, constitute a beginning of sorts that had some practical effects. Vital logistic preparations, needed before any such undertaking could be attempted, were begun. "The first of these was to reactivate some of the south and southeasterly commercial ports [the Falmouth, Plymouth, Southampton group, and some of the London docks]."[9] These facilities had been closed as part of British anti-invasion preparations in 1940. There was also planning, particularly the start of logistic planning regarding the troops that were expected to arrive.

ROUNDUP had a longer life but ultimately suffered the same fate, albeit for different reasons. When General Marshall presented the three concepts to the British COS, there was agreement in principle that planning should go ahead for a major cross-Channel operation in 1943 as well as the short-lived possible emergency operation in 1942. Agreements in principle do not, as a rule, include specific, detailed plans for their execution, and so it was in this case.

As plans began to be made, and without any agreed-on offensive operation planned against Germany for 1942 that involved U.S. troops, a series of debates began in Washington and London. The Russians needed support. The Western Allies were anxious to demonstrate that support. FDR was anxious, for domestic political reasons, to have the United States take the offensive against Germany in 1942. Britain needed to secure the Mediterranean, while gaining the whole of North Africa was part of Britain's plan from the beginning. The U.S. Army needed to have Europe be an active theater of operations to counter the U.S. Navy's demands for resources in the Pacific, especially after the victory at Midway.

This and more led to a decision by FDR and Churchill in July 1942, against the strong advice of the Joint Chiefs of Staff and counter to an earlier agreement between the CCS, to launch Operation TORCH, the invasion of Morocco and Algeria, in November of 1942. Churchill proclaimed that the operation would be cheap, that it was the "true second front of 1942 . . . the safest and most fruitful stroke that can be delivered this autumn."[10] A consequence of the decision, known at the time but not accepted by all participants, was that troops and material needed for a cross-Channel attack would now not be available before the spring of 1944. As U.S. chief of naval operations Adm. Ernest King and Marshall wrote into the Combined Chiefs of Staff document, "Options in 1942–43" dated 24 July 1942, "A commitment to this operation [TORCH] renders ROUND-UP in all probability impractical of successful execution in 1943."[11] Eisenhower held a briefing for Churchill in September of 1942. There Churchill "and certain of his close personal advisors" became "acutely conscious of the inescapable costs of TORCH."[12]

Eisenhower wrote to Marshall after the meeting:

> The arguments and considerations that you advanced time and again between last January and July 24th apparently made little impression upon the Former Naval Person at the time, since he expresses himself now as very much astonished to find out that TORCH practically eliminates any opportunity for a 1943 ROUNDUP.[13]

The planning for ROUNDUP to take place in 1943 became an academic exercise, and the code name with variations (ROUNDHAMMER, Super ROUNDUP) became a generic title for plans relating to crossing the Channel at some point. There was, of course, no agreed-upon plan for a cross-Channel assault, and the British particularly continued to hope that such an invasion would prove unnecessary or would occur only when Germany had been fatally weakened by air bombardment and defeats on the Russian Front. In part this was because the forces available in Great Britain were, in 1942, neither fully equipped nor particularly well trained.

In June 1942 now Major General Eisenhower was sent to London by Marshall to evaluate and report on the Special Observers Group, whose work was of some concern now that BOLERO had been approved and needed to be implemented. He returned with serious concerns about the leadership there and declared, "It is necessary to get a punch behind the job or we'll never be ready by spring [1943] to attack [that is, launch a cross-Channel invasion]."[14]

While there was not going to be a 1943 cross-Channel assault, Marshall took Eisenhower's advice to heart and sent him back to London to take command of the newly created European Theater of Operations, U.S. Army. By late July, with TORCH now the operation that was to be executed, the question of who was to command was raised. On the advice of Admiral King, newly promoted Lieutenant General Eisenhower was ironically designated the commander, and yet another new command was formed, Allied Force Headquarters, housed at Norfolk House, on St. James's Square, just off Pall Mall, in the center of London.

TORCH's shambolic but successful landings on 8 November 1942, fortunately opposed by Vichy French and not veteran Germans, got the United States into the war against Germany and allowed for the next meeting on the strategic direction of the war, code-named SYMBOL, to be held at Casablanca, in what was then French Morocco from 14 to 24 January 1943.

Much has been written about the strategic debates at Casablanca and the commitments reached to continue operations in the Mediterranean for 1943, setting aside potential opportunities in Northwest Europe.[15] The disagreements reflected those deeply held beliefs that showed themselves early in the coalition and were never fully resolved until the middle of 1944. The essential basis for the serious disagreements that continued to exist between allies stemmed from different approaches to the issues at hand.

Churchill, as demonstrated at a meeting at Chequers, the prime minister's country house, prior to the Casablanca conference, deliberately disdained all attempts to establish any overall strategic concept. He wrote, "In settling what to do in a vast war situation like this, it may sometimes be found better to take a particular major operation to which one is committed and follow that through vigorously to the end, making other things subordinate to it, rather than assemble all the data from the world scene in a baffling array. After the needs of the major operation have been satisfied . . . other aspects of the war will fall into their proper places."[16] As General Alan Brooke, chairman of the COS, noted in his diary in January of 1943, Churchill "often wished to carry out . . . sudden changes in strategy! I had the greatest difficulty in making him realize that strategy was a long-term process in which you could not frequently change your mind. He did not like being reminded of this fact and frequently shook his fist in my face and said, 'I do not want any of your long-term projects, all they do is cripple initiative.'"[17] Brooke, whose colleagues in Whitehall nicknamed him "Colonel Shrapnel," was described by Churchill as a "stiff-necked Ulsterman and there's no one worse to deal with than that." The historian Alex Danchev, in writing about the two, noted, "Where Churchill had an iron whim, Brooke had an iron will."[18]

It seemed to the Americans, as Admiral King explained to FDR during the Casablanca conference in January 1943, that "the British have definite ideas as to what the next operation should be but do not seem to have any over-all plan for the conduct of the war."[19] The same day King declared to the British chiefs, "It is important to determine how the war is to be conducted. Is Russia to carry the burden as far as ground forces are concerned? [Is] a planned step-by-step policy going to be pursued or are we relying on seizing opportunities . . . Germany's defeat can only be effected by direct military action and not by a collapse of morale." Marshall added the question, "Was the [proposed] operation in Sicily part of an integrated plan to win the war or was it simply taking advantage of an opportunity?" Hap Arnold, chief of the U.S. Army Air Forces, added, "We . . . have to decide not only what we are going to do in 1943 but also in 1944 since otherwise . . . our priorities in production might be wrongly decided."[20]

The British chiefs responded by saying that because there were too many variables, it was impossible to map out "a detailed plan for winning the war." The forces being built up in Great Britain should continue to be used as the "final action of the war as soon as Germany gives definite signs of weakness," and there would come a point (sometime in the future) "at which the whole [German] structure . . . would collapse." In the meantime, Allied policy should be to force Italy out of the war and to bring Turkey in.[21]

One meeting at the Casablanca conference clearly demonstrates the essential differences in approach. The Americans needed a strategic plan with what today would be called "milestones" and a "critical path" that would lead to direct action against Germany. The United States was still getting itself organized for war. Logistics and industrial production were at the top of the United States' planning list. The British position was that Allied ground forces were still too weak for a direct confrontation, and if Italy could be taken out of the war, if the ring around Germany could be tightened, if the bombing of German cities could be increased, and if the Russians could inflict defeats on German ground forces, then Germany would collapse. Once Germany's will to resist had been broken, invasion would either be unnecessary or weakly opposed, if resisted at all.

Concerning Turkey, the British chiefs were well aware that the primary benefit was geographic. According to Brooke, "The real value would have been the use of Turkey for aerodromes and as a jumping off place for future action."[22] In August of 1943, on the way to the Quebec conference, the War Cabinet's Joint Staff noted that "bomber forces based in Turkey would be in the best position to bomb Ploesti [the site of key Romanian oil fields], but other worth-while targets are few. . . . The moment . . . for Turkey to enter the war on our side is not yet ripe."[23] In truth, it would have been a net drain on Allied manpower and resources, yet the argument for Turkey continued to be made. It is also true that no one seemed to ponder the question of why Turkey would want to enter the war when their current situation as a neutral was so favorable for them. Geography was going to ensure that they would be the victor's friend regardless. In the end Turkey declared war on Germany when it was convenient, in February 1945.

For the Americans, the Pacific and European theaters were connected; strategy and domestic politics demanded offensive action in both at the same time. The British, with their home islands just twenty-one miles from the German-occupied Continent, thought more in sequential terms regarding strategy and focus: first Germany, then Japan. While the maintenance of India was strategically critical, the rest of Asia and the Pacific was of secondary value to the British, notwithstanding the political damage they suffered by their inability to defend Australia and New Zealand as well as the loss of prestige that came with the fall of Singapore. To them, most Asian issues could be negotiated and agreed on at the postwar conference table.

By the end of the Casablanca conference nine major decisions were made:

Winning the U-boat war
Increasing the strategic bombing offensive
Invading Sicily
Continuing support of Russia
Conducting limited offensives in the Pacific
Reopening the Burma Road
Increasing U.S. air presence in China
Concentrating forces in the United Kingdom for an *eventual* return to
    the Continent
Pursuing a policy of unconditional surrender[24]

The decisions to continue operations in the Mediterranean and in the Pacific had the anticipated effect of moving BOLERO to the bottom of the priority list, and there was no great buildup of U.S. troops in Britain for the first half of 1943. By the end of February 1943, "the European Theater of Operations had become a stand-by theater manned by a skeleton crew."[25]

Near the end of the Casablanca conference, on 22 January 1943, the Combined Chiefs discussed a paper presented by the Combined Planners called *Proposed Organization of Command, Control, Planning and Training for Operations for a Re-entry to the Continent across the Channel beginning in 1943*. The idea of some sort of staff had been discussed by the British chiefs at least since August of 1942. As they noted then, "The organization, planning and training for *eventual* entry into the Continent should continue so that this operation can be staged should a marked deterioration in German military strength become apparent, and the resources of the United Nations available after meeting other commitments, so permit."[26] An aide-mémoire written by the secretary of the COS committee before a meeting with the ROUNDUP planners during the same month noted that a joint and combined staff could be formed, headed by a "Brigadier or equivalent rank. This syndicate would have at their disposal the considerable quantity of information . . . which has already been collected for ROUNDUP."[27]

The Combined Chiefs agreed with the proposal to form a U.S./British staff to bring cohesion to the planning process for an eventual cross-Channel operation. Where, when, or with what forces was not specified. They intentionally did not appoint a commander or deputy commander to lead the operation, in part because no operation had been authorized. It was also likely that neither General Brooke nor General Marshall could identify a competent commander who, along with his staff, could be spared from more urgent assignments. FDR had proposed a British supreme commander while Churchill suggested that it was only necessary for someone to look to the planning at this stage. At a later meeting the Combined Chiefs proposed that a British officer be assigned as chief of staff for the time being.[28]

In examining this proposal FDR questioned whether "sufficient drive would be applied if only a Chief of Staff were appointed." General Brooke thought that "a man with the right qualities . . . could do what was necessary in the early stages." It was left at that.[29]

―2―

"NO SUBSTANTIAL LANDING IN FRANCE UNLESS WE ARE GOING TO STAY"

Shortly after taking command of 1st Corps in May 1942, Lt. Gen. Sir Frederick Morgan found that it was becoming difficult "to work up much enthusiasm in the preparations to meet so unlikely an event as a German seaborn invasion."[1] To rekindle interest and enthusiasm in the professional lives of his troops and subordinate commanders, who "had had their fill of manning coast defenses," he proposed that 1st Corps consider taking the offensive. What better offensive action to take than to plan a crossing of the Rhine and invading Germany?

As he wrote the outline for this map study / command exercise, he found himself "confronted with the problem of how to get 1st British Corps from Yorkshire to Hamburg and points east."

> Appalled by the immense difficulties of such an operation that the briefest consideration made only too obvious, this being an affair of the imagination only, we decided to solve the problem by means of a simple assumption. Starting with the heartening passage, "The British Army having successfully invaded Germany from the Northwest . . ." our prospectus went on to describe a situation of reasonable orthodoxy. But it was a refreshing change to be toying with German place names rather than those of our own home towns.[2]

Morgan was right to be appalled. There wasn't much history of large-scale amphibious assaults or of combined operations in the British terminology of the time (attempted landings from the sea against prepared enemy defenses) in the two hundred years or so before World War II. The one most people could remember, the Gallipoli campaign, didn't inspire confidence in the concept. Nor had attempts in Norway or Dakar in the current war done much to rebalance the record.

It's true that there were landings from the sea throughout history. The British had a particular fondness for "descents" or raids, but those were, in the main, unopposed landings, seeking to "hit 'em where they ain't" followed by either a brief action and return to the sea or by a set battle, as in the case of Quebec during the Seven Years' War, or at New York in the American War of Independence.[3] How to "kick the door in," fight one's way ashore, and stay with a modern army was a different matter. What could be said was that amphibious operations on a larger scale than ever seen or imagined were the only way for the Allies to take the fight to both the Germans and the Japanese. While there was some study of the subject before World War II, how to do it was largely worked out during the war as operations were conducted—and there was no one agreed-on way of doing it.

In 1938 the British created a modest establishment, the Inter-Service Training and Development Centre, staffed by four officers: a Royal Navy captain, a British Army major, a Royal Air Force wing commander, and a captain of the Royal Marines. Their task, as then captain L. E. H. Maund, the "chairman" of the center, put it, was to show that an assault from the sea "was practical, to indicate how the assault should go and to design and build the equipment that would make it practical."[4]

By the time war broke out they had managed to design and have built a small number of landing craft of various types, primarily for the raids they envisioned would occur. They had given consideration to what kind of beach organization there should be to handle troops and supplies that had landed, experimented with raids launched from submarines, examined what types of vessels could be converted into transports or assault ships, and put forth some general theories of operation, mainly regarding small "hit-and-run" operations with an emphasis on gaining tactical surprise, landing at night, and, consequently, the minimal use of naval gunfire support.

In 1940 and again in 1941 they placed what were at the time large orders with Andrew Higgins of New Orleans, whose boats were also being ordered by the U.S. Marines. Higgins, the inheritor of a great deal of money as well as a timber business, was a trained naval architect and had a great deal of experience building fast, light, wooden boats that were at home in the bayous and that had been highly desired by rumrunners and bootleggers during Prohibition.[5] The British preferred Higgins' thirty-six-foot version while the Marines opted for the thirty-two-foot size, the British and Higgins believing that the larger boat was a better sea boat and had the advantage of carrying a few more men.

For U.S. armed forces, the Marines had spent the most time thinking about amphibious warfare, beginning with America's pivot toward Asia that started in the 1920s. As with most projects in the interwar years, training and exercises were modest, as were the budgets, and much of what was considered was essentially theoretical. The Marines published the *Tentative Manual for Landing Operations* in 1934, which was adopted by the Navy in 1937; with modifications, it remained "the book" during World War II. The Marines rejected the idea of night landings and surprise, believing that the difficulties outweighed the advantages. Instead, they opted for the employment of naval gunfire support, close air support, and ultimately days or weeks of preparatory bombardment. "There was no ambiguity in the doctrine. Surprise was not significant. Battles were, ideally, to be won with the deliberate, methodical, sustained use of overwhelming firepower, followed up by a direct, mass infantry assault."[6] This was to be World War II in the central Pacific.

The U.S. Army was late in considering amphibious war. Notwithstanding the fact that projection of American power was going to require shipping to move forces to operational theaters, the Army was initially focused on hemispheric defense. As with so much else, Dunkirk and the fall of France changed the basic assumptions. While there had been limited exercises with the Navy in the 1930s, efforts became serious starting in 1941. In 1942 Army units that were to be part of TORCH conducted amphibious training in the Caribbean and on the Atlantic coast with the 1st Marine Division and with the Navy's Amphibious Corps. "The Army's experience in working with the Navy and Marine Corps did not persuade it that the Marine Corps doctrine was the best solution to amphibious warfare."[7] Indeed, Gen. George Patton reported after the TORCH landings, "Daylight landings are too costly and will be successful only against weak or no opposition."[8]

Obviously, there are differences between isolating and then capturing an island and invading somewhere on a continental shoreline. Still, there are viable options from which to choose and questions to answer—daylight or night, how long a preparatory bombardment, how to employ tactical and strategic aircraft, can isolation of the invasion area be achieved and how, use of airborne troops, speed of buildup, and so on. The amphibious assaults conducted in the Mediterranean and at Normandy were both joint and combined—more than one military service was involved from more than one country. Each one became a bespoke, one-off operation with the British approach dominating the planning. OVERLORD was, to a degree, the exception. In developing the outline plan for the cross-Channel attack, the COSSAC planners would be working with a narrow knowledge base.

Combined Operations

As the last British troops were being evacuated from France in June 1940, Churchill was hectoring the Chiefs of Staff (COS) to find some way to take offensive action. "The passive resistance war, in which we have acquitted ourselves so well must come to an end. I look to the [British] joint Chiefs of Staff to propose me measures for a vigorous, enterprising and ceaseless offensive against the whole German-occupied coastline."[9]

While more ambitious in concept than practical in execution, this exhortation led to the adjutant-general (the commandant) of the Royal Marines, Lt. Gen. Alan Bourne, being appointed by the COS as the first "Commander of Raiding Operations on coasts in enemy occupation and Advisor to the Chiefs of Staff on Combined Operations."[10] In addition to planning and conducting raids across the Channel, he was tasked with providing advice on the organization for conducting amphibious assaults, supervising all training relating to combined operations (including training the crews who would operate the special purpose craft that were to be built), and developing and issuing contracts for the production of those craft. As one might anticipate, the work of the Inter-Service Training and Development Centre became part of the Combined Operations domain. While all three services were involved, Bourne and his staff were headquartered in the Admiralty.

General Bourne was in the job for about a month, during which time there were some small raids that achieved little. In July Churchill's thoughts returned to the idea of large raids and imaginative enterprises. Having never approved Bourne's appointment, he now desired to see someone more senior and more unorthodox in the position.

Sixty-eight-year-old Admiral of the Fleet Sir Roger Keyes certainly fit that description. Early in his career, Keyes, as commanding officer of a destroyer in support of the efforts to rescue the legations besieged in Peking (Beijing) during the Boxer Rebellion of 1900, was eager to get into the fight. He "handed over command of his destroyer to his First Lieutenant and joined an army column [marching on the Chinese capital]. . . . He was the first man into the city [Beijing], climbing a 30-foot wall."[11] He survived the naval battles at Gallipoli in 1916 and was best known for planning and conducting the raid on German U-boat pens in Zeebrugge harbor in 1918. He had retired in 1935 but returned to active duty in 1940. He also served as a member of Parliament from 1934 to 1943. A friend of Churchill's, he became director of Combined Operations in July 1940.

Within a week, Churchill was asking Keyes for proposals for medium-sized raids using between five thousand and ten thousand men, to be launched in September or October at the latest. When Keyes received the memo, the strengths of the Commandos and independent companies that had been formed for raiding "were 500 and 750 respectively, and of the latter 250 were earmarked to go to Gibraltar."[12]

Keyes' fifteen months as director were contentious, at best. He set up Combined Operations Headquarters (COHQ) as an independent entity, moving out of Admiralty offices and into the newly built and as-yet unoccupied New Scotland Yard building in Richmond Terrace, near Downing Street. This was a mixed blessing. The benefits of an independent command are many, but "from the material, naval personnel and psychological aspects, separation at this particular time, when everything depended on Admiralty effort, was a misfortune and led . . . to a good deal more than separation. The day of private navies and armies had dawned."[13] Not just the famous Commandos, which were the COHQ's operational units, but eventually groups such as the Special Air Service, the Special Boat Service, the Long Range Desert Group, and even Gen. Orde Wingate's Chindits in Burma were all part of a range of special operators that siphoned off some of the best small-unit leaders to what were arguably peripheral operations. Whatever their value may have been, they certainly appealed to Churchill's late-Victorian sense of combat—just the thing for a former subaltern of cavalry who fought at Omdurman in Sudan in 1898 and who, as a war correspondent, was captured and then escaped from a Boer prisoner of war camp in 1899 and then wrote about the adventure for the newspapers.

While Keyes was in charge, there were advancements in the thinking about special ships and craft, particularly the LST (landing ship, tank), and the establishment of operational training centers. There were, however, few raids. "Plans were discussed, but the answer was always the same: you cannot assault an enemy coast without the proper number of special craft and until the crews have been trained."[14]

Keyes went to Churchill and proposed that Commandos take the small island of Pantelleria, just south of Sicily, in order to improve the sea transport situation in the central Mediterranean. Both the COS and the commander of the British Mediterranean Fleet, Adm. Sir Andrew Cunningham, doubted that the island could be held.

Churchill gave Keyes permission to conduct the operation with two thousand commandos under his direct command. At the last minute, in December 1940, the operation was cancelled. Keyes was furious and blamed everyone from the COS on down, venting his anger in a string of memoranda to Churchill.[15]

There was also a fundamental organizational disagreement that could not be resolved. Keyes believed that as "director" of Combined Operations, he should have control over the planning and preparations for any amphibious operation and should be responsible for the training of all the naval personnel involved. This meant that on occasion, the idea and the planning for a raid originated in Combined Operations, as was the case for Pantelleria, and then it had to be "sold" to the appropriate commander in chief for execution. Consequently, coordination with the joint planners and any connection with strategic goals was not always achieved. Additionally, Keyes' opinion of the COS bordered on contempt (in the midst of one meeting, he accused them of being "yellow"[16]), and he was inclined to give his opinions freely and directly to the prime minister, among others.

The COS took the view that only they were to give advice to the prime minister or the War Cabinet regarding strategy, that commanders of various operations or organizations were responsible to them not to COHQ, and, as for the reentry into the Continent, that "the planning and training for this must be the job of the Commander-in-Chief, Home Forces, with his appropriate naval and air opposite numbers" (soon to be called the Combined Commanders).[17] Consequently, the COS believed that the exact role of the head of Combined Operations needed to be redefined. Keyes was notified by Churchill that his title was now advisor of Combined Operations, not director. Keyes would not accept what he saw as a demotion and resigned.

On 27 October 1941 Lord Louis Mountbatten, captain in the Royal Navy, cousin to King George, and longtime friend of the Duke of Windsor, took over as advisor of Combined Operations. Selected by Churchill without consulting the COS, he was "many ranks and 27 years junior to Keyes, but all this was reckoned an asset."[18] Mountbatten brought great energy and enthusiasm to the project and set about building up his staff and strengthening his hand, ensuring that the COS and everyone else knew that he had the full support of the prime minister. While no expert in combined operations, he was a fast learner, able to effectively represent the amphibious warfare views at major interallied conferences, had great charm, was liked by the Americans, and had what in different circumstances could be described as a knack for effective presentation.

The exchanges between the COS, Keyes, Mountbatten, and Churchill had the seeds of future difficulties embedded. The Commander-in-Chief, Home Forces, and his naval and air equivalents were, according to the COS, responsible for the planning and training of forces related to some future, as-yet-unplanned or agreed-on reentry into the Continent. They would report directly to the British COS. When the Americans arrived, planners at ETOUSA had an informal liaison relationship with the planners of the Combined Commanders, but all plans still went through them to the British COS.

Mountbatten and COHQ felt, as had Keyes, that they existed as the depository of all knowledge and doctrine related to amphibious operations and, as the duty experts, would have to play a major role in the planning and conduct of any amphibious attack launched from Great Britain. After the entry of the United States into the war, some American officers served at COHQ, but it remained a British organization.

The Casablanca conference established a planning staff related to cross-Channel operations, initially to catalog and bring some organizational structure to whatever studies and concepts had been put forth so far. Headed by a British staff officer but without a commander, this staff, near as anyone knew, was to report to the CCS in Washington and was tasked with planning both a deception operation in the Channel and reentry into the Continent under two possible sets of circumstances. The resolution of this tangle was neither easy nor quick.

In March of 1942 Mountbatten was promoted from captain (acting commodore) to vice-admiral, with the additional ranks of lieutenant general and air-marshal. His title was changed to chief of Combined Operations and he now joined the COS as an equal member whenever either combined operations or the general conduct of the war were discussed, which is to say, for almost every meeting.

By now there were trained troops, specialized assault craft, and experience from smaller raids in the Mediterranean and Norway. From the relatively simple and straightforward creation of small landing craft that began in 1938, by 1943 there developed an entire range of specialized craft types, each designed and built to address a specific need or provide the means of moving some of the various components of an invasion force from ship to shore. There were the LCA (landing craft, assault), which were small craft for infantry initially designed for raiding; the LCC (amphibious command ship), which were control craft; the LCH, the headquarters craft; the LCI(L), landing craft infantry (large), which carried up to two hundred men and their equipment; the LCM, which were for mechanized equipment like vehicles and tanks; the LCP(L), also for personnel; the LCS (Landing Craft, Support); the LCT, which carried fifty-five men plus vehicles; and the LCVP, landing craft designed for either vehicles or personnel. There was also the LSI(L), the landing ship, infantry (large), which carried assault craft and men. And there were the LSM (landing ship, medium), a larger, oceangoing version of the LSI, and the famous LST. This was in addition to the AKA (amphibious cargo) and APA (attack transport) ships, which carried craft and men for the assault, and the MT (motor transport) ships, in which forty vehicles or mechanized transport could be loaded.[19] By 6 June 1944 there were even close-support craft like the LCT-R, or landing craft tank–rocket.[20]

In some cases, assault ships would have both men for the assault and the craft needed to land them. If so, then it was a matter of proper coordination so that the troops would be loaded into the assault craft at the proper moment, take their place in the correct assault wave, and land on the right beach. If the craft were on one ship and the troops on another, then the boats had to be loaded out in the correct sequence, be gathered in assembly areas, be directed to the right transport at the right time, pick up the troops, and then head to the right beach. In both cases, there were often subchasers, control craft, or mine sweepers helping with the navigation.[21] It took a great deal of training before young men, most of whom had no sailing experience, were proficient in the art of laying a small craft alongside a large ship, loading troops, and delivering them on the beach, then turning around and doing it again.

Between January and June of 1942, ten raids of various sizes were conducted; the planning for some had started under Keyes. The raid on the radar station at Bruneval, France, and the raid on the dry dock and other facilities at Saint-Nazaire are among the most well known in this period.

Operation JUBILEE, the Dieppe Raid, might well have been controversial even if it hadn't been a spectacular failure. It would seem to have violated Churchill's requirement of "no substantial landing in France unless we are going to stay," as well as having a long list of questionable planning and operational decisions associated with it. Whatever else can be said about the tragedy of 19 August 1942, one perceived accomplishment (which turned out to be false) was the "massive fighter battle in the skies. . . . Convinced that a great air victory had been won at Dieppe, and that at last a way had been found to inflict severe wastage on the Luftwaffe, the head of Fighter Command, Sir Trafford

Leigh-Mallory, wrote Mountbatten shortly afterwards urging more raids of the same kind, making only one common-sense observation . . . : 'When attacking the enemy on land, one does not generally strike at his strongest point.'"[22] That is to say, don't attempt to seize a defended port by direct amphibious assault without substantial air and naval gunfire support, which would likely damage the facilities that one would hope to seize intact.

Mountbatten was encouraged to think of other raids or feints that would continue to bring the Luftwaffe up into battle with the Royal Air Force under favorable conditions. The fact that well-trained troops might be the bait to attract the Germans did not seem to enter into the equation, nor did the possibility of the Germans deciding to not take the bait as offered.

A Plan for What Might Be Done Next

Summer and fall of 1942 were, of course, also the time of the debates over SLEDGEHAMMER, which was put to rest before the Dieppe Raid. The North African campaign also put an end to the discussion about any major cross-Channel effort in 1943. Additionally, TORCH drew off most of the small group of experienced American planners who had been in London working on the question of reentry into the Continent and who were now assigned to Eisenhower's Allied Force Headquarters (AFHQ) at Norfolk House. Soon Lieutenant General Morgan and his 1st British Corps would become part of the TORCH campaign.

Morgan enjoyed challenging his staff to consider some of the larger issues confronting them. He felt that with the Americans now in the war, some sort of offensive action—certainly not across the Channel, but somewhere—should be considered. The question to his officers' mess was—where? In early autumn 1942 their collective answer was somewhere between Casablanca and Tunis. This was, as it turned out, a pretty good guess, but for Morgan it also marked the beginning of what became a very different assignment.

In October 1942 1st Corps was renamed 125 Force, assigned to TORCH, and was initially intended to be deployed in case the Germans drove into Spain and attempted to close the Strait of Gibraltar. Morgan's force was to conduct an amphibious landing and occupy what was then Spanish Morocco so that the strait would remain open even if Gibraltar was captured. Morgan observed that, "on paper, in London, there seemed to be a certain rough logic in the idea but, the more deeply one went into it, the more I became impressed with the lack of our knowledge of the conduct of such affairs in general."[23]

Morgan traveled from his headquarters in Yorkshire down to London to meet General Eisenhower, arriving the same day as Maj. Gen. Mark Clark, Eisenhower's deputy, returned from his clandestine negotiations with the French military in North Africa. While Morgan was impressed with his new commander, he encountered one significant problem almost at once. His written orders, conveyed to him by the AFHQ staff, were totally incomprehensible. While it had been "compiled according to the best War College standards . . . the whole document as it stood meant not a thing to any of us."[24] As a result, one of his first steps was to become acquainted not only with "American English" but with that specific subset known as U.S. Army staff language. (COSSAC later took this into consideration with their communication. Memoranda, for example, would employ "combined" terminology for clarity. Thus, reference would be to "L of C/Communications Zone," "Formations/Units," or "Stores/Supplies.")

Morgan set about to train his force for amphibious operations. The two divisions were stationed in the Scottish Lowlands, from where it would be relatively easy to embark from the River Clyde around Glasgow. Among the training areas used were those associated with various COHQ facilities, notably the Combined Training Center in Largs, a small summer resort town near Glasgow.

Morgan also grew to know and respect Eisenhower's chief of staff, Walter Bedell Smith, who stayed in London while Eisenhower went to Gibraltar for the final planning of the North African invasion. "By the time he [Smith] in turn left for Africa we had established an understanding which stood us in good stead later on."[25] By December of 1942 Morgan was obliged to travel to North Africa, as the hypothetical planning questions of October had become a more complex reality and the details of employing 125 Force could no longer be dealt with at long range. He took the injunction of Marshal Ferdinand Foch seriously: "Don't phone, go and see."[26] Interestingly, Morgan's command was joint and combined, with "his sailor" being Commo. W. E. Parry of the Royal Navy and "his airman," Brig. Gen. Robert Candee of the Eighth U.S. Army Air Force.[27]

The trip to North Africa connected Morgan with many of those involved in TORCH. He demonstrated little of the standoff reserve so often attributed to British officers, on one occasion enthusiastically entering into a very American debate about the American Civil War that flared up during an evening's festivities. Seeing that those arguing for the "South" were outnumbered, he entered the fray with such good effect that Adm. John Leslie Hall, USN, made Morgan an honorary Southern Democrat. The same Admiral Hall was to be the commander of Amphibious Force "O" at Omaha Beach, the force that put the U.S. 1st Division ashore on D-Day. More importantly, Morgan saw an allied operational headquarters that worked. He "had been able to talk with old British Army friends who formed part of Ike's team, to catch from them the spirit of the thing . . . to appreciate to what an extent . . . integration of the two forces had already taken place."[28]

His flight back to the United Kingdom was not without incident. When the pilots sighted land an hour earlier than planned, Morgan was summoned to the cockpit of his loaned B-17 for a consultation. He was able to confirm that the land in sight were the Isles of Scilly and not the Brest peninsula of occupied France. Successfully landing outside London, one member of his staff "sought confirmation of our good luck by means of the slot machines in the bar, from which he quickly derived a small fortune. It was not all luck. Acquaintance with [this B-17's crew] taught one a lot."[29] (Had they missed the Isles, they might have missed landfall altogether as they were flying on a northerly heading.)

The potential threat for which 125 Force was formed never appeared, and by early 1943 Morgan was ordered to plan an invasion of Sardinia, for which his force would be reinforced by two American divisions and the Royal Marines division. As planning for that operation developed, he was then told that the next operation would now be Sicily and to start planning for that operation. "It became evident that the conquest of Sicily would be an affair far larger in scope than either of our previous projects, larger in fact than could be contemplated with the use of so small a body as a corps."[30] The responsibility for planning that operation was transferred to AFHQ and to the commanders responsible for the operation. By March 1943 both his divisions had been stripped away and fed into the Mediterranean battle. His 1st Corps, now reduced to just a headquarters, was to be reformed with the assignment of training as part of the spearhead for the eventual cross-Channel attack.

Having given the matter some thought, Morgan began to press higher authorities to be more specific. Where are we to attack, when, and with what? He fully understood and advocated for troops to get used to the idea of fighting "in some country in which they would arrive after a long sea voyage and where they would find strange conditions among a population which might range anywhere from demonstratively friendly to definitely hostile."[31]

He noted from his contact with COHQ and in planning for the various deployments of 125 Force that no two beaches are alike. Therefore, it seemed to him, that some correlation between training and operations needed to exist. As he said, "it was essential to narrow down the various possibilities with which one might be confronted on some future D-Day."[32] In a conversation with his old friend from their service together in India, Gen. Lord Hastings "Pug" Ismay, Morgan expressed his strong opinion that someone should be appointed who would do something about this lack of direction and clarity. Ismay was now deputy secretary to the War Cabinet and military advisor to Winston Churchill. He suggested that Morgan write a paper on the subject, which Morgan then did and sent off to his old friend.[33]

In early March Ismay invited Morgan down to London to discuss the matter further, and, upon reporting to Ismay's office, Morgan was handed a stack of documents that represented the work done by various people at various times related to a cross-Channel attack. Morgan was asked to review the material and to produce for presentation to the COS his concept of "a plan for what might be done next." It was due the next day. Morgan submitted a memorandum but admitted that he didn't think much of his first attempt "nor did the Chiefs of Staff, so I was given a second chance."[34]

Not yet having new divisions assigned to 1st Corps and being free from any attachment to any potential project, Morgan, on his second attempt, gave the chiefs a straightforward and honest analysis of what he thought, which was also witnessed by Ismay and Mountbatten. He then left the meeting.

Not long after, on 12 March, standing in an elevator at New Scotland Yard, while heading to a meeting at COHQ, Morgan got an indication of what was to be his fate. Just as the elevator door was starting to close, Mountbatten jumped in and offered his enthusiastic, if premature, congratulations, notwithstanding the fact that the elevator was jammed full of people of all ranks. As far as Mountbatten was concerned, Morgan, with his presentation, had apparently talked himself into a job. One problem for Morgan was that he wasn't sure he wanted to transition from being a corps commander, albeit one without any troops at the moment, back to a senior staff officer for what sounded like a decidedly dodgy and not yet clearly defined project. "As soon as I could emerge from Combined Operations Headquarters I . . . made for the nearest open space, the Temple Gardens, where I walked with Bobbie [his aide] to regain composure, a process that was completed shortly afterward at the bar of the Cavalry Club."[35] How he traveled from Richmond Terrace, across from Downing Street, to the Temple Gardens, just beyond King's College London, and then back to the Cavalry Club in Mayfair is not explained. With his composure regained, at least for the moment, Morgan began to reflect on what needed to be done, if he were to be given this new assignment.

— 3 —

"FOR WHAT ARE WE TO PLAN?"

Fifteen months before General Morgan's fateful day at New Scotland Yard, the British Joint Planning Staff in December 1941 submitted an analysis to the COS that was a general outline of what a reentry into the Continent might look like. The COS then asked the Commander-in-Chief, Home Forces, the newly appointed Gen. Sir Bernard Paget, to review the paper and to consult with the commanders of Bomber Command, Fighter Command, and the Royal Navy's Commander-in-Chief, Portsmouth, in providing his evaluation.[1]

In January 1942 the COS gave further guidance to Paget:

German morale and strength in the West may deteriorate at any time in the future to a degree that will permit us to establish forces on the Continent. You are, therefore, to plan and prepare for a return to the Continent to take advantage of such a situation. . . .

You should continue your study of a major raiding operation against one of the main French Atlantic ports in case it becomes desirable to carry one out but preparations for such an operation are not to be allowed to delay your preparations for your primary task.

The Advisor on Combined Operations [is] to be consulted at all stages of the planning.[2]

Around the same time, Mountbatten and Commo. John Hughes-Hallett, representing Combined Operations, were invited to join General Paget in attending a staff exercise conducted by the various Home Forces commanders. Each of the generals and their staffs were instructed to prepare and present "an outline plan for the seizure of the Cherbourg Peninsula, to hold it for a week, and then withdraw back to England."[3] In other words, to plan something similar to SLEDGEHAMMER, or IMPERATOR, but in Normandy, not the Pas-de-Calais.

Lt. Gen. Bernard Montgomery, commander of South Eastern Command, presented last, and "after explaining the hazards of such an operation, went on to point out that it would be easier and more worthwhile not to withdraw the troops but to flood the Carentan Marshes and hold the Peninsula."[4] Although this would create a lodgment and a base for future offensive actions, Montgomery did not address how the troops were to break out and drive toward Germany through the German troops that undoubtedly would be in strong defensive positions on the other side of the marshes. Still, it made a change from considering the Pas-de-Calais.

From these modest beginnings emerged the Combined Commanders, sometimes called the Combined Commanders-in-Chief. The Commander-in-Chief, Home Forces, Sir Bernard Paget; Air Officer Commanding Fighter Command, Sir Trafford Leigh-Mallory; and Sir Charles Little, Commander-in-Chief, Portsmouth, had many duties. Being the Combined Commanders was a somewhat informal collateral duty as the British armed forces slowly reoriented themselves from a purely defensive posture to consideration of offensive action from the British Isles. The RAF's Bomber Command went its own way as a result of a directive issued by the Air Staff in February 1942. It was authorized to bomb Germany "without restriction," and Air Chief Marshal Sir Arthur Harris went at it with a will.[5] He waged his own offensive against German cities, believing that charring enough German acreage would make a cross-Channel attack unnecessary.

The Combined Commanders were required to consult with Combined Operations Headquarters when developing their plans. Mountbatten's unique position of being both head of an independent headquarters and a de facto member of the COS created problems on occasion, particularly if he disagreed with the Combined Commanders, although perhaps less often than it could have done.

The Combined Commanders took up the question of crossing the Channel and reached the conclusion that the Pas-de-Calais was the proper landing area, for one chief reason: in 1942 RAF fighters were unable to provide air cover in any meaningful way over other possible beaches. The Pas-de-Calais was also the closest viable landing site to Antwerp, which was identified as a critical port of supply for a drive into Germany. Mountbatten argued instead for the Cherbourg Peninsula (and, by extension, for the French Atlantic ports)—having seen the merit in the idea presented by General Montgomery and made it his own. He also thought that air cover could be provided by fitting the fighters with auxiliary fuel tanks.

Gen. Sir Alan Brooke, chief of the Imperial General Staff and chair of the COS, also believed that the Pas-de-Calais was the proper location. On 10 March 1942 Mountbatten attended the COS' weekly meeting for the first time. As noted in Brooke's diary, they discussed "the problem of assistance to Russia by operations in France, with [a] large raid or lodgment. [It was] decided [the] only hope was to try to draw off air forces from Russia and for that purpose [the] raid must be carried off on Calais front. Now directed investigations to proceed further."[6] Still, Mountbatten was keen to go his own way.

He continued to press for Normandy and the Baie de la Seine in meetings with the Combined Commanders. He next brought this up at a meeting of the COS on 28 March. Mountbatten, having a choice of sitting either with the COS or with the Commanders, sat with the Commanders and, when his turn to speak came, "roundly denounced their plan [for the Pas-de-Calais]. . . . In the end the Commanders left the room with orders to work on the Normandy plan."[7] However correct he might have been, the Commanders had no great appreciation for the assistance that Mountbatten had given them. There was, as a result, some amount of friction between the various headquarters, and both Paget at Home Forces HQ and the RAF still believed in the Pas-de-Calais.

Early British planning for crossing the Channel was also informed by their preparations for a German invasion in 1940. Hughes-Hallett was Mountbatten's naval advisor at Combined Operations and was as expert in the details of amphibious assault as almost anyone in Britain. He noted that the experiences of anti-invasion planning in 1940–41 brought to light "the enormous magnitude of problems to be overcome before even a minor amphibious operation could be . . . successfully carried out."[8] The tides in the Channel are difficult, particularly for small craft. Both the RAF and the German air force, the Luftwaffe, had major forces that would have to be brought to the fight. Logistical support, specialized training for the crews operating the landing craft if not the assault troops as well, and timing issues were staggeringly complex. In Hughes-Hallett's opinion, there were few army officers who had any real understanding of the magnitude of the problem, except perhaps for those few who had been personally involved in planning amphibious attacks or training troops for them.

The Combined Commanders had planners, of course. Brig. Colin McNabb for the army, Commo. Cyril E. Douglas-Pennant for the navy, and Air Marshal Sholto Douglas were the head planners. As General Morgan later observed, "Just as no nobleman of olden times was apparently a nobleman unless he employed his tame jester, so in 1943 no commander was alleged to be worth his place in the field unless he retained his own planner."[9] This was a comment on the proliferation of planners, not their quality. McNabb worked well with the Americans at ETOUSA and went on to serve as brigadier general staff for Kenneth Anderson's First Army in Tunisia, where he was killed in combat. Douglas-Pennant commanded the naval assault forces for GOLD BEACH on 6 June, and Sholto Douglas became the commander of Coastal Command in January 1944, after serving as the senior RAF commander in the Middle East.

A principal problem for the planners was the custom of the COS to require them to examine problems and design plans without a specific operation associated with the plan they were asked to create. Consequently, their work was subject to constant revision by higher authorities. "Each such revision was liable to call for variation or amendment of the plan put forward, in many instances necessitating cancellation or re-execution of work already put in by troops on the ground."[10] Another problem was that the fighting was going on in the Mediterranean, was likely to remain there, and, consequently, planners in London were far removed from any possibility of action.

The "Planning Racket"

In early 1942, with the U.S. Army's Special Observer's Group in London and its evolution into ETOUSA, the Americans arrived, full of enthusiasm and lacking experience.

On 7 February 1942 Col. Ray Barker, USA, commander of the 30th Field Artillery Regiment at the newly built training facility of Camp Roberts in California, received orders to report to the New York port of embarkation. He stopped in Washington, D.C., on the way and discovered that he was to take over the artillery section of the Special Observers Group in London. This meant that his promotion to brigadier general was deferred, but he told the chief of field artillery, "Never mind about the promotion part of it, if I can just go where the war is."[11] Having spent some amount of time in England in the interwar years, and being a student of British history, Barker thought that he could be effective there.

In a bit of cloak-and-dagger work, the group traveling to England were given civilian passports and wore civilian clothes on the trip, as they went by Pan American Clipper from New York to Bermuda, to the Azores, and then to Lisbon. From Lisbon they went to Shannon Airport in Ireland on a British Overseas Airways aircraft, then flew to Poole (near Bournemouth on the Channel coast) and went by train into central London.

The London they encountered had adapted to war. In a series of "Letters from London" for the New Yorker magazine, journalist Mollie Panter-Downes sketched out what life in the British capital was like during the Blitz.

Life in a bombed city means adapting oneself in all kinds of ways all the time. Londoners are now learning the lessons, long ago familiar to those living on the much-visited southeast coast, of getting to bed early and shifting their sleeping quarters down to the ground floor.[12]
. . . For Londoners, there are no longer such things as good nights; there are only bad nights, worse nights and better nights. Hardly anyone has slept at all in the past week. The sirens go off at approximately the same time every evening, and in the poorer districts, queues of people carrying blankets, thermos flasks, and babies begin to form quite early outside the air-raid-shelters.[13]
. . . Things are settling down into a recognizable routine. Daylight sirens are disregarded by everyone, unless they are accompanied by gunfire or bomb explosions that sound uncomfortably near. A lady who arrived at one of the railway stations during a warning was asked politely by the porter who carried her bag, "Air-raid shelter or taxi, Madam?"[14]

In London Barker joined what was then a group of about ten officers. While initially tasked with planning the deployment and training of artillery units expected to be arriving as part of BOLERO, he was quickly named head of the war plans section. While that may not have seemed an obvious assignment for a field artillery officer, he explained that he was picked "because I happened to be standing there and no one else [was] available."[15] From then on, he was involved in what he called the "planning racket."

Initially there were only a couple of U.S. Army officers involved in planning relating to the eventual reentry into the Continent. While he requested and got additional support, he felt that the first thing he needed to do was "to find out what the British were doing in this field."[16] This is when Barker discovered the Combined Commanders and their planners. While building his own staff, Barker worked in close daily cooperation with the British planners. Asked if he had been assigned to work with the British, Barker replied, "No one actually told me that I should associate myself or collaborate with these people; it was just the obvious thing to do."[17]

Barker and his group got to work on preparations for BOLERO as well as plans for SLEDGEHAMMER and ROUNDUP. In July, there was what his then boss, Dwight Eisenhower, described in his diary as a day that might become "the blackest day in history."[18] SLEDGEHAMMER was cancelled. But not entirely. The COS decided at its meeting of 22 August 1942 that "for purposes of deception and to be ready for any emergency or a favourable opportunity, all preparations for 'SLEDGEHAMMER' continue to be pressed . . . and [recommended] that a Task Force Commander be appointed with authority to organize the force, direct the training and maintain a contingent plan for execution."[19] Both Paget and Mountbatten were at the meeting, as was Pug Ismay.

At the same meeting, Air Chief Marshal Sir Charles Portal, acting as chair in the absence of General Brooke, quoted from a Combined Chiefs of Staff (CCS) memorandum written the prior month, saying in effect that as a result of TORCH going forward, "we have accepted a defensive encircling line of action for the continental European theatre . . . but that the organization, planning and training for *eventual* entry in the Continent should continue [in case there was] a marked deterioration in German strength . . . and that the resources of the United Nations available *after meeting other commitments*, so permit."[20]

General Paget noted that the planning for ROUNDUP would be based on working out the minimum requirements for forcing an entry into the Continent against weakening opposition. He also felt that, at this time, there was "no need for the Supreme Commander-in-Chief or his Deputy to be nominated." Mountbatten added that TORCH would employ every available landing craft and trained crew, and no operation of any scale could be mounted from the UK before March or April of 1943.[21]

The vision in August 1942 was to prepare contingency plans for an operation that could not occur before the spring of 1943, using the minimum force available after all other commitments were met, assuming that German resistance had weakened, and without identifying a commander or his deputy or identifying units that would be involved.

After the Dieppe Raid, planning continued. In late September 1942 a deception exercise, Operation CAVENDISH, was postponed for a second time and the Commander-in-Chief, South Eastern Command, Lt. Gen. J. G. Swayne, wrote to Paget arguing that the operation should be cancelled. Originally planned for October 1942 and now proposed for early November, the operation was an attempt to convince the enemy "that an invasion was being staged, though this deception was always difficult on account of the small number of modern landing craft available." General Swayne pointed out the obvious fact that the "enemy must know that the possibility of sufficiently long periods of suitable weather being obtainable in November are extremely remote. . . . I am informed by A.O.C. 11 Fighter Group that from the air point of view November would be very unsuitable for this enterprise."[22] We can infer that the operation was another attempt to lure the German air force into battle while a sea-based feint approached the Pas-de-Calais. As the general noted, weather over the Channel in November is rarely favorable for such operations; indeed, it was a basic principle (at least for experts like Hughes-Hallett) that the Channel's "invasion season" ended in September. The operation was cancelled.

Another operation, titled OVERTHROW, was to be a major cross-Channel effort and required coordination with Bomber Command to ensure that pre-invasion targets like gun emplacements and all forms of transport were attacked, which meant that Bomber Command would have to stop bombing cities and start bombing tactical targets. In part, this was to test if bombers could hit targets like gun emplacements and to find out what the level of damage might be. That operation also didn't get past the planning stage.

By now the long-considered operation to capture the Cherbourg Peninsula had a code name as well, and by September 1942 outline plans for a similar operation focused on Brittany were being considered.

By the end of September 1942 the Combined Commanders and their planners were considering the sixth draft of a memorandum to the COS, "Future Planning for Operation ROUNDUP" and the third draft of a similar memo, "Offensive Combined Operations in North-West Europe in 1943–1944." The memo for ROUNDUP outlined what the planners believed a theoretical phase 2 would look like—assuming the Allies had successfully reestablished themselves on the Continent. They identified three main goals: the capture of Paris; the capture or peaceful occupation of the Atlantic ports of Brest, Lorient, Saint-Nazaire, and Nantes, in part for a secure rear area to build up forces and in part because they expected the French would have to be fed with food shipped into the country; and a drive to capture Antwerp.

The commanders and planners requested that the COS grant them the authority to "frame an outline plan . . . basing it on the assumption that the full number of divisions included in the [previously] approved outline plan for Phase I will be available; and to prepare this outline plan in cooperation with the staff of the Commanding General ETOUSA, on the distinct understanding that the completed plan is subject to his approval and may therefore require revision."[23] That is, they asked for permission to plan given a certain set of assumptions, knowing that the American commander might modify or reject their plan after the work was completed.

The second memo recommended that "raids, whether designed primarily to provoke air battles under conditions favourable to ourselves or for some other purposes, must be closely co-ordinated with the approved strategy for 1943 and 1944" and not just be done for their own sake (a reference, perhaps, to Dieppe) and that "a plan for moving an Army into Europe in the event of serious deterioration in German morale should be prepared in outline."[24]

In the memorandum the planners also proposed consideration of an alternative to the existing ROUNDUP plan. Noting that the capture of the

Pas-de-Calais might be a "very hazardous operation," the planners proposed the capture of Le Havre, Rouen, and Cherbourg at the earliest opportunity. If German forces in the Pas-de-Calais could be contained by a series of major raids, then a "land and sea attack on the Cotentin [Cherbourg] Peninsula (could be) increased in strength." They went on to state that while prior planning had been based on the idea of simultaneous assaults over a wide front, consideration should be given to launching a series of assaults, "timed and directed to take advantage of the then existing circumstances, and supported in each case by a maximum possible concentration of air and naval effort. . . . We might hope to deceive the enemy as to whether he was still faced with major raids, or feints or with our main effort."[25]

The concepts in these memos were put forward as a basis for operations in 1944. The Combined Planners then asked the COS if they agreed in principle with the concepts and if they wished the planners to begin a detailed study of the proposed alternatives.

In broad terms, these ideas were not far off from Churchill's vision of what a cross-Channel attack might look like. In his note to the British COS regarding Operation IMPERATOR, Churchill noted that "if this were one of a dozen simultaneous operations of a similar kind, very different arguments would hold" versus those against the operation in question.[26] His vision in June 1942 was of "at least six heavy disembarkations at various points along the north and west coast of Europe, from Denmark and Holland down the Pas de Calais ['where a major air battle will be fought'] to Brest and Bordeaux. He also advocated 'at least a half a dozen feints' to mystify the enemy. These armoured landings would be followed by a second wave of heavier attacks at four or five strategic points, with the hope that three might be successful."[27] He envisioned a third wave once a port had been captured and opened.

There was, of course, no calculation of resources needed or resources available, nor any particular target date for the operation, nor any force commanders to lead beyond the roles to be played by the Combined Commanders.

The Combined Planners suffered from being a British, as opposed to an Allied, group. While it was true that there was ongoing, informal collaboration between Barker's group at ETOUSA and the planners, they reported to the Combined Commanders, who then reported to the British COS. The blunt-speaking Hughes-Hallett (who was called Hughes-Hitler behind his back[28]) said of the planners, "I could not take the work very seriously. The combined staffs of the Combined Commanders were so large that when they had plenary meetings it resembled a meeting of Parliament itself—with no equivalent of Mr. Speaker to enforce rules of order."[29]

The questions the planners had were not being answered. The projects were beginning to feel like exercises that were never to be executed. In addition to the fighting in North Africa, initial plans for attacks on either Sardinia or Sicily were being considered, which left few resources for the planners to use for any cross-Channel operation. It seemed that the Allies were going to stay in the Mediterranean for a long time.

At the end of October 1942 the COS accepted a memorandum from the Joint Planners, which was a statement of the British military's strategic outlook. Among the analyses was the following:

Despite the fact that a large-scale invasion of Europe would do more than anything to help Russia we are forced to the conclusion that we have no option but to undermine Germany's military power by the destruction of the German industrial and economic war machine *before* we attempt invasion. For this process, apart from the impact of Russian land forces, the heavy bomber will be the main weapon, backed up by the most vigorous blockade and operations calculated to stretch the enemy forces to the greatest possible extent. . . .

Even when the foundations of Germany's military power have been thoroughly shaken, it is probable that she will be able to maintain a crust of resistance in Western Europe. We must have the power to break through this crust when the time comes. We must therefore continue to build up Anglo-American forces in the European Theatre in order that we may be able to re-enter the Continent at the psychological moment.[30]

As for amphibious operations against France, the paper suggested more "Dieppe"-type raids (obviously with better outcomes) as well as large raids of longer duration against high-value targets and smaller commando raids.

Operation SKYSCRAPER

According to Barker, now a brigadier general, he and the other U.S. and British planners grew increasingly frustrated throughout the fall of 1942. In December a British major general, John "Sinbad" Sinclair, an officer in the Royal Horse Artillery who had started out in the Royal Navy, joined the planners. Sinclair and Barker finally got down to what Barker felt was constructive planning.[31]

On New Year's Day 1943 Barker and Sinclair agreed that they had accumulated large amounts of data, information, intelligence, and tentative plans, and they felt it was necessary to "produce something that would bring it all to a head and come up with a definite conclusion and a definite recommendation."[32] What they produced on their own initiative became known as Operation SKYSCRAPER.

SKYSCRAPER, an outline plan submitted to the Combined Commanders on 18 March 1943, was an impressive document and unambiguous about its purpose. The first sentence reads, "The object of this paper is to obtain decisions on certain major points which must govern not only the planning for a return to the Continent against opposition, but more particularly the organization, equipment and training of the Army in the United Kingdom during 1943."[33] Barker and Sinclair note that the plan had not been approved by the Combined Commanders nor had all the details been worked out. That is, they acknowledged that it was their idea to create the document and send it up the chain of command, and it was not the result of a directive to generate another study.

They go on to make the point that "it is generally agreed that the original 'ROUNDUP' plan is not a feasible one and some other basis is therefore necessary." Unlike earlier plans, Barker and Sinclair proposed a landing concentrated on the beaches in front of Caen in Normandy as well as landings on the Cherbourg Peninsula. Starting with the premise of a landing against determined resistance, not a weakened or demoralized enemy, they estimated the initial assault force at ten divisions afloat and up to four or five airborne divisions, plus commandos, engineers, and other special troops. They also estimated the numbers of all the specialized landing craft that would be needed.

While their scenario involved three distinct phases from initial landings to the capture of Antwerp, the key message to the Commanders and the COS comes toward the end of the summary. First there is an acknowledgement of the size of the force contemplated or the "bill" for the operation. They acknowledged that the bill "is a large one, and obviously not to be accepted lightly." They go on to state, "A warning must, moreover, be sounded with regard to the degree of opposition which could be overcome if the 'bill' is met, and the resources provided. The 'bill' is for THE MINIMUM RESOURCES LIKELY TO PROMISE SUCCESS AGAINST APPRECIABLE RESISTANCE.... The margin between success and failure would be very narrow."[34] Because they were not presenting a plan to deal with weakened German forces on the brink of collapse, the margin would always be narrow for troops fighting their way ashore from the Narrow Sea.

The most remarkable part of the plan comes at the end of the summary, when Barker and Sinclair demand that the COS make a clear and unequivocal choice:

> An invasion of the Continent in the face of German opposition is such a specialized problem that there is no chance of undertaking it successfully without careful preparation over a long period.... The decision as to whether or not we prepare the Army specifically for this purpose cannot be deferred.... The rock bottom of it all is, however, this: knowing the very great difficulties in provision of resources, for what are we to plan and prepare?
>
> If we are to plan and prepare for the invasion of Western Europe against opposition it must be on the understanding that the resources considered necessary are fully realized and that it is the intention to provide them. Given that knowledge, we can go ahead on a reasonably firm basis.
>
> If, on the other hand, it is clear that such resources can in no circumstances be provided, then it would seem wise to accept at once that invasion against opposition cannot be contemplated....
>
> In conclusion, a decision on the points raised ... is a matter of urgency as a basis for planning and preparation. As already pointed out, to defer the decision is to decide not to be ready.[35]

Paget sent the plan to the COS, who did not respond directly, although they noted that some of the assumptions regarding the scale of German resistance were vague. With the dramatic changes in circumstances that were occurring across the broad European Theater in 1943 (which are addressed in chapter 7), it could hardly have been otherwise. Paget believed that the COS were "unfavourable to the plan because of the huge bill for resources."[36] SKYSCRAPER did, however, make up a significant part of the stack of papers that Ismay gave Morgan to read before presenting to the COS. Morgan, having read SKYSCRAPER and the other material, made a recommendation in mid-March that clearly convinced the august body of senior officers that he was the person for the job. What exactly did he say?

While he made no attempt to delve into strategy or tactics, Morgan argued that it was necessary for the staff to be a completely joint and combined British-American effort in every detail from the very beginning. It needed to be slotted into the existing chain of command but be independent enough to seamlessly become an operational headquarters when the time came. More importantly, Morgan stressed that the prior habit of separating planning from execution could not continue. It would be necessary "for all concerned to throw their hearts over the jump and make up their minds there and then that the campaign had already begun, that there should be no question of producing just another plan to be a basis for future argument."[37]

In the absence of a supreme commander, all that the commander would need must be provided for: forces, a supply system, command and control systems, and, most importantly, "a plan of action both basically sound and yet sufficiently elastic to admit of variation as might be necessitated by developing circumstances."[38] This was a somewhat elaborate way of saying that the plan needed to be good enough to be approved but capable of modification by the commanders as needed without disruption to the basic concept. Morgan also recommended that the senior planners hold the rank of major general and not brigadier as they would have to interact on a daily basis with the War Office and other ministries. To get those ministries to respond, it would be necessary to have sufficient rank to gain and keep their attention.

Morgan had trained troops for amphibious assaults and had planned amphibious operations. As commander of 1st Corps, he was known to Mountbatten and Combined Operations. He had also successfully, if briefly, worked with American forces, and that was not a universal accomplishment. At the time it was widely believed that the supreme commander would be

British, with an American deputy, and so it made sense for the chief of staff to be British as well. All of this led to the British COS agreeing on 1 April that Morgan was the man for the job, however the job was going to be defined.[39]

Notwithstanding Morgan's impression of the COS' reaction to his recommendations and Mountbatten's congratulations, his appointment to head this new planning staff did not come at once. It took about a month to work out details of Morgan's appointment and for the CCS to issue the directive to him that outlined his responsibilities. Formally issued on 26 April, it was made available to Morgan in draft form in advance, and the British COS authorized him to act on the assumption that approval of his appointment would occur. The key elements of the directive read:

> The Combined Chiefs of Staff have decided to appoint, in due course, a Supreme Commander over all United Nations forces for the invasion of the Continent of Europe from the United Kingdom.
>
> Pending the appointment of the Supreme Commander or his deputy, you will be responsible for carrying out the above planning duties. . . . You will report directly to the British Chiefs of Staff. . . .
>
> You will accordingly prepare plans for:
>
> (a) An elaborate camouflage and deception scheme extending over the whole summer with a view to pinning down the enemy in the West and keeping alive the expectation of large scale cross-Channel operations in 1943. This would include at least one amphibious feint with the object of bringing on an air battle employing the Metropolitan Royal Air Force and U.S. Eighth Air Force.
>
> (b) A return to the Continent in the event of German disintegration at any time from now onwards with whatever forces may be available at the time.
>
> (c) A full scale assault against the Continent in 1944 as early as possible.[40]

Morgan asked for clarification regarding the last point, feeling that "as early as possible" was not particularly precise from a planning standpoint. His question went up to the CCS, and their answer—1 May 1944—came back in mid-May, after being discussed at the next interallied conference in Washington, D.C. (TRIDENT).

At the Washington conference, the basic Casablanca priorities were restated. Under "Basic Undertakings in Support of Overall Strategic Concept," there was listed, in conjunction with the use of the heavy bomber weapon in what was named the Combined Bomber Offensive, the resolution "that forces and equipment shall be established in the United Kingdom with the object of mounting an operation with a target date of 1 May 1944 to secure a lodgment on the Continent from which further offensive operations can be carried out."[41] This was far short of being an ironclad commitment to a cross-Channel assault. It was still just one available option of many, but it did allow Morgan to move forward.

The Combined Chiefs noted in their response to Morgan that his report was to be considered at the Quebec Conference (QUADRANT) in mid-August. Working backward from that date, the CCS would need to have the outline plan for both the cross-Channel assault and the "return to the Continent in case of German disintegration" by 1 August to allow time for them to consider the recommendations. Following from that, the due date to the British COS would be 15 July—Morgan reported to the Combined Chiefs who had authorized the staff, but through the British COS, his immediate superiors, who therefore had a right of first veto on any proposal.

While waiting for the official directive formally appointing him, Morgan knew he had the choice of either waiting for the paperwork to arrive or to "indulge in intense activity guided by common sense and one's personal predilections."[42] He chose the latter course. He found an unoccupied room in Norfolk House, which was a modern, purpose-built office building, and talked the management into assigning it to him. It happened to be the room where he first met Eisenhower. He also prevailed upon the various organizations located in Norfolk House to provide him with clerical help when needed. At this point his staff consisted of "Bobbie, my aide-de-camp; my motor driver, Corporal Bainbridge, whom together with his car I had frankly stolen from 1st Corps headquarters; and two batmen [personal orderlies]."[43] Morgan would readily confess to a weakness for the unconventional, and this new assignment was certainly beginning in a most unconventional way.

Morgan was summoned to a lunch at Chequers on 4 April so that Churchill could take the measure of the man. The prime minister showed his guests the film *Desert Victory* and insisted that this demonstrated the way to defeat the Germans. Morgan demurred, noting that while war in the African desert and war in northwest Europe may have things in common, there were also certain differences to be considered. Churchill let the comment pass and notified the War Office that Morgan "would do."

In his room at the Mount Royal Hotel one evening during this period, Morgan gave thought to his new situation as he took his bath. His new title was unwieldy; those with whom he was to work and to lead needed to be motivated and to sense that there was real change. This group would clearly need the creation of some esprit de corps. One element that would help would be a name that would unify the small band that was to be formed. It needed to have a martial sound yet needed to be vague enough that no one would be able to figure out what the job was by the name alone. His mid-bath inspiration was to title himself and his group COSSAC (Chief of Staff, Supreme Allied Commander). And so COSSAC he became.

—4—

TO PLAN THE RECONQUEST OF EUROPE

As Morgan surveyed his office in Norfolk House on the first day of his new assignment as COSSAC, he noted that he had taken possession of "a couple of desks and chairs . . . a few sheets of paper and a pencil that someone had dropped on the floor."[1] He was starting from zero, which, under the circumstances, at least meant a fresh start.

Morgan was an enthusiastic "Westerner" who believed that an early reentry into the Continent starting in northwest France was the proper strategic direction. He did not agree with the more opportunistic approach of senior British leaders. While he believed the principle of "flexibility" can have many advantages, "especially when one's resources are slender . . . [,] it is well to be flexible only if, [in the end] there is the firm intention to do something definite." He went on to say that he and some of his colleagues suspected that the "British authorities had at this time no real plan for the day when they would have to stop being flexible."[2] His approach made it easier to work with his American allies and to recruit like-minded officers from both the British Empire and the United States.

While he was temporarily reliant on the kindness of strangers for his clerical needs, he moved quickly to recruit the highest level of planners for the jobs at hand, trusting that they, in turn, would attract others with whom they had successfully served. Morgan had been in the Staff Duties Directorate in the War Office in 1936–37, so he knew or knew of most of the officers who might be both available and desirable for these positions. His long service in India would also be useful as fellow veterans of Indian service would make their mark. As he said, "When it came to creating the British Army portion of the COSSAC staff the War Office . . . [gave] me practically carte blanche, with the result that the British Army component was able to hit its stride in amazingly quick time."[3]

He did have a fight with Brooke to get Maj. Gen. Charles West for operations (whom Morgan knew well from their long service together in India), and it took some time to get Maj. Gen. Nevil Brownjohn, who took over supply and came over from Paget at Home Forces. Brig. Kenneth McLean, the senior British Army planner, was another old friend of Morgan's from India—he married the woman who had looked after Morgan's children there. All three played important roles in creating OVERLORD. West and McLean were both engineers and combat veterans. According to Ray Barker, West had a "keen analytical, engineering mind that could analyze a problem and get to the roots of it . . . [,] an ability to reduce it to fundamental terms at first. . . . McLean was a hard, pragmatic Scot," while West had a calmer temperament.[4] McLean was described by Morgan as someone who knew all the tricks of the trade and was a "weaver of plots beyond compare and, moreover, an expounder of same, who appeared in the next few months before crowned heads and chiefs of state, justifiably earning universal applause."[5] He had previously spent time on the Planning Staff in Whitehall and at Combined Operations Headquarters (COHQ).

Representatives from the other services of both nations, particularly the U.S. contingent, arrived more slowly and suffered from higher turnover rates for a variety of reasons. McLean noted that in the spring and summer, "the American Air Force and Navy came very little into the planning picture. They changed quite frequently and had little continuity in their work."[6] Barker agreed with this assessment, noting that the U.S. Army Air Forces sent over good men who didn't stay for very long. Of the U.S. Navy's representatives, Barker's evaluation was that they didn't send their best men.[7]

Morgan observed that while senior British officers were noticeably less enthusiastic about the project than their American counterparts, it was just

the opposite among the more junior officers. The British officers signed on
at once while some Americans didn't see the point in associating with what
looked like a predominantly British staff for a possible operation that could
become a dead end. Still, most of those who joined soon shared the enthusiasm
and sense of common purpose that comes from being part of a group that
must produce something of importance and is given not quite enough time
or resources to produce it.

General Brooke had discussed the organization of what was evolving into
the COSSAC staff with Gen. Frank M. Andrews, commanding general of
ETOUSA, on 26 March.[8] This in turn led to soon-to-be major general Barker
being designated as deputy chief of staff for COSSAC (or Deputy COSSAC,
as he was called), although for a while he also continued as the operations
officer at ETOUSA.

Barker and Morgan met for the first time at Norfolk House in early April. As
Barker explained, "As a natural thing the small group that I had been working
with on the planning for ROUNDUP—the 'ROUNDUP Planners' they called
us—we just re-designated ourselves and were absorbed into COSSAC. And a
group of Britishers moved in, and so the thing just flowed together without
any formal thing."[9]

The staff's initial formation clearly had a certain air of informality to it.
There were, of course, requests to British, British Empire, and American
authorities for staffing, but there was also a tone that suggested the unconventional approach that Morgan enjoyed. Perhaps it helped that COSSAC took
over Norfolk House, which is where many of the planners already worked.
Still, because so many plans conceived there were stillborn, all it took was a
mention that one worked at Norfolk House to evoke both pity and disregard
from one's audience. This was so noticeable that Morgan asked, unsuccessfully, if they could rename the building Suffolk House. This was not possible
because of the history attached to the site. The old Norfolk House, a most
palatial structure of the dukes of Norfolk and the birthplace of George III,
dated back to the mid-1700s. The original building had been demolished in
1939 and replaced by the modern office building.[10] Morgan took consolation
in the fact that it made security easier—no one would expect something as
dramatic as a cross-Channel assault to emanate from such a place. Security

was a particular concern as COSSAC was explicitly forbidden to have contact with the many allied governments-in-exile located in London, and the French headquarters was also on St. James's Square just a long block away from Norfolk House.[11]

Thanks to Morgan's friendship with Canadian general Andrew McNaughton, with whom he had served in World War I, COSSAC was able to gain meaningful support from a cadre of highly trained Canadian staff officers. South Africa was also well represented, as was Australia.

Morgan wanted his staff to be as small as possible—mirroring what he believed was the approach taken by Marshal Foch at the end of World War I—and to function more as a coordinating body, not duplicating efforts but taking advantage of the knowledge base that already existed. In this he was partially successful. Because COSSAC considered all aspects of a cross-Channel assault and the campaign that was to follow, the range and scope of issues to be addressed required that expertise be added to the staff, both formally and informally. There was no useful precedent for a multinational planning staff that was also intended to be the foundation of a coalition's operational headquarters for the major campaign being planned. As Barker noted, "We didn't start out with any table of organization. . . . There was no one to prescribe it for us. We had to develop it as we went along. . . . There was a certain amount of trial and error."[12]

Morgan was well aware of the inherent political challenges of being the chief of staff to an unnamed supreme commander and having to report to the CCS, but through the British COS. His life now changed from that "of a simple British soldier to that of the international half-world wherein there is no simplicity. It had been one thing to serve as a British commander under foreign orders. It was quite another to owe primary allegiance, as [he] now had to, to an allied committee."[13]

An early example of this allegiance was demonstrated when he received a memo from the British War Cabinet that sketched out an idea about applying "the whole united strength of Britain and the United States to the Mediterranean" and that asked Morgan to respond with the advantages of a northwestern European strategy compared with the Mediterranean. He understood that this represented just a late-night conjecture of the prime minister, but he was nonetheless obliged to answer. As COSSAC was an Allied staff, neither American nor British, he also felt obliged to share the memo with Barker, who in turn felt obliged to share the memo with ETOUSA. The net result, after everyone calmed down, was that it became clear that if "there should be anything that the British authorities deemed unnecessary for the American authorities to hear about, then they must not send it to COSSAC."[14]

To be fair, there was at least one occasion when Americans in Washington, talking over a secure line to compatriots in London, exhorted their colleagues: "Don't tell the British for God's sake." Which provoked laughter from the London end of the line as "every word had been keenly listened to by two British generals and one British admiral."[15] For Morgan, building trust among COSSAC's staff as well as a strong sense of unit identity were among the highest priorities. In today's parlance, it was clear from the very beginning that they "had each other's backs."

By the time of the first weekly staff meeting on 17 April, Morgan had gathered enough officers to fill in the top levels of the organization. It helped that he reduced the Combined Commanders' planning structure from twenty-nine sections down to four, plus an administrative section.[16]

COSSAC was initially formed with an operations planning branch, with army, navy, and air force sections; an intelligence branch; and a logistics (administration, in British Army usage) branch. Major General West was the operations branch head. There were American and British components to each section, each headed by a principal staff officer or deputy chief of staff. For the British Army, that was McLean. The three components of the planning branch (army, navy, air force) were also split into three sections: one for broad concepts, one for cover plans, and one for detailed tactical planning, each with about four officers. There was a parallel American structure. The exception was the intelligence section, which was headed by a British Army officer and provided reports and analyses to all the operations sections. In addition, a central secretariat was established that served all the branches as well as Morgan.[17]

This arrangement quickly proved unwieldy, and modifications occurred along the way. By November Barker, in consultation with Morgan, completed the reorganization into an operational staff with the structure completely integrated, the principal staff officer of each section being either British, American, or Canadian on merit, without regard to national identities. As Barker wrote at the time, "In contemplation of the transformation of this staff from a planning to an operational headquarters, any division along national lines should be abolished."[18]

Later, sections for civil affairs, press relations, and coordination with governments-in-exile (which was established after the Quebec conference) were created, among others. (On 6 June 1944 the Supreme Headquarters Allied Expeditionary Force [SHAEF], building on COSSAC's foundations, had expanded to include the following sections: G1, G2, G3, G4, G5 [civil affairs], psychological warfare division, public relations division, signals division, engineers division, adjutant general, medical division, air defense division, political officers as well as naval and air staffs and a European Allied contact section.[19])

In general, U.S. officers serving in all the sections and RAF officers seemed to rotate through more often than did British Army officers, with the Royal Navy having periods of stability. The shortest tour of duty was that of then rear admiral Sir Philip Vian, RN, who was present for the first COSSAC meeting and back in an operational command the next week, replacing a commander who died in an air accident. One of the most effective combat officers in the Royal Navy, Vian later became the Eastern Task Force Commander for OVERLORD.

He was replaced by John Hughes-Hallett, who retained command of a small amphibious assault force named Force J, located aboard HMS *Vectis*— the converted Royal Yacht Squadron facility on the Isle of Wight—while also being Admiral Little's representative at COSSAC. Morgan noted that Hughes-Hallett, among his other credits, was well known for his motorcycling achievements on the London to Portsmouth road. Barker considered him to be excellent, combat experienced, and "intensely practical."[20] McLean, the practical Scot, thought Hughes-Hallett to be "obstinate and determined. An exceedingly capable man who succeeded in getting everybody's back up."[21] Another writer with knowledge of combined operations described Hughes-Hallett as someone "whose respect for entrenched rank when it was wrong was not conspicuous."[22] The discussions between McLean and Hughes-Hallett must have been interesting. Hughes-Hallett stayed at COSSAC for the critical initial planning period, being replaced by Rear Adm. George Creasy, RN, in the fall of 1943.

Hughes-Hallett gave an evaluation of the naval planners he encountered in Norfolk House in April 1943: "There was no officer with the authority, or indeed the knowledge and experience, to make even a provisional decision on where the landings should be made or how they should be followed up. . . . They had become rather cynical and had ceased to believe in the reality of their work."[23] This cynicism could be found among many of the COSSAC planners as they started working with their new commander.

It was this serious morale problem that Morgan addressed head on in his first address to COSSAC staff in mid-April. He gathered everyone, including the cooks, on the ground floor of Norfolk House to let them know what was going on.

Until recently, of course, the initiative remained in the enemy's hands. I think that we can now say that recently the initiative passed to us, although it must be confessed that hitherto there have not been many signs of our knowing exactly what to do with it now that we have it. . . .

About a year ago it became possible to regard the invasion of Europe as a practical proposition, and attempts were made to define the problem in terms that really meant something. These were not entirely successful, and then, while they were still under discussion, came a sudden change of policy that brought about the campaign in North Africa that is now drawing to a successful conclusion in its first phase.

. . . I need not go into too much detail with regard to the many vicissitudes that have overtaken this planning. A large number of very able people have done an immense amount of work and have at least produced what is going to be very useful to us, an immense amount of invaluable data bearing on the job in hand. They have produced no plan worthy of the name, but that, I should like you to understand clearly, was no fault of theirs; it was simply because they lacked direction from above.

. . . I want to make clear that, although the primary object of COSSAC is to make plans, I am certain that it is wrong to refer to it in any way as a "planning staff." The term "planning staff" has come to have a most sinister meaning—it implies the production of nothing but paper. That (which) we must contrive to do somehow is to produce not only paper; but ACTION![24]

Morgan then reemphasized that they were not a planning staff but the beginnings of an operational staff serving as the vanguard for a powerful army being gathered in the United States, which would join with British, Canadian, and American forces already in Britain. Their mission was not to plan another raid or just to cross the Channel. His job was "to plan nothing less than the re-conquest of Europe."[25]

He accepted that the planners were frustrated, but time was short, the work would be hard, the expected standards of performance were high, and he was depending on them. He made it clear that while the initial challenge was to get across the Channel, their goal was Berlin. As a reminder of the full scope of the effort facing them, Morgan announced that the map in his office would not be the routine view of the English coast facing northern France but one that featured San Francisco to the west and Berlin to the east.[26] He finished his remarks by showing everyone a draft organizational outline so each person could see where they fit in; he let them know that regarding both the plans and Morgan's obligation to keep his superiors informed as to the progress of their work, "I rely entirely upon you."[27]

Morgan knew that while organizational charts were necessary, "the more highly coloured the better, for purposes of academic argument and for bulldozing the personnel-supply authorities, it is the chaps not the charts that get the job done."[28] He worked hard to motivate "the chaps" and the women who joined COSSAC. Molding this disparate group into an effective, motivated team, and quickly weeding out those who couldn't work in a multinational environment was one of his great accomplishments.

Morgan, Barker, and the senior officers worked six and half days a week, with Morgan sometimes sleeping next to his desk. As one might expect under the circumstances, there was no "routine" day for them. As Barker described it, they "free lanced." They met each morning to share information. Barker might go to one of the British ministries or to ETOUSA, and Morgan might head for a meeting at the War Office or at COHQ. Both were well known at many of the ministries by this time, with Barker on a first-name basis with many British civilian and military officials. The schedule for one week of Morgan's meetings in June shows him visiting HMS *Vectis* and Force J at Cowes for an inspection of a new landing craft, the LCI(S), and then meeting Admiral Little in Portsmouth; a visit to Gen. Ira Eaker, Eighth U.S. Air Force; meeting Lt. Gen. W. D. Morgan of General Headquarters Home Forces to discuss the relationship between COSSAC and Home Forces; meeting with Gen. Sir Ronald Adam, adjutant general, who told Morgan that it had been proposed to transfer four U.S. and three British divisions from the Mediterranean back to England for OVERLORD, adding veteran units for the assault; an interview with Sir Percy James Gregg, the secretary of state for war, to discuss civil affairs; a visit to the Civil Affairs School in Putney; an interview with the head of the French department of the Foreign Office; and a visit to Fighter Command headquarters to hear General Montgomery and Air Marshal Sir Harry Broadhurst speak about air-ground cooperation in North Africa.[29] Some weeks were busier.

They also spent a great deal of time working with the planners "on the next lower level, giving them our ideas, checking on what they were doing."[30] They worked late into the night, either working on a specific problem, on sets of figures produced by the planners, or "just having a bull session on how things seemed to be going—trying to size up the situation."[31]

Out of many of those late-night conversations would come questions about the feasibility of a project or issue. Morgan and Barker would gather the people concerned and get their views. Then Morgan or one of the planners would draft a paper on the subject, which would be circulated for comments to the appropriate sections. As Barker said, "It was quite informal." Even though Morgan and Barker were both experienced staff officers, they were still trying to find the most effective ways of making the machine work—which, they discovered, came from consultation, mutual respect, and a shared sense of purpose.

There was barely enough time to accomplish their three assignments: the feint attack across the Channel, the plan to cope with German collapse, and the cross-Channel assault. The reentry into the Continent in either guise was going to occur sometime in the first six months of 1944. The plans for both those operations were subject to evaluation and approval in slightly less than three months. In less than five months COSSAC also had to plan, organize, and execute the feint toward the Pas-de-Calais. The operation needed to be large enough so the Germans would feel compelled to respond and the German air force could be engaged and damaged, notwithstanding the fact that there were now fewer amphibious resources based in England than there were for the Dieppe Raid.

The feint was named Operation STARKY, which was part of a larger deception effort called COCKADE. The COS hoped that COCKADE would hold the German forces in northern France in place, preventing the reinforcement of the troops that would be facing the Allied invasion of Italy. The quick reentry across the Channel with whatever forces were on hand in case of German collapse was code-named RANKIN. The outline plan for the reconquest of Europe was initially called Operation RUDGE, but from 5 June 1943, when the report from the Washington conference (TRIDENT) reached COSSAC, they knew it as OVERLORD.

Morgan decided to take an approach that was the opposite of what had been attempted before. Earlier plans started by trying to estimate what it would take to conduct a successful landing against opposition, with SKYSCRAPER being the clearest and most detailed example of that method. After coming up with a plan, the planners would then be told resources on that scale were not available and their estimates of German opposition were off the mark. Consequently, the plan would be shelved. Morgan took the other approach: he demanded to know a specific force level up front as well as the intended date of its use. He then considered whether the assigned mission could be accomplished with that force and how it could best be employed. This way COSSAC arrived at a practical plan.

In addition to all this, the "shop" had to be established. All the daily details of a functional office needed to be organized. This led to at least one relatively lighthearted adventure amid the pressure to produce the plans that could change the course of the war in Europe. Space was at a premium in London. The COSSAC team was scattered in billets all over the city. The normal work-week was five and half days—more for Morgan and Barker. Additionally, the

British and Americans had different work habits. The Americans preferred a workday that started at 9 a.m. and ended at 5 p.m. The British would start at 10 a.m. and quit at 6 p.m. Rather than dictate a start and end time, Morgan allowed the Americans to keep to their schedule and the British to theirs.

For Morgan it was not about "control"; it was about motivating a remarkably diverse group to work together to produce a workable, "sellable" plan against the odds. One thing that would greatly help this process and that was clearly needed was a secure place for COSSAC personnel to relax and associate in their off-duty moments. Perhaps inspired by the successful mess that COHQ was running, Morgan decided he would create an eating-and-drinking establishment within Norfolk House.

Having found the funds to make the necessary changes to the top floor of Norfolk House (being joint and combined had the advantage of being able to call on almost every U.S. and British command for funding), Morgan then set about looking for the kitchen and dining equipment necessary for the task. "A high official of the Office of Works [and Buildings], a department not usually notable for its charitable outlook[,] . . . was apprised of our proposal. 'Your proposal,' said he, 'is the most outrageous I have ever heard and appears . . . to involve total disregard of all our most cherished regulations. So, let's do it. Incidentally, somebody will have to pay for it one day . . . with any luck it won't be you or me.'"[32] Not only were refrigerators, stoves, tables, chairs and the other requirements of an eating establishment procured but also a complete cocktail bar previously housed at Selfridge's Department Store.

Morgan's luck held in terms of catering staff as well. There was an official of one of the many newly created government agencies who lived with his wife in a small flat in Norfolk House. Her great passion was catering, and she had friends who shared her passion. There were members of the COSSAC staff whose civilian professions had given them the necessary knowledge to draw up contracts covering this sort of activity, "even when the contravention of countless government regulations was involved."[33] Consequently, the kitchen was fully staffed almost at once.

While the difference in work hours did much to prevent overcrowding at mealtimes, the difference in ration sizes and in food preferences created challenges. "Luckily the management of our club seemed to be effectively in touch with unauthorized sources of supply. We took scrupulous care not to investigate this."[34] Thus the COSSAC Club was born, contributing greatly to the morale of everyone in the organization.[35] While waiting on the answers to the questions regarding the timing of the assault and size of force for OVERLORD, the staff began work on the September feint. This introduced them into the world of deception planning, and while the particular operation that was mounted achieved little by itself, it helped lay the foundation for later successes.

STARKY was the one element of COCKADE that required substantial resources. The other two schemes were notional, using agents and wireless traffic but not requiring assets such as real units or ships. One (TINDALL) was pointed in the direction of Norway from bases in Scotland with British forces, and the other (WADHAM) was supposed to suggest a threat to Brittany and the port of Brest by U.S. forces.

COCKCADE was an attempt at deception and as such required Morgan to work with Col. John Bevan, head of the London Controlling Section, which coordinated all Allied deception efforts in Europe. Bevan and Morgan established a deception planning group within COSSAC with Maj. Roger Hesketh serving as link between COSSAC and the London Controlling Section. Hesketh, an Oxford-educated barrister and amateur architect, served in intelligence throughout the war and wrote an excellent postwar account of the FORTITUDE deception campaign that remained classified until the 1980s and was not published until 1999.[36]

Deceiving the enemy is a bit of a black art, and Morgan needed to learn at least some of it for STARKY. As he discovered, the goal is not to make your enemy *think* something: it is to make your enemy *do* something specific that will help your plans. The more one understands the enemy's worldview, beliefs, preconceptions, and strategic concerns, the more likely it is that the actions you persuade the enemy to take will be desirable ones. The enemy may or may not "actually believe in the false state of affairs that you want to project. It is enough if you can make him so concerned [about the possibility] that he feels that he must provide for it."[37]

The deceiver also has to choose which channels of information that lead to the enemy's decision makers he or she is going to use. They must be channels that the enemy has established and trusts, that can be manipulated by the deceiver and can be monitored to measure success. As we will see, STARKY did not contribute to the Germans' belief in an immediate Allied attack across the Channel, nor did it fully use the best communications channels for selling the story to the Germans.

Morgan's outline plan for STARKY was finished within a week or so of his formal appointment with help from Bevan and the London Controlling Section. It was submitted to the COS on 3 June and approved on 23 June.

This was the first, but not last, instance of Morgan encountering the fundamental problem of his assignment. He was the chief of staff to a supreme commander who did not exist and for operations whose plans were not yet approved. As such, he had authority to plan; his command encompassed Norfolk House. He could not issue orders to combat units or operational commands—often commanded by officers senior to him. Additionally, the British Army at the time did not generally recognize the use of "by direction" authority in the same way as did the U.S. Army. In the U.S. military, a commander could delegate certain responsibilities to subordinate officers—the issuing of routine orders, for example. Additionally, the commander's chief of staff could, on many occasions, act in the name of the commander, serve as an ambassador or envoy to other senior commanders or political decision makers, and issue orders in the commander's absence. This is "by direction" authority, as the orders are signed by the subordinate with the notation "by direction." In 1943 the British Army had no equivalent process; commanders issued orders, and staff officers did not.

Morgan could cajole, request, suggest, and plead, but he couldn't order. Neither Bomber Command nor the Eighth Air Force diverted squadrons from their missions over Germany for STARKY—although some training missions were flown over France. The Royal Navy declined to provide two old battleships for shore bombardment purposes—their response to Morgan's request was described as an "explosion that shattered the cloistral calm of the Chiefs of Staff committee room."[38] Courtesy of Combined Operations, there were eight small commando raids carried out on the Channel coast in July and August, out of fourteen planned, that were intended to suggest that information of the sort needed just before an invasion was being sought.[39]

"D-day" for STARKY included a major British Army exercise, HARLEQUIN, centering on an embarkation rehearsal and using troops from the British XII Corps and Canadian I Corps, a total of four divisions.[40] Morgan ordered that the troops be told that they were participating in an exercise, not the invasion. This drew strong protests from those responsible for propaganda directed at the Germans. They argued that telling troops the truth undermined efforts to persuade the Germans that an invasion might be imminent. Morgan "stood firm by his policy of telling the truth to the troops."[41]

More than eighty squadrons of Fighter Command and Eighth Air Force fighters were assembled for the anticipated air battle. "The civilian economy of southeastern England was disrupted by pulling together the genuine light shipping needed," real landing craft being in short supply. The necessary security measures restricting the movement of civilians and shifting troop locations were put in place for parts of the South of England starting in August.[42]

Wednesday, 8 September 1943, was fine and fair. The troops for the operation gathered in their assembly points and were marched to the embarkation sites, where they were promptly turned around and marched back, as there were not enough assault ships or craft available for the trip across the Channel. The fifty-ship convoy that had been collected, commanded by Hughes-Hallett, formed up and headed toward Boulogne, mine sweepers in front. Squadrons of fighter aircraft roared overhead looking for the enemy. At the appropriate moment everyone turned around and headed back to England. It all worked perfectly. In short, everyone did their job . . . except the Germans, who were nowhere to be found and who apparently barely noticed the effort. What the Germans had noticed was what Field Marshal Gerd von Rundstedt's staff called "somewhat too obvious preparations for attacking the Channel front, which are at the same time conspicuously slow in reaching completion."[43] The fact that the little convoy was sailing at the same time as a series of landings in Italy were occurring, culminating with the amphibious assault at Salerno the next day, meant the Germans were paying much more attention to the Mediterranean.

If the goals of the operation were to create an air battle over the Channel and to hold German divisions in northern France, it must be ranked a failure. The other two components of COCKADE (TINDALL and WADHAM) achieved even less. It seems fair to conclude that the Germans had seen enough of these demonstrations to not be deceived by another convoy sailing in broad daylight in the general direction of the French coast without any of the preliminary "softening-up" attacks by air and naval forces. Additionally, as Hesketh pointed out, on 6 June 1944 the German air force was not committed to the battle until after the first landing had occurred.[44]

Rundstedt, the German commander in chief in the West, expressed concern about the preparations going on in England in general and viewed STARKY as a very real rehearsal for invasion. However, the German High Command recognized that "the *Schwerpunkt* [main effort or primary focus] of the enemy attack on the mainland of Europe lies in the Mediterranean and in all probability will remain there."[45] It pulled out ten of Rundstedt's divisions between May and October. It wasn't until 3 November that the highest levels of German command changed their mind with the issuing of Fuehrer Directive 51, which attempted to shift the emphasis for defense to the Western Front.

Furthermore, using the Pas-de-Calais as the target for a deception effort at the same time it was being presented as the intended site of the invasion was problematic. As Hesketh points out, "To conduct and publicise a large-scale exercise against an objective that one really intended to attack during the following year would hardly suggest a convincing grasp of the principle of surprise."[46] There were, however, many benefits and lessons that accrued to operations in 1944, some of which did not directly affect COSSAC, as a result of STARKY.

The first was Barker's introduction to Morgan of the offices and work of Sir Samuel Findlater Stewart, chair of the Home Defence Executive, located in the attic of Norfolk House and hitherto unknown to COSSAC.[47] Born in Largs, Scotland, he had joined the India Office in 1903 and spent the majority of his career there. He had been the permanent undersecretary of state for India from 1930 to 1940. In 1939 he was transferred on a temporary basis to become the director general for the Ministry of Information and in 1940 left the India Office to be the chair of the Home Defence Executive. It was in this capacity that he "became involved in the work of Britain's intelligence agencies. In 1941, he was invited to join the Twenty (or XX) Committee, supervising British wartime deception policy."[48]

Stewart also chaired a committee under the COS, called the BOLERO Combined Committee, on which served representatives of ETOUSA, including Barker; Commander-in-Chief, Home Forces; Minister of War Transport; Minister of Home Security; and Combined Operations, among others. Sub-committees had representation from the Ministry of Production, Ministry of Supply, the Railway Executive Committee, the War Office Director of Movements, and other agencies.[49]

Stewart had an unrivaled understanding of how Whitehall worked and was "apparently intimately acquainted with every individual in British Government employ and, with the aid of an absurdly small staff, able to adjust any matter needing coordination of any kind, however vast and complicated."[50] Sir Findlater provided immeasurable support to OVERLORD throughout 1943 and 1944, notably by chairing an ad hoc committee on the security arrangements for the invasion.[51]

For the actual invasion, under Stewart's direction, a secure area was created around the coast from Hull in the east to Penzance, plus the areas of Milford Haven in Wales and Portishead in the Severn estuary, near Bristol, as well as the estuaries of the Forth, Tay, and Clyde Rivers. This resulted in some 600,000 people being prevented from visiting the coast each month. In some places, this ban was kept in effect through August 1944.[52]

In July of 1944 Stewart became responsible for deception operations against the Germans relating to the threat of the V-1, creating the impression that the bombs were overshooting their targets. He also chaired a committee that attempted to resolve disputes between the Secret Intelligence Service and Special Operations Executive. In 1945 he was asked to examine and make recommendations regarding the postwar assignments and structure of the Security Service.[53]

Another lesson was that the value of the British Double-Cross System of agents run by the Twenty Committee was underscored. In particular, agent Tricycle was able to send a great deal of information about troop movements and other details gleaned from his notional network of agents in Britain during the STARKY period, elevating his status with his German handlers and relieving them of some anxiety about his qualities as an agent. Agent Garbo was also incredibly busy, sending reports from his fictitious agents and burnishing his reputation with German intelligence. Other Double-Cross agents were put into play as well, all helping build up the picture that London Controlling Station wanted Berlin to see. The creation of two fictitious armies in Britain for Double-Cross agents to discover and report on as part of the operation also paid dividends in 1944 as part of the FORTITUDE deception campaign, which was largely dependent on controlled agents' reports.

An additional benefit to the Twenty Committee was the realization that extensive use of double agents for deception required a procedure that would ensure there was a standard method of handling the traffic that was produced. Each "story" that was created was broken down into a set of "serials." Each "serial" then had an alternate story for the Germans along with a date on which it was to be provided to the enemy along with the real and notional evidence that would support the story. The evidence would then be "assigned" to the notional subagents that the Double-Cross agent was running, depending on their profile and location. This was used with particular success in the handling of agent Garbo.[54]

Morgan had specifically identified the attainment of air supremacy as a prerequisite for the invasion. STARKY showed that feints and demonstrations in the Channel were not going to lure German day fighters into battle, and the British stopped trying. As a consequence, in COSSAC's outline plan, emphasis was placed on the Combined Bomber Offensive's potential to engage and destroy German fighters in large numbers. The task fell largely to the Eighth Air Force, whose daylight raids certainly attracted fighters. It also became necessary to solve the problem of long-range fighter escort for the bombers (which came from British-suggested modifications to the P-51 Mustang and adding increasingly larger drop tanks to Allied fighters). By the spring of 1944 the Allies controlled the skies over northwest Europe.

COSSAC also learned a valuable lesson in press relations. They had failed to properly inform reporters, and, consequently, a range of stories about the operation were written. Morgan noted after the fact that "we had to content ourselves with a very lame communique to the effect that an enjoyable time had been had by all and many useful lessons had been learnt."[55] COSSAC and later SHAEF learned how to organize positive relations with the press, get their story out, and gain the trust of the reporters.

The second part of this press relations lesson was that whenever cover stories were put out in London or Washington, a sensitive awareness of the emotions, morale, and planned actions of the various resistance groups in occupied countries had to be maintained. Later, when COSSAC was able to communicate to the partisan groups, it was made clear to them that accurate information would only come from one source, and it wouldn't be the daily newspapers.

The most important lesson from STARKY was the realization that the Allies needed to reconsider how best to deceive the Germans about Allied intentions and what channels of communication to manipulate. Bevan, Morgan, and the planners realized that they had to find a solution to the problem of "how do we work out a deception plan using the idea of a cross-Channel assault on one part of the French coast when our actual plan is—a cross-Channel assault against another part of the French coast?" They abandoned the concept of raids and demonstrations designed to distract and confuse the defenders in favor of the expanded use of the Double-Cross network of double agents to exaggerate the size of the assault, positioning forces so as to appear to threaten as many targets as possible, using visual misdirection (as opposed to camouflage), phantom formations and other measures, such as dummy radio traffic, designed to "induce the enemy to make faulty strategic dispositions in relation to operations by the United Nations against Germany."[56] Their deception planning also included a timing component, trying to create an environment where the Germans would be caught off guard by the assault.

As we'll see in chapter 11, COSSAC continued to work on the invasion's deception plan, particularly from the period of September 1943 onward. That plan ultimately became the famously titled BODYGUARD (which included FORTITUDE North and FORTITUDE South), approved on 23 January 1944. Unlike STARKY, BODYGUARD was, in the words of British historian Sir Michael Howard, "perhaps the most complex and successful deception operation in the entire history of war."[57]

——5——

THE INDIAN ARMY AND
CHASING PANCHO VILLA

The oldest of nine children, Frederick Morgan didn't come from a family with a military background. There were none of the evocative scenes of the ancestral country estate filled with generations of military glory as portrayed in films like the Korda brothers' 1939 version of *The Four Feathers*. Morgan's father came from a succession of timber merchants—importers of soft woods from Russia and North America. As a result of World War I and the Russian Revolution, the business disappeared—leaving his father to "the management of the dwindling family estate . . . [which] in turn also became a casualty of the First World War. Whereafter the family migrated to Chichester."[1] Consequently, Morgan, who relied on his military pay to live, was keenly aware of the ebb and flow of his finances.

He was not a graduate of Sandhurst, as was Churchill, but of Woolwich, where Royal Engineers and Royal Artillery officers are trained. While he did not gain a placement that would have led to service with the engineers, he did well enough to enter the "real gentlemen's life in the Royal Field Artillery." Morgan quoted the Duke of Wellington in this regard. "The Horse Artillery would be the finest cavalry in the world if it weren't for their bloody guns."[2] In July of 1913 nineteen-year-old Second Lieutenant Morgan joined his first unit, stationed at Aldershot, on Salisbury Plain. He had barely settled in when he was sent out for more training in the emerging art of firing artillery accurately at targets beyond visual range—which seemed "pretty far-fetched" at the time. While on the course at the Royal Garrison Artillery installation at Shoeburyness, Morgan encountered gin for the first time. One day, after a particularly gin-flavored lunch, there came a call for volunteers for service in India. "Put me down for India said the gin, speaking through my lips. And so began . . . an experience that lasted over twenty years."[3]

On the sea voyage to the subcontinent he met a woman also on her way to India. Her father, from an Anglo-Irish family, was a doctor in the Army Medical Service and had spent his career in India. Just over three years later Morgan and Marjorie Whaite were married. They had two daughters and then a son.

The unit he joined in early 1914 was one of those old-school batteries of field artillery, "living in a constant state of readiness for whatever may befall." The young lieutenant felt quite incapable and at a loss as to what to do. "It was, as ever, the soldiers who made it possible. They were typically kind to this young whipper-snapper . . . with some six months of not very helpful service behind him."[4] He had only a few months to settle in. With the start of what became known as the Great War of 1914–18, his unit and much of the Indian Army was sent to fight in France, leaving India in mid-October and arriving at Marseilles a month later.

Morgan admitted that this first, brief experience of India did not expose him to any profound observations or deeper understanding of India or the Indian people. He was focused on mastering the details of the center section of 84th Battery, Royal Field Artillery. He was happy to later unlearn "most of what I had learnt about India and Indians . . . for in some odd way, in spite of it all . . . somewhere inside the East registered its call."[5] He was a product of his time and saw India as part of the empire, but he was observant and thoughtful enough to recognize that the presence of the British was possibly a mixed blessing for those whose country it was.

Morgan's unit joined the Lahore Division in France, and he spent the war on the Western Front. He participated in most of the major battles, including the Somme and Passchendaele, and was mentioned in dispatches twice. He had the full experience of being a junior officer in that great industrial conflict.[6] It was at the Second Battle of Ypres in 1915 that he had his first experience in international military relations, being picked by his commanding officer to contact the French troops on their flank, upon whom the British would have to rely if the Germans renewed their attack. He stayed with the French unit for a few days. Once the danger had passed, he returned to his battery and was almost immediately wounded and concussed by a German shell. Upon his return from the hospital, Morgan had the good fortune to be made aide-de-camp to the commander of Divisional Artillery, Brig. Gen. Edward Spencer Hoare Nairne. For the rest of the war he served as a staff officer, ending the war as brigade major of Divisional Artillery, in which position he was the principal staff officer at the Divisional Artillery's headquarters.[7]

When the Indian Divisions were deployed from France to the Middle East in December 1915, the artillery of the Lahore Division remained behind and was attached in turn to various infantry divisions as they formed up, giving the inexperienced divisions the advantage of having veteran artillery, without which they would not have been ready to enter that desperate struggle on the Western Front. They served with the 2nd and 3rd Canadian Divisions, the 4th Australian Division, then the 4th Canadian Division for the capture of Vimy Ridge (along with Alan Brooke, who was a senior artillery officer in the Canadian Corps), and finally the 42nd East Lancashire Division.[8] It was with the last unit that Morgan experienced firsthand the kind of inspirational leadership that had a direct impact on him. There were other fine officers that Morgan encountered, but Micky Walshe, the 42nd's general of Divisional Artillery, was in a class by himself for Morgan.

Walshe, "the archetype of fighting Irishman," would today be called a true warrior. If he had a weakness, it was, "from the point of view of his staff, that he would not go and be recklessly foolhardy by himself. We were honoured in rotation with invitations to accompany him on his expeditions which rarely bore any relation to the operation of his artillery."[9] Morgan later claimed that it was only Walshe's inspired and passionate leadership that gave him the impetus to overcome his hesitancy and the lack of self-confidence he had felt all too often for most of his service life up to then.

Now twenty-four, Morgan ended the war by surviving the Spanish flu epidemic. While recovering near Charleroi, Belgium, and watching the division slowly disband after the Treaty of Versailles was signed, he was not certain what he should do. He was unconvinced that a military career was the right direction for him but knew nothing of the civilian business world. He had married the year before, when in England on seven days leave after Ypres, with Marjorie having gone home to family in the United Kingdom with the advent of war.

At first he thought going back to England was the solution. "Then, out of a dark and dismal winter sky, came the brilliant solution to all my troubles. The call came for volunteers for service in India. . . . Anyone who would volunteer for a normal tour of six years in India would be eligible for two months leave in England. . . . No price was too high to pay for such a boon after all that had gone before."[10]

He served in India until 1935, with just a brief period back in what he called "the Home Establishment" in Great Britain. It was in India that Morgan encountered the experiences and remarkable personalities that shaped his approach to his profession. He returned to India after the Amritsar massacre but served in the same area, albeit nearer what is now Islamabad, about 280 kilometers farther north.[11]

This next phase of his career began with assignment to a brigade of field artillery in England that was reforming from a cadre left over from the war into a full-strength unit to be stationed in what was then northern India. Now a captain, he served as the adjutant for three years. Here he experienced firsthand what it took to take a mob of unwilling soldiers and turn them into a fully equipped, well-trained, motivated, combat-ready unit. He credited his commanding officer, who was "never ruffled, never hustled, always with something in reserve," and who had the ability to reduce complex problems to simple terms so that a solution could be found. It was through his leadership that Morgan and the others were able to "rekindle the sacred flame of disciplined endeavour that has carried the British Army undefeated through centuries of mismanagement and disaster."[12]

From there he moved to a base at what was then Campbellpore (now Attock, Pakistan, about seventy-eight kilometers from Peshawar), where he was placed in command of Indian troops. There, in addition to learning how to lead men from a different culture and often in a different language, he began to have what he later described as a nagging doubt as to "the infallibility of the British overlords, the 'heaven-borne' who ruled India."[13] In that area, hard by the North-West Frontier Province, keeping order was more akin to the small wars of peace on a daily basis than anything else.

In 1924 he was transferred to the staff of the 1st Indian Division, whose commander was also in command of the Rawalpindi District, in the Punjab, through which ran the main road to the Khyber Pass. The commander, Maj. Gen. Sir Herbert Uniacke, was another major influence on Morgan. Uniacke, a field artillery officer considered a progressive and modernizer, spent four years on the Western Front in World War I and was senior artillery officer for the British 5th Army for two of those years, developing innovative methods of employing artillery.[14] He was a most unconventional character, of a type that seems sometimes to flourish in places far removed from strictures of the "home office." It can be said that he did not suffer fools, however senior to himself, gladly or otherwise. In his memoirs, Morgan observed, "In today's drab world of sadly bureaucratized uniformity, he would not have lasted five minutes in any position of authority."[15]

Perhaps because he was a highly competent professional, high on General Uniacke's list was the care of the troops under his command. One project that was important to him in this regard was the creation of a recreational facility in the Himalayan foothills for the enlisted men under his command, where they could get relief from the brutal summer heat. There was no chance of government funding, of course. So, the general drafted Morgan into his scheme of the "Order of the Golden Oriole," with a goal of raising the £25,000 needed. Approaching the local merchants, professional classes, and minor potentates of the area, the general and his accomplice offered each the opportunity to join the Order at one of three levels of membership. In exchange for their generous donation, they would receive a signed parchment scroll, highly decorated in impressive colors and suitable for framing, presented with a flourish and a handshake. In this way the enlisted men's club was built in short order.

There was one footnote. For the ceremony marking the laying of the cornerstone, it was unclear until the last moment which high official would be present. So, on one side of the stone it noted that the honor was done by Field Marshal Sir William Birdwood, Commander-in-Chief, India; on the other side, the name of Gen. Sir Claud Jacob, commander of the Northern Army was inscribed. Morgan's job at the ceremony was to cover the side of the stone that was not needed.[16] The campaign was both unconventional and effective.

From the 1st Indian Division, the now thirty-one-year-old Morgan went on to the staff of General Jacob, where for the first time he was able to see the point of view of a theater commander, particularly a commander who had the North-West Frontier as part of his area of operations. While attached to Northern Command in 1925, Morgan was given the task of organizing the annual training maneuvers—that year they were to be the largest maneuvers since the end of World War I. Morgan chose the Attock Fort, near Campbellpore for the exercise's center. Working with a young captain of the 6th Royal Gurkha Rifles stationed at the fort named William Slim (later, Field Marshal William Viscount Slim[17]), the exercise went like clockwork. Field Marshal Birdwood told Morgan that he would be delighted to nominate him to the Staff College at Quetta, if Morgan could pass the entrance exam.

Although overdue for his posting back to the United Kingdom, Morgan stayed long enough to complete the exams (his last chance to pass before he became overage to apply and having already failed the test once). Before the results were published, Captain Morgan boarded ship for England. He arrived amid the general strike of May 1926. Adding to the disorientation was the fact that he suffered the fate of many people who have lived for years in "foreign" environments. Upon the return to one's home country, things aren't quite like one remembers, and there is a sense of displacement. This was made all the more difficult for Morgan because the last memory he had was of prewar England and seen through a teenager's eyes. Plus, "the army of 1926 in England . . . was hardly comparable with the tough, trained troops I had just left in India."[18]

Shortly after being assigned as commander of an artillery battery near Portsmouth, he received word that he had passed the exam "by an extremely narrow margin" and was eligible for nomination—with one problem: those officers who Morgan knew and who were willing to nominate him were all in India. This meant they could nominate him to Quetta but not to Camberley, conveniently located in Surrey, England. While his colleagues in the Northern Army were willing to help, the War Office, predictably, was less accommodating.

The War Office gave Morgan the choice of either going back to India for only the two-year course—in which case he would have to pay his own way out and back (as well as that of his family, if he chose to take them along)—or he could agree to another six years in India and travel at government expense. It took perhaps seconds for him to decide. Money was absolutely a major consideration. "There were days of the month when I didn't own the price of a tram ticket, let alone a passage to India."[19] He had sold some of his possessions, including an old fowling piece, to raise the cash to get back to England. Staff College was the ticket to a career, India was preferable to England for both him and his wife, and so the decision was easily reached.

The next two years at Quetta were more than a step on the ladder up. "They constituted a period of gestation toward rebirth into an altogether new existence."[20] In the words of Field Marshal Claude Auchinleck, "Quetta in those days was ahead of Camberley in the practical nature of its teaching, the greater realism of its exercises and its generally liberal and forward outlook."[21] When Morgan arrived in 1927, the lessons of World War I had been incorporated into the curriculum and, as he said, it was possible to look back on his past fourteen years of experience with a different, more constructive viewpoint. The two-year course ended with a student-and-staff exercise planning and executing (on paper) an attack by the Japanese on Singapore, with the students in the role of the Imperial Japanese Army. The rules of the exercise, of course, made it highly unlikely that the "Japanese" would succeed. For the outcome to demonstrate anything other than British superiority would have been inconvenient in the extreme. In the interwar years, Quetta and Camberley combined to produce about fifty trained staff officers per year. One major criticism of the curriculum at both staff colleges was that the courses placed too much emphasis on strategy and not enough on learning operational techniques.[22]

Quetta still serves as the Command and Staff College for Pakistan's army. Pug Ismay had been a student there five years earlier. In Morgan's class was his colleague from Attock, William Slim. John Crocker, who had risen from the ranks during World War I and later succeeded Morgan as commander of 1st Corps in 1943, was in the class as well. He made significant contributions to the development of the OVERLORD plan and led 1st Corps in northwest

Europe with distinction. There was also Kenneth Anderson, later commander of the British First Army in Tunisia as part of TORCH.[23] Morgan would have likely encountered and possibly worked with Anderson while making plans for his 125 Force. Bernard Paget was the chief instructor there in the 1930s, and Bernard Montgomery was an instructor at about the same time.

After Staff College Morgan returned to the field artillery for just over a year. He was concerned that he had not been immediately selected for a staff position, but he was finally sent for on a temporary basis to be staff officer to the major general of Royal Artillery, the senior artillery officer in India. Upon arrival Morgan discovered the general and his permanent staff officer were set to go on a trip for three weeks. Morgan asked if the general had any orders, or at least a suggestion as to what to do. The response: "My boy . . . there are serving in India some six hundred officers and twenty thousand men of the Royal Artillery. Until I get back in three weeks' time you can do what you bloody well like with all of them. Goodbye. Have fun!"[24] Captain Morgan was thus introduced to the concept of command on behalf of an absent commander and of being in a position of authority beyond what would be justified by his rank.

His first permanent posting was as the Royal Artillery staff officer at the headquarters of Western Command, back at Quetta. There he came under the considerable influence of Lt. Gen. Sir Henry Karslake, the senior artillery officer there. During World War I Karslake served on the Western Front and became known as an outstanding trainer of troops—he brought several divisions up to necessary levels of readiness. "Being the man he was he had exploited to the full the value of personal example and had himself 'gone over the top' with the leading waves of riflemen. His accounts of the mechanics of the business, his dissertations on 'the anatomy of Courage' . . . were beyond price."[25] Karslake was promoted to be major general of the Royal Artillery and took Morgan with him. Morgan served as staff officer there for his last three years in India. After nineteen years of service and at the age of thirty-eight, he was promoted to major in 1932, and eighteen months later he received a brevet promotion to lieutenant colonel.

At that point he had served for almost sixteen years in India and four on the Western Front during the war. Morgan was ready to move on, and he knew that to continue his career he was obliged to "make a determined effort to cope with the business of peacetime soldiering in England."[26] So in 1935 he returned to England, noting that, with the rise of Hitler, the chances of a major war were likely to increase.

Knowing that air war was adding a new dimension to the battlefield and that it was an area where doctrine and weapons were still being worked out, Morgan sought out and was given command of an antiaircraft battery stationed at Portsmouth. Here he came face to face with all the limitations and deficiencies of the British Army circa 1935. These deficiencies were the result of many factors. As a result of substantially reduced spending since 1919 following Churchill's "Ten Year Rule," the specialized armaments industry in Britain was reduced "to a skeleton by 1933."[27] An officer serving in the British Army had written in 1928, "As regards disarmament for the British Army, the problem is simplified in that the Army is so really small, and is maintained so obviously for non-aggressive duties, that no step that can seriously reduce its power is conceivable."[28]

Expert commentators like B. H. Liddell Hart insisted that France's army was sufficient to cope with Germany's army and that the British did not need to create an army for employment on the Continent. In Parliament, the formal Opposition's position in 1936 was, "Not a single penny for this government's rearmament programme."[29] The government had no choice but to seek understandings with Nazi Germany and emphasize the strengthening of the Royal Air Force and Royal Navy as potential deterrents, even at the expense of the army.

Morgan next spent two years at the War Office, working under the general director of staff duties, where he was responsible for overseeing the selection of officers for staff training, their training at staff colleges, and the appointment to staff positions of graduates up to the rank of brigadier. "He later described his term at Whitehall as a nightmare as there was so little sense of urgency to prepare for the impending war."[30]

In 1938 he became a staff officer at the headquarters of the 3rd Infantry Division. This was at the start of the period when the British government's approach to its army changed and the strategy of avoiding any continental commitments fell apart. Particularly after the Germans occupied Prague in

March of 1939, it was clear that a British expeditionary force would be required to fight alongside their new French allies.

One of the 3rd Infantry Division's brigade commanders was a certain Bernard Montgomery. At one point Montgomery put on a short course for officers in his brigade and invited Morgan to join him. Morgan spent more than a week as Monty's house guest, and they became friends as well as colleagues.

The centerpiece of the division's training for 1938 was an amphibious exercise conducted in early spring. Surprisingly for such an obscure event, there are at least three full descriptions of the experience.[31] Montgomery's brigade, with Morgan along for the ride, was embarked on destroyers. They went out into the Channel almost to France then turned around and landed on Slapton Sands, later used during the war to train assault troops for OVERLORD. The scene that early morning did not invoke any suggestion of the 1944 Normandy landings. It did, for at least one observer, conjure up visions of Julius Caesar or images from the medieval Bayeux Tapestry. There were, of course, no purpose-built landing craft in existence, and troops were put ashore before dawn in ships' lifeboats, with oars muffled, as in the eighteenth century. It was said that the life of one colonel was saved by a flask of whisky brought to him as he floundered on the beach. After landing, many of the troops charged up the beach with great enthusiasm. The umpires ascribed this to the great spirit of the troops; the naval officers observing the charge attributed it to the army's desire to never be in a ship again.

The general commanding the operation disregarded the navy's warning, late in the afternoon, of an approaching gale. The navy was obliged to move its ships out to sea; the brigade, Morgan and Montgomery included, was obliged to march just over eight miles in wind and rain along the coast to the Britannia Royal Naval College at Dartmouth, arriving after 11:00 p.m., taking over the cadets' quarters and eating the cadets' breakfast the next morning. It cannot be said that great lessons were learned, but it undoubtedly created memories for some of the participants of the inherent difficulties in amphibious operations.

In August of 1939 Morgan was promoted to brigadier general and took command of a new formation, the support group for the 1st Armored Division.

He commanded the division's artillery, infantry battalions, and engineers. The support group had existed for less than a month when Morgan arrived, and it was an ad hoc setup, made up on the fly with much finding of ways and means not necessarily envisioned by those in the War Office in order to get the job done. He had missed by one month being appointed as chief of staff to Montgomery, who had become commander of the 3rd Division and in 1940 took it to France and then back from Dunkirk.

It was the support group that Morgan led into combat in France in May 1940, landing at Cherbourg and encountering the Germans near Abbeville. At one point he climbed into a scout car to engage in a personal reconnaissance only to realize that he had no idea how to work the Bren gun that was their only defense. He ordered the driver to pull over and give him a few minutes instruction on the basics. Fortunately, he had no immediate need to use the Bren.

He thought the orders he received—to fight his way through German lines to join the British and French trapped at Dunkirk and be evacuated from there—were not realistic. He chose to ignore them. Instead, he moved his unit west, with part of it leaving from Cherbourg in the Cotentin Peninsula and the rest from Brest, even farther west. At Brest he inherited what he described as "1,500 drunk Canadians" and got them back to England as well.[32]

Upon his return to England he re-formed his unit under General McNaughton, another artillery officer, as part of the Canadian Corps. In October he was transferred to the staff of II Corps in Norfolk and then in February 1941 was promoted to major general and took command of the Devon and Cornwall County Division. To his left was Montgomery's V Corps, and there were some boundary issues between the units that were settled over a decent lunch in a hotel near the border.

We can get a sense of the urgency to find officers to command by the pace at which Morgan moved from unit to unit. October 1941 saw him transferred to command of the 55th Lancashire Division, which was at the lowest equipment and manning level. He created a divisional battle school, where realistic training for infantry could occur. General Paget, newly appointed as Commander-in-Chief, Home Forces, opposed Morgan's decision as he felt that General Headquarters should run all battle schools to ensure uniformity.

Morgan was finally able to set up the divisional school, which "saved [the division] from disintegrating."[33]

In May of 1942 Morgan received promotion to lieutenant general and took command of 1st Corps, soon to be part of the planning for TORCH and whose story we have already told.

Morgan had both command and staff experience in a variety of settings and with a variety of formation types. Service in India was certainly adventurous and offered opportunities that were more "operational" than garrison or office duty. Serving on the frontier gave him the experiences and opportunities to work with outstanding characters whose personality and approach were allowed to mature far from metropolitan Britain and the strictures of that small island. He learned from them and adapted those lessons to his own personality. He also had the experience of command, albeit at the battalion and brigade levels, of units like antiaircraft artillery and the support group of an armored division, where doctrine, tables of organization and equipment, and the means of employment were still being worked out. In units like this, there was no one agreed way of proceeding, and a penchant for innovation was required.

The army also taught him how to ride a horse, and he was good enough to be in the top echelon of his class at Woolwich. Early on, of course, the field artillery was all about horses, and he spent much of the time mounted when serving with the artillery in India. Unlike many of the British in India, he was no great enthusiast of game hunting or pig-sticking—Morgan claimed that he had enough of that sort of thing in France during World War I. He did have a lifelong love of playing cricket and was a decent batsman.

Morgan had a wonderful, if slightly droll, sense of humor that served him well throughout his career. Indeed, even as the demands of COSSAC mounted, he would stop for thirty minutes each Wednesday evening and listen to a radio program, "It's That Man Again."[34] Judging by some YouTube clips of films made by the "It's That Man Again" team, the show was a combination of the pun-filled British music-hall comedy of the period with a dash of early Marx Brothers surrealism and a touch of the later British *Carry On* films. His sense of humor combined with an innate graciousness served him well in his dealings with Americans, who in turn enjoyed his company.

Ray Barker's description of Morgan is typically direct and clear: "Here was a great character: Here was a man who above everything else was honest and straightforward. And it was apparent right away that he was a man of great ability, but the outstanding impression that one gained was that 'here is a straight shooter.'"[35]

Barker was five years older than Morgan and was born in upstate New York. He enlisted in the 15th Cavalry Regiment in 1910, at the age of twenty-one. Three years later he was commissioned in the Cavalry, going through an officer candidate school, not West Point.[36] He joined the U.S. Army during a period of great reform. In 1902 Secretary of War Elihu Root established garrison schools at all Army posts. This provided a uniform basic professional educational structure for Army officers, a two-year program that included "a basic knowledge of administrative and drill regulations, weapons, tactics, law, field engineering and the care of horses."[37] The next school to be established was the General Service and Staff College at Fort Leavenworth. This quickly evolved into a two-year course, with the first year becoming the Infantry and Cavalry School (later called the School of the Line) and the second year becoming the Staff College.

Unlike at Quetta or Camberley, at Fort Leavenworth, "the approach was German. Far from being theoretical, the emphasis was on application—problems that called upon the student to grasp the essential principles involved and to produce the appropriate course of action."[38] The coursework also included a background in military history. One instructor published his lectures as *American Campaigns* in 1909, which was used as a textbook at West Point until 1959. The competition among students was fierce, and grades were marked to the third decimal place.[39]

A system of professional schools evolved from this beginning, with Leavenworth the keystone of the system. There were branch schools (tanks, infantry, air, artillery), the Army Industrial College, the Command and General Staff School, and the Army War College all running by the 1930s. The branch schools trained company grade officers; only a few of those graduates would go on to Command and General Staff School, and perhaps half of those graduates might attend the War College. "In 1936, one estimate was that only 75 of 1000 eligible infantry officers could go to the CGSS."[40]

The American response to the 6 March 1916 attack on the town of Columbus, New Mexico, by Pancho Villa and his men gave Second Lieutenant Barker an introduction to campaigning in the field. The Woodrow Wilson administration sent an expedition into Mexico, commanded by Gen. John Pershing, to seek out and punish Villa. Barker rode with the expedition. There were four cavalry regiments, two infantry regiments, two field artillery batteries, and the first-ever aviation unit deployed with eight unarmed training aircraft, plus ten trucks.[41] Supplies couldn't keep up, and both men and horses went hungry in the southwestern desert. George Patton was Pershing's aide and gained some headline fame by killing the head of Villa's personal guard detail. They never did find Villa, and Pershing was ordered back across the border in February 1917. By the time the troops were back, the United States had broken relations with Germany, with Congress declaring war in April. At the time, Barker was one of 5,800 regular Army officers.

The same year, Barker transferred to the Field Artillery; it was with the 153rd Field Artillery Brigade of the 78th Infantry Division that he went to France, arriving in June 1918. The division took part in the Saint-Mihiel offensive and the Meuse-Argonne drive, suffering significant casualties.[42] After the war the division returned to the United States and was disbanded, but Barker remained overseas and participated in the American occupation of Germany for about a year. He then returned to the United States and attended the Cavalry School. The Arlington Cemetery website lists a Bronze Star as one of his decorations, likely dating from World War I.

His career appears to be typical for a U.S. Army officer of the period. He didn't leave any published memoirs or diary, so there is less detail about his postings than there is for Morgan. U.S. Army posts were typically isolated, unglamorous little communities. He was an avid reader of history, particularly British history. That Barker was highly regarded by the Army can be seen by his progress though their professional schools. In 1927 he graduated from the Advanced Field Artillery School, and in 1928, from the Command and General Staff School. By 1935 he had reached the rank of lieutenant colonel. In 1940 he graduated from the Army War College. Between 1940 and early 1942, he commanded two field artillery regiments, was promoted to colonel in June of 1941, and in early 1942 went to England.[43]

If Morgan had an innate sense of charm and diplomacy, Barker was direct to the point of occasionally being blunt and was inclined to cut to the heart of the problem. They had a common background as field artillery officers, as officers who had spent time on the frontier, and as combat veterans on the Western Front in World War I. They both focused on practical solutions to problems, and as artillery officers they were used to working in an environment that required both the mastering of technical matters as well as leading troops, with perhaps a different sense of what the relationship between officer and enlisted man would be than if they had been infantry officers. This would have been particularly true of the ex-enlisted Barker.

Barker had ample professional schooling and may have been more technically proficient than Morgan, a result of the U.S. Army's approach of creating a series of professional education opportunities. Even though there was a significant lack of budget in the interwar years, officers like Barker demonstrated a high level of professionalism and prepared for the future as best they could. As one future general officer said, "It was our schools that saved the Army."[44] Morgan may have had less professional schooling and more on-the-job training, but his intellectual curiosity, common sense, and leadership ability more than compensated for any shortfall in coursework.

Morgan and Barker worked together with a marked degree of informality, mutual respect, and support. They realized almost at once the qualities that each brought to the demands of COSSAC. One small symbol that meant something to both men came from Morgan's idea that they should exchange and wear one of each other's uniform buttons on their tunics. At least until the end of the Quebec conference, each day the British Army was represented on an American uniform, as was the U.S. Army on a British one.[45] Gestures large and small went a long way to building the sense of team that was so important to COSSAC's ability to produce high-quality plans with incomplete information and with little time for reflection.

Both men could express their views to senior officers and policy makers without excessive concern about their careers. Morgan expressed more awareness regarding pay. He made a point in a postwar interview to bring up the fact that he took a pay cut when he went from commanding 1st Corps to COSSAC since he didn't rate combat pay in that position. He did get it restored plus an allowance for entertaining that lasted until Eisenhower arrived. Once Morgan was part of SHAEF, his pay was cut again. Three years later he still brought it up.[46] Barker didn't mind having a promotion delayed if it meant getting to be part of the fight.

Barker's commonsense view can be illustrated by a short conversation he had with General Marshall when the latter was visiting London in 1942. Marshall said to Barker, "I hear that you're pro-British." Barker replied, "I don't know what you mean by 'pro-British' but certainly under the current circumstances here I shouldn't be anti-British. That would be fatal to our cause. I do get along with them. I understand them and I understand their point of view."[47] The answer suited Marshall.

One example of the way Barker and Morgan worked together can be found in a memo Barker wrote on 18 June 1943. Hughes-Hallett had written a memo expressing some concerns about the planning process, particularly the supply problems caused by the lack of port facilities.

In response, Barker gave Morgan this advice:

I believe that Commodore Hughes-Hallett has in mind the restrictions which administrative [logistics] planners have always placed on operations, by severe limitations on port capacities. I do not feel that this factor is to be taken too seriously. What is needed in this field is for the operational planners, being guided by common sense, shall [sic] determine what our port requirements are, and then demand that the Engineers, and others concerned, find ways and means to produce them.[48]

Fate or, if you prefer, random chance put these two officers together at exactly the right time. Together they found the ways and means to accomplish a great deal.

— 6 —

"FOR THE FIRST TIME
I REALLY BELIEVE IN THIS OPERATION"

In June 1943 Gen. Sir Bernard Paget relinquished his position as Commander-in-Chief, Home Forces to assume the newly created position of Commander, 21st Army Group. The creation of 21st Army Group marked the formal reorientation of the British Army in the home islands to a more offensive stance. Paget's first task was to train the British forces that would eventually cross the Channel and reenter the Continent. In mid-1943 he held the view that he was as likely as anyone else to command those forces in that assault, so he examined any proposed plan that came his way with a most careful eye. (Appendix B has a brief description of the structure of the British Army's Home Forces after Dunkirk.)

The COS had tasked the Combined Commanders with examining the issues and any plans related to the reentry of the Continent. As one of those commanders, Paget had given a great deal of consideration to the problem. While he wasn't convinced that an assault across well-defended beaches could be successful with the forces available, he held to the view that if there was to be an attack, Pas-de-Calais was the correct place. The reasons are familiar. It was an easier crossing, and landing craft could be "turned around" more quickly, meaning that fewer would be needed. It was closer to Antwerp and Germany's industrial center. There were many airfields concentrated in the south of England, therefore protective fighter cover would be able to stay over the battlefield longer. Also, in 1943 many of the landing craft crews had not reached the level of training necessary to be successful in the difficult waters around the Normandy coast while the Dover Straits were considered to be within their capabilities.[1]

Paget held this view possibly because the conclusions reached in SKY-SCRAPER suggested an assault force much larger than the COS were willing to contemplate would be needed, and he had firsthand experience from Norway that showed what would happen when forces without adequate resources or a fully thought-out plan engaged a well-trained enemy. He also cared deeply about the individual infantry soldier and worked hard when he was Commander-in-Chief, Home Forces to establish realistic training programs to improve infantry performance. The battle schools were run at the division level and gave soldiers a sense of the reality of battle as well as some live-fire training. There was some inevitable variation from unit to unit, notwithstanding the fact that the instructors for each school were all trained at General Headquarters' battle school at Barnard Castle, but it marked a great improvement on what had gone on before.[2]

Paget, whose father was the dean of Christ Church College, Oxford, was a distinguished and conventional soldier. A light infantryman and Sandhurst graduate, he fought with distinction on the Western Front for three years in World War I, having served in India from 1911 to 1914. In World War II he led a reduced division in the Norway debacle, was chief of staff to the Commander-in-Chief, Home Forces, Field Marshal Edmund Ironside, and then held the same position when General Brooke took command of Home Forces. From there, in January 1941 he became the commander of South Eastern Command, covering the counties of Kent and Sussex, and then Commander-in-Chief, Home Forces in November of 1941.[3]

The chief of Combined Operations, Lord Louis Mountbatten, held the view that Normandy was the better choice. The shelter from the unpredictable Channel weather was better, and the German defenses were not as strong because the Germans expected the attack at the Pas-de-Calais. The port of Cherbourg, along with Le Havre, had more capacity than the ports farther east until one got to Antwerp. The road net behind the beaches was more suitable than at Calais, and the Cotentin Peninsula could be used for the buildup of forces. The major French Atlantic ports were within reach (although too far to be of significant use in any sustained offensive). Fighter cover was possible, and, in any case, air supremacy was going to be required before any invasion was attempted, so one didn't need to plan for dogfights over the invasion beaches on D-Day to wrest control from the German air force, and expeditionary airfields could be built once forces were ashore. Because Combined Operations were the experts on all things amphibious, this point of view also had strong support.

As a result of one of the conclusions at the Casablanca conference, COSSAC was formed and instructed "to prepare plans for . . . a full-scale assault against the Continent in 1944, as early as possible."[4] Mindful that the resources that were identified at the Washington conference in May were insufficient for the task—particularly in terms of shipping and landing craft—and knowing that without a commander they "would have no real means of influencing priority, competing in the open market with established commands already committed to major campaigns," the COSSAC team, led by Morgan and Barker, got started.[5]

Barker pointed out to Morgan in his 18 June memo:

Since the writer bases his argument largely on the factor of time and the non-availability of the S.A.C. [Supreme Allied Commander], we must consider these factors in relation to the question of the mission implied in COSSAC's directive to prepare an outline plan for a 1944 operation. . . . As to the former, COSSAC's directive leaves no room for equivocation. As to the second, . . . the plan [should be] presented as the *outline* of what COSSAC and his Staff consider to be a practicable operation, designed to accomplish the indicated object.

. . . Be it remembered that this outline plan is, in fact, no more than a "proposal" until it has received the sanction of the Combined Chiefs of Staff, and that it cannot be implemented until that sanction has been obtained. However, after that event, it is imperative that COSSAC be given a considerable degree of plenary power . . . or we shall lose much valuable time. . . .

Time presses. Much remains to be done in every field. Nothing constructive will be accomplished until at least an outline plan has been approved.[6]

Knowing what was desired (a reentry into the Continent), and knowing when it was required (May 1944), COSSAC set aside issues like landing craft and executive authority for now and got to work on figuring out where it should happen, going back to the beginning. This wasn't because Morgan didn't trust those who had done all the planning up to now—indeed, many of those planners were now part of COSSAC—but because there needed to be a positive, active recommendation from them, not just agreement with one of the previously submitted points of view, neither of which were universally accepted.

Morgan and his staff spent the first few weeks reviewing all the possible landing beaches from Spain to Denmark, concluding without much surprise that, however desirable other possible locations might be, practical considerations reduced the choices to Normandy or Pas-de-Calais. One thing Morgan was able to do by cutting and pasting together some RAF charts was to lay out a view of Western Europe as it looked if one were standing in Berlin—a view from the other side of the hill, so to speak. It helped him to see the problem "through enemy eyes" and understand the challenges they faced in preparing to defend against invasion. While the Allies might feel themselves constrained to a cross-Channel approach, the Germans had to consider the defense of their entire "frontier."

With the alternatives reconfirmed, the U.S. Army planners were directed to make the case for Normandy and the British for Calais. The ensuing debate was "observed" by Morgan; Barker; Paget; Lt. Gen. Jacob Devers, who had replaced General Andrews at ETOUSA when Andrews was killed in a plane crash in Greenland; and Mountbatten. At the point at which a decision had to be made, passions began to rise on all sides.

It gradually appeared that adverse criticism centred in the British Home Forces headquarters, whither had gravitated several senior officers who had greater experience, greater than any of us, in the study of this that was now *our* problem . . . the general conclusion reached [by them] was that the whole affair represented an undue risk, all things considered, but that, if it were ordered, the proper scene of action lay in the Pas de Calais. Were they right in contending that it was out of the question to attempt anything at all with the meagre resources placed at our disposal? . . . Was it wrong to listen to such die-hardism, as was contended by the Americans in particular?[7]

Morgan hesitated to decide. It may have been because of Paget's seniority, or perhaps Morgan was sensitive about his position as a staff officer, albeit a chief of staff, and Paget's as a commander. He was certainly well aware that he would have to continue working with both Paget and Mountbatten as well as being keen to protect the rights and prerogatives of his unnamed commander. Morgan felt COSSAC didn't have a sympathetic ear at the COS, either. As he later wrote, "Whenever one was forced to refer to them [the COS] there always seemed to be an air of thinly disguised impatience with the upstart amateurs from over the way. And to me there is always a tone, a rather blush-making mendicance about many of the Former Naval Person's telegrams to the President."[8]

The answer to the question "Who gets to decide?" or, more precisely, "Who is to approve the recommendation to be submitted to the British Chiefs of Staff?" had yet to be answered. It was routine that COSSAC would have to work closely with Combined Operations and that COSSAC planners would have ongoing informal conversations with their colleagues from British Home Forces and the joint planners. There wasn't time for reliance solely on formal or official channels of communication. All the relevant planning staffs were kept up to date and gave their opinions, if for no other reason than to prevent surprises and misunderstandings. However, that also muddied the waters when it came to understanding who, exactly, was ultimately responsible for the plan. Another complication was that Paget, very much senior to Morgan, felt that Morgan had "too little experience of actual command."[9]

Would it be wise to submit a proposal to the COS or to the Combined Chiefs over the strong objections of the likely commander of the British forces for the proposed operation? Could Morgan submit such a plan, or did Paget have the authority, formally or informally, to approve the plan in advance? The answer was not made explicit. If he was to be the commander of the operation, Paget certainly would have substantial authority when it came to the execution of the plan. It seemed unlikely that the British COS would accept a recommendation from Morgan with which Paget disagreed. Personally, Morgan agreed with Mountbatten, Combined Operations, and most of the COSSAC planners that Normandy was the correct choice. The exact relationship between COSSAC and Combined Operations, however, was not explicit. Were they to be expert advisors or supervisors and instructors? It had only been late May, after the

Washington conference, when Morgan's questions regarding the details of OVERLORD were answered. In early June he was still seeking a broader consensus, and the outline plan was due to the British COS on 15 July.

In part, the concerns were the result of having to imagine or comprehend a method of operation that was untried on the scale contemplated. There had been raids and landings of various sizes, but neither TORCH nor the Dieppe Raid could be called encouraging precedents. Guadalcanal was not an opposed landing, and Tarawa was still in the future (November 1943), as was HUSKY, the invasion of Sicily (July 1943). In any event, few thought that the experiences in the Pacific would be of any use in a European context.

It was only at Sicily, less than a year before OVERLORD, that one first saw mature Allied amphibious technique. "HUSKY involved seven Allied divisions ... and several thousand ships ... [as well as] the first wide-scale use of purpose built landing vessels (LSTs, LCTs, LCIs) and amphibious trucks (DUKWs)."[10] It was difficult for some to envision how it would all work, and all were aware that failure might have well meant that the British Army would have been unable to make a second attempt, at least not within a reasonable time.

Another crucial aspect that would continue to dog all of Morgan's efforts was the multifaceted problem of COSSAC's lack of a commander. Morgan was able to lead the COSSAC planners as if there was a commander, to convince them that they were not just producing papers and studies, as had so many before them. But when in contact with outside organizations, either operational commands, ministries, or theater commands, the empty chair at the top of COSSAC's organization was an ongoing hindrance.

Finally, there were those who believed that German coastal defenses "seemed to consist of an unbroken line of impenetrable wire, backed by a serried line of pillboxes proofed in ferro-concrete of unprecedented thickness, bristling with automatic weapons of every caliber, manned by bullet-proof human wildcats to whom raw meat was regularly fed."[11] Hence the desire to gather forces far beyond what was physically possible for the initial assault, notwithstanding the recognized need for additional amphibious ships and craft.

These barriers were threatening the whole enterprise. The resolution of these conflicts was Operation RATTLE, held on board the not very seaworthy HMS Warren, at the end of June and in early July 1943.

Exactly how RATTLE came to be is a story that depends on who's telling it. According to Mountbatten:

> Freddie Morgan . . . did absolutely nothing when he arrived. That is the reason why, in desperation, I called the Largs Conference [RATTLE]—to try and get something done. When I tried to persuade Freddie to call [the conference], he simply said that he wasn't the Supreme Commander— that he was only the Supreme Commander's Chief of Staff—and that he couldn't ask all the other commanders-in-chief who were superior to him. I then said, in that case, I'd call it myself.[12]

It is understandable that Mountbatten would have been impatient, and it had been clear for some time to the chief of Combined Operations that Normandy was the preferred choice for the assault. It is inaccurate, however, to say that Morgan had done "absolutely nothing." Morgan and his small team were being pushed to provide plans for three operations, with neither the resources, support, nor time to allow for thoughtful deliberation and consideration of all alternatives. Furthermore, Morgan was highly sensitive to the absence of a supreme commander, perhaps excessively so, but the greater risk would have been to err too far in the other direction, to be seen as attempting a sort of power grab and offending those whose willing cooperation he needed. Walter Bedell Smith, Eisenhower's chief of staff, could be Ike's alter ego, could give orders and speak with the authority of his commander. Freddie de Guingand could represent Montgomery and let it be known what it was that Monty wanted. Both commanders were known quantities. Morgan had none of those advantages. He was in a situation where he had to be a diplomat and a negotiator as well as a soldier. Nor would it have been helpful for Morgan to call a meeting and have several senior officers decide not to attend.

Mountbatten—admiral/general/air marshal, confidant of the prime minister, member of the Royal family—had a different perspective and didn't face Morgan's challenges. His involvement cut the Gordian knot that Morgan wrestled with in ways that only someone like Mountbatten could have done. The two were very much in league with each other in making RATTLE a success. For his part, Morgan believed that the chief of Combined Operations didn't get the full credit he deserved for his involvement in the early planning stages.[13]

Hughes-Hallett remembered that Mountbatten wrote a letter to Morgan in early June, suggesting that COHQ put on a course for the "benefit of senior staff officers and junior commanders who would be taking part in the invasion."[14] He offered to make HMS Warren, formerly known as the Hollywood Hotel in Largs, Scotland (a summer resort town on the Firth of Clyde, near Glasgow), available for the course. Largs was the home of Rear Admiral Combined Operations Bases, North as well as being a combined training center that was fully staffed and in the business of providing combined operations courses for selected officers of all services. It had all the equipment and spaces that would be needed. Indeed, "the [combined training center] at Largs was looked upon from a Combined Operations point of view in much the same way as the Staff College at Camberley was from the point of view of the army."[15]

According to Hughes-Hallett, on 9 June 1943 Mountbatten invited Morgan, Leigh-Mallory, and Paget to COHQ at Richmond Terrace to discuss the idea with him and to work out the details. Hughes-Hallett always felt that Mountbatten was disappointed at the relatively minor role that Combined Operations was now playing in what was to be the ultimate combined operation, and that their expertise and experience was not being fully taken advantage of. There were other difficulties.

Hughes-Hallett recalled that "General Paget was furious. At first, he flatly refused to attend the meeting, but in the end was persuaded by Leigh-Mallory."[16] Paget was giving Leigh-Mallory and Hughes-Hallett a ride to the meeting and continued to denounce the whole idea during their drive; he "urged that [they] turn it down flat. Leigh-Mallory continued to maintain that much good would come of Mountbatten's idea . . . and that the first course should be attended by ourselves and our most senior staff officers. Paget was taken aback by this astonishing suggestion."[17] Hughes-Hallett suggested that it be called a conference, not a course, and that it could consist of a series of short lectures and discussions presented by experts in their fields, dealing sequentially with all the issues relating to the assault. The three sat in Paget's car debating while parked in front of New Scotland Yard, making them late for the meeting. Finally, Paget reluctantly agreed.[18] He apparently thought either the conference or his attendance unnecessary.

At the meeting Mountbatten quickly accepted Leigh-Mallory's and Hughes-Hallett's suggestions. Morgan and Mountbatten then worked out the agenda and conference details. Mountbatten presented the idea of a "study period" to the COS on 11 June. General Devers was present, and he asked if he and his staff could be included and, of course, they were.[19]

A letter from Morgan to Mountbatten, dated 16 June 1943, asked for some corrections to the 9 June meeting minutes, noting that the purpose of the proposed conference was changed from Mountbatten's original proposal (as they had discussed at the meeting) and was now "for the benefit of Commanders and *Senior* Staff Officers of all services who are interested in operation 'OVERLORD.' It was this alteration, if you recollect, that 'ipso facto' dealt with a large number of the successive items on the Agenda." Morgan went on to note that the minutes unwittingly misrepresented the role of the chief of Combined Operations in the training of assault troops. "We re-affirmed at the meeting that the only authority that can be responsible in any way for the training of an assault force is the commander destined to command that force in the assault." He ended by saying that he attaches "such importance to the course that you are so kindly organizing for us on the 28th June that I feel we should spare no pains to see that the event gets off to the best possible start."[20]

The final agenda for the meeting was issued by COSSAC on 22 June 1943. With the agreement and support of Leigh-Mallory, Admiral Little, and General Paget, Morgan stated in a letter to Mountbatten that the proposed conference would not be the time or place to discuss the strategical problem or to talk about a system of command and control (at the operational level) as those attending would not be the ones making final decisions on those matters. But he (Morgan) would present a paper on the "Strategical Background," which would provide the basis for discussion. The agenda for the four-day conference included at least one field trip to examine various landing craft types. It also covered every technical aspect of the amphibious assault, a review of improvements made, and lessons learned as well as demonstrations of new equipment.[21]

As Morgan later wrote, RATTLE was the opportunity to gather everyone in one place and insist that all points of view be talked through. "The object ... was to give all concerned the opportunity to discuss openly with each other the whole subject of a cross-Channel operation, its feasibility in general and the practicality of all the many detailed points of execution. . . . We must hear the conclusion of the whole matter argued out in comparative public."[22] There was to be no sulking in one's tent, as he put it. It was also essential for Morgan to make it clear that COSSAC was now charged with the responsibility of developing the plan. "Experts abounded, many of whom were convinced . . . that he had in his little black bag the secret of the infallible system. The price of such an article was very often simply control . . . of the whole operation. That belonged by definition to our Supreme Commander-to-be, whose interests COSSAC must jealously guard."[23]

Mountbatten did not disappoint Morgan when the conference began. "Domestic arrangements were perfect. . . . As there were suspected to be savage breasts among us, the pipe band of the local Home Guard appeared at intervals to rend the atmosphere with the indigenous substitute for music."[24] Even the Scottish summer weather cooperated, providing an unusually long period of four consecutive days of warm, sunny weather.

The first session started at 10:00 a.m. on Monday, 28 June, with Mountbatten as chairman and Adm. Sir Charles Little, Gen. Sir Bernard Paget, Air Marshal Sir Trafford Leigh-Mallory, Gen. Andrew McNaughton, Lt. Gen. Jacob Devers, and Morgan front and center. The more than seventy attendees included representatives from the Admiralty, the War Office, the Air Ministry, RAF Air Groups, 2nd British Army, Canadian Army, 1st Corps (British Army), 6th Airborne Division (British Army), Fighter Command, ETOUSA, COHQ, and COSSAC. Some of those present would have operational commands on D-day, like Leigh-Mallory and Brig. Gen. Norman Cota, USA, who would go from COHQ to assistant divisional commander of the 29th Infantry Division on Omaha Beach. Cota had been the G-3 (operations officer) of the First Infantry Division in 1941–42 and had been deeply involved in the amphibious training of the division before TORCH. ETOUSA had the additional advantage of having the participation of one lieutenant colonel, R. O. Bare of the U.S. Marine Corps, as well as two representatives of the U.S. Navy. "There were twenty assorted generals, eleven air marshals and air commodores, eight admirals, and brigadiers galore. . . . There was one solitary Paymaster-Lieutenant, Royal Navy."[25]

Mountbatten started by explaining that the conference was called because it had become apparent that there "was a need for guidance from COSSAC

and the Commanders-in-Chief concerned on a number of important points."
He went on to say that he hoped that the conference would come to some
definite conclusions on which the provision of equipment, future training,
and planning could be based and added that "the Prime Minister and the
COS placed great store by this Conference."[26] All of which was true, but this
implicitly meant they were there to get "buy-in" from all concerned on the
correct target for the assault, which for Morgan and Mountbatten meant
Normandy, and to accept that COSSAC was the agency responsible.

The agenda was complete, detailed, and in chronological order. It started
with the assembly and embarkation of troops, then the cross-Channel voyage,
the beach assault (including the use and timing of naval gunfire support), the
consequent buildup of forces, and the use of airborne forces and signals. There
were visits to a headquarters ship and landing craft, and there was discussion
of the scope and location of combined training for both British and American
troops, control of the air, recognition of air forces, uses of air transport, the
need for working ports, artificial harbors, and supply over the beach. Other
issues included the number of divisions available for the assault, characteristics
of available craft and weapons to cover the assault, neutralization of coast
defense batteries, pros and cons of daylight or night assault, waterproofing
of vehicles, logistic aspects of the buildup, use of "Blossom" (chaff), technical
developments, and special equipment. Mountbatten's reports of each day's
work to the British COS after the conference ran to 130 pages.[27]

Twenty-three briefing papers had been prepared in advance. Morgan presented
his overview. Others produced by COHQ and British Home Forces addressed
issues such as the problems of attacking prepared defenses, typical German
fortifications, command and control of the assault, training establishments,
and courses to be run or developed—each matching up with an agenda topic.

The first day's meetings included a review of the German defenses in the
West "and a survey of the problems confronting the Movements Directorate
of the War Office."[28] From the point of view of the Movements Directorate,
the assault across the beach was relatively straightforward. To them, the real
challenge would be planning for the movement of troops to embarkation
sites and loading men and equipment into craft, which would have to begin
approximately two weeks before D-day. They would need three months' notice
to be ready on time. Once the troops left their marshalling yards, they were

committed to the operation, as far as the directorate was concerned.[29] In other words, it was not an operation that could be delayed or rescheduled on short notice to take advantage of other perceived opportunities, or because operations to seize those opportunities were taking longer than planned.

The next discussion was about the training of the assault forces, led by Admiral Little. After a fair amount of discussion, the American assault force was assigned to the Plymouth area with the follow-up force centered around Milford Haven in Wales. It was more difficult to find areas for the British assault forces—it being desirable that the sea and beach conditions have some resemblance to those of the Normandy coast. Ultimately, training areas in the Cromarty Firth, at Rosyth, and at Harwich were chosen. Hughes-Hallett and Little noted that while the two navies were in agreement, they would also like the armies to agree with the choices because the divisions to be landed on D-day should train with the same naval assault force that was to carry them in the attack.

Paget immediately rose and expressed his "vehement opposition to the proposals. Why [he asked] must the Navy choose areas where there are no accommodations for troops on anything like the scale visualized? [Hughes-Hallett] replied that it was not really the Navy who had chosen the areas, but rather God when he had sited the harbors and landing beaches round the Kingdom."[30] Around midnight, Little, Mountbatten, Leigh-Mallory, and a small group of Combined Operations staff officers were able to persuade Paget that the recommendation was the right one.

Leigh-Mallory also presented on the first day, discussing tactical air operations and warning that the Allies ought not to count on having total air superiority from the onset. This was followed by a discussion regarding the possible uses of airborne troops, with Leigh-Mallory noting that currently there were not enough transport aircraft, and it was hard to say when the numbers available for the assault would be known.

Monday evening Morgan and Mountbatten met to compare notes. Morgan was not encouraged; Mountbatten remained optimistic but admitted that the debate had yet to be won. To Morgan, after observing what he called "the opposition" closely, "it looked as if there was no hope."[31] Still, they decided to give it one more day—and, in fact, they had until the end of the conference, which gave them three days.

At some point on Tuesday, amid presentations about the assault, starting with pre-assault air and naval bombardment and finishing with advancing inland and building up forces, the tide turned favorably for Morgan. Perhaps it was the combination of a Scottish setting far from ministry offices, the ongoing expert and thorough presentations covering all the details, or a deeper appreciation that all were trying to solve the same interconnected problems, each from their own perspective, that started the change. Or, possibly, the sense started to take hold that every voice would be heard and that a real final decision would be made. Alternatively, it might have been that they began to see that the plan just might work.

On the third day, Wednesday, Major General Brownjohn, COSSAC's logistics chief, presented on the supply and logistics challenges related to the buildup of forces after a successful assault. The discussion centered around the familiar topic of the likely capture of a working port with sufficient capacity to be of use. It was in this presentation that the idea of artificial harbors was put forth to the group, what was to become the famous MULBERRY operation.[32]

The basic problem was well known. It was obvious that any invasion would need substantial port facilities. Few ports along the Channel's French coast had such facilities. Those that did would be strongly defended, and their facilities would be destroyed before the Allies could capture them. Additionally, ports rarely present themselves at places that are convenient to the beaches that are best for amphibious assault. Both TORCH and the Dieppe Raid showed that attempting to seize a port by direct assault was a difficult proposition. COSSAC planners had gone around and around to no effect until one hot June afternoon just before RATTLE, when, at the end of yet another frustrating meeting, Hughes-Hallett exclaimed, "Well, if we can't capture a port we must take one with us."[33] So he and others put the known together with the unknown and addressed the issue of artificial harbors, pulling together the results of various studies and experiments that had been going on for over a year.

MULBERRY was a system consisting of "break ships" that formed a breakwater plus various types of piers and pontoon bridge–like components, portable bridge spans, reinforced concrete caissons (some of which had light antiaircraft guns installed) as well as other items that were developed by the Royal Navy's Directorate of Miscellaneous Weapon Development (also called the Wheezers and Dodgers).[34] It was the innovation that made it possible for those studying the problem to believe that a solution to what had been an intractable problem had been found. Without such a solution, there would not have been an invasion.

After Brownjohn presented, one of the engineers described the technical details to the audience, then Hughes-Hallett explained in a straightforward manner that what was needed was a "stretch of water deep enough to accept large ships, but shallow enough to take blockships to form a breakwater. Inside these you set up your floating piers."[35] The one place he later found that met these criteria was Arromanches, in the middle of the OVERLORD beaches. Interestingly, the American site at Omaha Beach did not have quite the same combination of shore, shoal, and bottom conditions and was, perhaps, inevitably doomed to be wrecked by the great storm that roared in on D+13. (The storm lasted from 19 June through 21 June, subsiding on 22 June. The British harbor was damaged but repairable, unlike the American one.)

It was agreed at RATTLE that an artificial harbor system was necessary, both for OVERLORD and RANKIN. Work began quickly on the design of a variety of systems that became the famous harbors, the remains of which can still be seen at Arromanches. As LSTs were just coming into use, the idea of cross-beach supply of the assault force was not discussed. To the conferees, the scale of the challenge suggested that port facilities of some sort were needed.

Admiral Little's contribution to the conference was critical. He was one of the most senior officers in the Royal Navy, having served in submarines, cruisers, and battleships. He had been deputy chief of the Naval Staff, Commander-in-Chief, China Station from 1935 to 1938, the Second Sea Lord until 1941, and was Commander-in-Chief, Portsmouth from 1942 through the end of the war in Europe.[36] He spoke with authority and common sense. At RATTLE, he developed a useful and diplomatic method for dealing with the more self-important brigadiers who attended and who were fond of protesting vigorously whenever their recommendation or point of view was overruled. They would announce: "I can accept no further responsibility for the Operation." "But Brigadier," Sir Charles would reply, "nobody is asking you to accept any responsibility. Our orders are to make the best possible plan. If you feel that you can make a better one without exceeding the available forces, please let us hear about it. But responsibility for carrying out the plan will rest with the Combined Chiefs of Staff in Washington, together with Mr. Churchill and the President."[37]

On the last day there was a long discussion about the timing of the assault. The last period was set up as a "free-discussion" period with topics being brought forward from the floor. Lt. Gen. Gerard Corfield Bucknall of XXX Corps (later replaced by Lt. Gen. Brian Horrocks[38]) rose and suggested that the standard amphibious assault tactics of landing before dawn were not desirable. The conventional British doctrine was for infantry to approach before dawn, land at first light or just before, punch a hole in the first line of defense, and then land armor and self-propelled artillery in daylight to exploit the situation. The problem was that the tactics didn't seem valid for a major assault against a determined and prepared defense "for the simple reason that if the beaches were resolutely held, the unfortunate infantry seldom succeeded in securing them . . . thus making the landing of armour and artillery exceedingly hazardous."[39] Bucknall argued for a combined arms approach, with tanks, artillery, engineers, and flail tanks to clear mines and obstacles in addition to infantry, all landing together. (Interestingly, the U.S. 1st Infantry Division and General Cota had come to the same conclusion after training operations along the U.S. Atlantic coast in 1942.[40])

Bucknall's remarks gained the support of some of the senior officers there, including Morgan's Quetta classmate, Gen. Kenneth Anderson, freshly returned from commanding the British First Army in North Africa.

Admiral Little took the floor and assured Bucknall that the navy would carefully study his suggestion. He then invited Hughes-Hallett to stick his oar in, as it were. Hughes-Hallett expressed appreciation for the comments and then went on to point out the many, but not insolvable problems related to the suggestion. The first was the different speeds at which the various craft approached the beach. The LCTs that would carry the tanks moved at not more than seven knots. The infantry's LCAs could make perhaps five knots. There was no time to build a new type of landing craft that could accommodate all the forces the general envisioned. The alternative was to figure out new ways to use the craft they did have. That would require some amount of experimentation and a complete revision of the training program for the operators of the craft. There just might be enough time to train enough people and be ready by the following May. Hughes-Hallett added that he felt that such a combined approach could only work in daylight and, based on his experience at Dieppe, that it was feasible.

At this point, Leigh-Mallory took the floor and welcomed the idea of daylight landings with enthusiasm. At last, he said, the RAF could give effective close-air support at the most critical point of the operation. He agreed that, with air superiority, a daylight landing was possible. General Paget also supported the concept, with the proviso that the navy could sort out the details in time.[41]

While the question of day or night landings and the related one of increased shore bombardment and naval gunfire support were not resolved at RATTLE, it did lead to a prolonged discussion about these issues. It was clear that the benefits of a daylight landing against a prepared defense included more accurate naval gunfire support, the ability to use air power effectively, the greater likelihood of finding the right beach, and, if tactical surprise was achieved, of not having German reserves starting to move until late on D-day, when they could be interdicted by aircraft, delayed by airborne forces, and possibly harassed by partisans as well.

This led to a change in doctrine for OVERLORD and a daylight assault, which had mixed results. COSSAC and SHAEF sought to provide overwhelming fire support primarily with strategic and tactical aircraft and not by using prolonged naval bombardment. In part this was because a prolonged period of bombardment of the target beaches was considered impractical for a continental invasion due to the obvious alert it would give the enemy. On 6 June the naval bombardment was intense, with specific targets assigned based on detailed intelligence gathering and analysis, but relatively short. It was also true that doctrine regarding this subject was still evolving, and the presumed effects of air bombardment were overrated. Naval gunfire support was provided by five battleships and two 15-inch gunned monitors as well as heavy and light cruisers and destroyers.[42] Close-in support was provided by landing craft modified to serve as gunboats or as rocket-launching vessels that were designed to saturate a small area of the landing beach. It should be noted that Royal Navy, Royal Canadian Navy, Royal Netherlands Navy, and Free French Forces warships joined the U.S. Navy in providing naval gunfire support on Omaha and Utah beaches.[43]

Morgan's view on the subject was clear. After the conference he was approached by an admiral who insisted that OVERLORD must be a night assault. Morgan replied, "In that case, I can only say that the assault will not take place."[44]

One of the great benefits of RATTLE was the creation of a list of specific items to be addressed, each assigned to someone for action. It was distributed with the issue to be resolved on the left-hand side of the page and those responsible for resolution on the right-hand side.

Examples include:

Aircraft recognition	
An early decision is required as to the method by which— (a) Our own aircraft British and U.S. will be recognized by the Naval and Land Forces engaged in the operation. (b) Our own aircraft British and U.S. will recognize our own troops on the ground	(a) *Action to be taken by*: C-in-C Fighter Command in collaboration with: C-in-C Portsmouth, C-in-C Home Forces, CG ETOUSA (b) *Action to be taken by*: C-in-C Home Forces and CG ETOUSA in collaboration with C-in-C Fighter Command
Timing of the assault	
Pending a decision being reached as to whether the assault should be launched in daylight or in darkness, all Forces concerned should be organized and trained so that they could land in daylight, darkness, or smoke.	*Action to be taken by*: C-in-C Portsmouth, C-in-C Home Forces, C-in-C Fighter Command, Chief Combined Operations

Other tasks were assigned to COSSAC, the War Office, the Admiralty, and other agencies, as necessary.[45]

Mountbatten reported to the British COS that the "subjects dealt with at this Conference were discussed against the background of the German defenses and dispositions as they exist today." He went on to say that the Combined Commanders and COSSAC were aware that the "eventual plan may have to be put into effect against a lesser degree of opposition or a lower state of morale that that which exist now. . . . All our preparations for OVERLORD [will] take into account this possibility"[46] That was his nod to the ongoing hope held by the COS that RANKIN would be the operation that would occur. Or at least that there would be RANKIN-like conditions in 1944. He didn't mention the other possibility—that German defenses might be stronger in 1944.

His topline summary to the COS emphasized three points.

The assault area required a much greater period of bombardment than previously attempted, probably conducted by the RAF.

The most critical period will be the time between the lifting of supporting fire by ships and aircraft and the time when the army can get its own supporting arms into play. He hoped that HUSKY would shed additional light on the subject and noted that 1st Corps was working on the problem.

If the army wants to land a combined arms force, it will have to be landed in daylight. "In those circumstances it will be all the more necessary to soften the area before the assault and for airborne troops to tackle the enemy forces from the rear."[47]

General Paget, speaking at the end of the conference, said that while he still hoped that an amphibious assault would not prove necessary, the 21st Army Group would devote its attention "to the problems which had been considered at the Conference."[48] Morgan's old 1st Corps was directed by Paget to take on the work.

RATTLE succeeded in breaking the logjam because everyone could be briefed by those with detailed knowledge of the issues. Then there could be open and honest discussion and debate unencumbered by deference to rank or politics, with specific, practical recommendations as outcomes, each assigned to an officer or agency for next steps.

By the end of the conference there was general agreement that Normandy was the better choice, and the Pas-de-Calais was finally laid to rest. The participants could see a practical operational plan start to take shape, of particular interest to those in the room who would be going across the beach on D-day. COSSAC was recognized as the body responsible to the CCS for the operation in question. It could be said that after RATTLE those tasked with planning OVERLORD again believed in the reality of their work. The conference ended in "a mutual exchange of public verbal bouquets, but . . . more significant was a private remark by a very senior pessimist: 'For the first time I really believe in this operation.'"[49]

—7—

THE PRIMARY U.S.-BRITISH
GROUND AND AIR EFFORT IN EUROPE

As the COSSAC team worked to create the outline plan for OVERLORD, a series of events were changing how senior commanders and political leaders considered the war and their available options to gain victory.

In the first half of 1943 the Western Allies suffered from a shipping crisis caused by poor estimates of available shipping being made by planners at the Casablanca conference along with the desire to take the offensive against both the Germans and the Japanese at the same time. The Americans supported military operations in the Mediterranean and Pacific at the expense of BOLERO. The British tried to keep BOLERO alive but could only do so by reducing support of British forces earmarked for HUSKY and reducing supplies for the population of the British Isles below the bare minimum needed. The American Joint Chiefs of Staff (JCS) were disinclined to provide support for anything other than military operations and didn't think that feeding their ally was their problem. It took an intervention by FDR and reallocations of resources to redress the balances, although BOLERO did suffer as a result. The hoped-for targets were missed, with roughly 76 percent of the planned troop movements to the United Kingdom being realized by 31 December 1943.[1] If the cross-Channel attack was to occur the next year, the rate of buildup would have to be accelerated, including the transfer of divisions from other theaters, or there might be fewer divisions available than what was needed to have a reasonable chance of success.

In the Pacific, the struggle for Guadalcanal ended in February with the Japanese pulling off a mini-Dunkirk to evacuate their troops. The fighting continued in New Guinea and in the Solomons. Maj. Gen. George Kenny's Fifth Air Force, a mix of U.S. and Australian squadrons flying American- and British-made aircraft, showed what air power combined with skill, ingenuity, and field modifications could do when they inflicted a serious defeat on the Japanese navy at the Battle of the Bismarck Sea in early March. *Essex-* and *Independence*-class carriers started to join the Pacific Fleet, Corsairs entered combat in February 1943, and Hellcats first saw combat in August. The oft-cited Washington conference in May authorized the launch of the drive across the central Pacific. Landing craft and amphibious warfare ships were going to be at a premium, with increased demand in both the Pacific and European theaters.

The war against Germany was also changing dramatically. "The final act of the 'organized mass death' of the German 6th Army at Stalingrad opened on 22 January."[2] The final surrenders occurred between 31 January and 2 February 1943. At the same time, Russian troops lifted the siege of Leningrad, although bloody fighting would continue there for a year.

In early May German and Italian forces in North Africa surrendered, with more than 275,000 becoming prisoners of war. "In victory, even the French began to work together, with Giraud and de Gaulle forming the French Committee of National Liberation."[3] The committee worked as the authority in those areas under French control located outside of continental France. The committee was considered a provisional authority by the Allies, but at least there was a French authority with which to talk.

At the end of May Adm. Karl Dönitz withdrew his U-boats from the North Atlantic after losing forty-one boats in thirty days. From 1 June to 18 September 1943 only one Allied ship traveling in a convoy was lost, and only fifteen ships total were lost in the North Atlantic.[4] This change was not immediately obvious to the Allies, and the Battle of the Atlantic continued until the end of the war. The buildup for OVERLORD, which began in earnest in the last six months of 1943, occurred without meaningful German obstruction. Now there were some who thought that construction might be shifted from escorts and subchasers to landing craft without severely dislocating industrial planning or increasing the threat to Atlantic convoys.

The Battle of Kursk, which started on 4 July, was either the greatest tank battle in history or it wasn't. Robert Citino, in *The Wehrmacht Retreats*, describes it as "the incredible Shrinking Battle of Kursk" and makes a compelling case that the battle has been overhyped.[5] Not that it wasn't a big battle. Located roughly 283 miles almost due south of Moscow and 645 miles east of Warsaw, Kursk was the German army's last major offensive attempt on the Eastern Front. For the first time, the Red Army won a summer battle. Coming on the heels of German defeats at Stalingrad and in North Africa, it contributed greatly to the feeling in the West that Germany might be, if not on the ropes, perhaps just a push or two away from collapse, notwithstanding the fact that they were clearly still deep inside Russian territory. There were some in London and Washington, D.C., who thought that rate of German losses couldn't be sustained. Maybe there would be no need for a cross-Channel assault. Maybe RANKIN would be the operation that took place. Or maybe a successful assault by itself would be the catalyst for German collapse.

On 10 July 1943 British, Canadian, and American forces went ashore in Sicily. Barker had traveled to North Africa to be briefed ahead of time and observe the planning. Mountbatten witnessed the landings. While not fully successful—substantial losses by the 82nd Airborne Division to friendly fire and the failure to prevent German forces from escaping the island are two items that are often mentioned—capturing the island opened the Mediterranean to west–east shipping, and Mussolini's government fell from power on Sunday, 25 July. For Hitler, losing his one major European ally was a significant political and diplomatic blow. Surely, the Allies thought, the German people must be starting to understand that they were isolated and the war wasn't going to go their way.

On the night of 23–24 July, the RAF and the Eighth Air Force bombing campaign against Hamburg began. By 2 August nearly 50,000 people had died, and there was a relatively short period of significantly reduced output from the industries in the city. Air Chief Marshal Harris claimed that 6,200 acres of the city had been destroyed.[6] On 17 August, at the same time as the Quebec conference, Peenemünde was attacked by Bomber Command, delaying the development of the V-2 by almost a year. Perhaps the bombers would provide the final shove to the whole system, and that would be how Germany would collapse.

If the period through 1942 had been one of ad hoc measures to make sure the war wasn't lost, 1943 seemed to offer great opportunities in almost every theater of operations. This changed the context for the discussions and decisions taken when the Combined Chiefs of Staff (CCS) met for TRIDENT in Washington D.C., and, more importantly, for the Quebec conference (QUADRANT) just three months later, where the OVERLORD outline plan was to be considered.

COSSAC was now writing essentially a "proof of concept" proposal. They were aware of the many other details that would have to be examined and considered at some point as it evolved into a detailed operational plan, but now their goal was to answer the question "can it be done?" with the forces specified. For example, Morgan warned the Combined Chiefs in May that while the specific requirements for landing craft had not yet been determined with precision, they "would be large enough to present a very serious problem, which has no precedent."[7]

The Washington conference in May 1943 marked progress in the evolution of a coherent strategy, and the creation of COSSAC obliged the Combined Chiefs to start talking in specifics about the cross-Channel assault. British and American chiefs continued to disagree over strategy, but there were points of near convergence, even if the emphasis was stressed differently. The Americans would agree to continued operations in the western Mediterranean after Sicily, provided they did not interfere with the planned Combined Bomber Offensive, the buildup of forces for the reentry into the Continent, and offensive action against the Japanese. For the British, taking a more optimistic tone compared with earlier proposed plans, it was important to maximize the exploitation of Mediterranean successes, which they believed was the best way to prepare the ground for a cross-Channel assault in 1944.[8] Also on the table for the Combined Chiefs to consider was increased support for China (in order to keep the bulk of the Imperial Japanese Army occupied), action in Burma, and the already mentioned offense across the Pacific.

In terms of a European strategy, Italy (and, by extension, the eastern Mediterranean) was the core point of disagreement between the Western Allies. The invasion of North Africa had been a better choice than a cross-Channel assault at the time, given the state of the U.S. Army, although the buildup in the United Kingdom suffered. Taking Sicily and opening the Mediterranean would free up thousands of tons of shipping, as General Brooke had argued. Sardinia and Corsica could provide bases for tactical air closer to the European mainland and could facilitate an amphibious assault on Southern France. It was difficult, however, for many Americans and some British, including Morgan, to see the merits in going farther in Italy than the line from Naples on the west coast to the Foggia complex of airfields roughly opposite Naples on the Adriatic side of the boot. Perhaps there was political advantage to taking Rome and to using the airfields north of Rome for fighters and other tactical aircraft. However, COSSAC observed that Foggia seemed to be the northernmost useful base for heavy bombers, given their rate of climb and the height of the Alps.[9] From Foggia the bombers could reach the Romanian oilfields at Ploesti as well as targets like aircraft production plants in southern Germany.

The Americans argued that the cross-Channel attack had to have unquestioned priority over any operation in the Mediterranean and that offensive actions in southern Europe should be shut down or at least restricted when the buildup of forces for the cross-Channel assault required it.

The British argued that invading Italy would put Germany on the horns of a dilemma. Taking Italy out of the war would place additional demands on German forces by obliging them to replace the Italians on the peninsula. To do that would mean taking forces from France or the east, unless they chose to withdraw to the north, to Milan, or perhaps to the Alpine passes. If they did withdraw, the Allies would have an easy advance to what the British called useful air bases at least as far north as Florence, perhaps even Milan and the plains of Lombardy. Brooke particularly talked about the utility of the Mediterranean in "wearing out German forces."[10]

In truth, while the fighting in Italy contributed to an overall weakening of Germany's ability to defend her territories, the degree to which it made a substantial impact on the German defenses in northwest Europe—which is the key consideration from the standpoint of the cross-Channel assault—is open to discussion. The Germans had troops enough to man the Atlantic wall, albeit of lower quality and often in static defense divisions. They had enough high-quality mobile divisions in France to be of concern to Allied planners. They fought an effective defensive campaign in Italy without drawing formations from other theaters and with a relatively small deployment of their own forces.

Certainly, the Mediterranean was where the British and Americans were in land combat against the Germans and Italians in 1943. As late as November 1943, there was one more U.S. Army division in the Mediterranean than in the European Theater of Operations.[11] But there was no easy drive to Milan. Brooke, when discussing the advantages to the attacker in Italy, was fond of pointing out that there was only one double-tracked railway running north to south on the peninsula.[12] Hence, the Germans would have great difficulty in moving supplies and reinforcements. He apparently didn't take the time to consider that once Allied fighter-bombers had repeatedly bombed the railway, it would have to be repaired before being of any use to Allied forces. It turned out that it was as difficult for the Allies to supply forces heading north up the Italian boot using that one railway as it had been for the Italians and Germans to move supplies south, down the boot to North Africa. To put it mildly, the terrain favored the defense.

As for actions in the eastern Mediterranean, it is difficult to see from this distance what increased impact would have accrued to Allied chances for winning the war, particularly at the cost of delays in OVERLORD.

For Churchill, however, as British historian David Reynolds points out, the collapse of Italy was the great opportunity of 1943, one that Churchill and Brooke found difficult to let go.[13] If the Germans withdrew from Italy or retreated toward the Alpine passes, Churchill thought there would be opportunities to be had in moving quickly north and then east to Trieste. From there, he thought, a path would be open to Vienna. It was not clear that the Allied armies could get there, if they could be supplied, or if the complex Balkan political situation was conveniently supportive of (largely) British foreign policy goals. (Not that anyone explicitly advocated the use of ground forces in the Balkans, at least not yet.) The prime minister again raised the possibility that the Allies might even be able to convince Turkey to enter the war. To what end was never quite clear.

At TRIDENT, the debate got to a point where, in a move similar to Morgan's approach to the question of Normandy or Pas-de-Calais, the Anglo-American Combined Chiefs decided that agreement "could only be reached if each side were to spell out in detail exactly what plan they had in mind for the conduct of the war against Germany, and how they proposed to overcome the difficulties which seemed to each inherent in the other's proposals."[14] American planners, with support from their British colleagues, developed a plan that emphasized BOLERO and argued that attacking Italy would make no difference. British planners, with American support, presented a plan that included knocking Italy out of the war as a necessary prior step.

Both sets of planners used a ten-division force for the initial cross-Channel assault, possibly accepting the basic premise of SKYSCRAPER. However, the Americans thought that 4,600 landing craft would be necessary, while the British used COSSAC's estimate of 8,500. That number had been submitted to the Combined Chiefs with the concurrence of ETOUSA.

It didn't help that the standard plan for loading used by COSSAC was different than the one used by planners in Washington. Even something that seemed as simple as the definition of "vehicle" could cause problems. Was a "vehicle" for planning purposes a jeep, a tank, or a standard-sized truck? What constituted a reasonable average in terms of lift, given that divisions might need more of some equipment initially (tanks for example) and less of other equipment, with the elements not in the initial assault waves arriving perhaps days later? There was, as yet, no standard answer to these and other questions. In any event, the 8,500 number for landing craft was so far beyond what was possible to produce and put into use by spring of 1944 that the Americans first suspected that this was a British attempt to sabotage the plan, forgetting that it came from an inter-Allied staff (COSSAC) with the agreement of the U.S. theater command.

After a fair amount of debate and to convince the British that the attack was feasible, the Americans tied the assault to the known production schedules for 1943, reducing the size of the assault to fit the number of craft.[15] This gave Morgan about 4,500 landing craft to work with. He was also given two airborne divisions, with enough transport aircraft to lift less than one division at a time. The British COS admitted that the ten-division number was picked because of the need for overwhelming strength, but that it wasn't quantifiable, and they accepted the American estimate. The specification of twenty-nine divisions total for COSSAC was an estimate that fell between the minimum and maximum number of divisions projected to arrive by spring 1944. The estimate of landing craft available yielded the five-division initial assault number, with three in the initial attack and two for immediate follow-up.

The Combined Chiefs also agreed to the transfer of seven veteran divisions from the Mediterranean, giving COSSAC not only combat-experienced troops but troops already trained for amphibious assault. The transfers were to occur in November, and Eisenhower, the Supreme Allied Commander in the Mediterranean, was limited to twenty-seven divisions in theater.

In addition, TRIDENT saw agreement to conduct a four-phase Combined Bomber Offensive, each phase intended to strike deeper into Germany, ending in April 1944, and considered a necessary preparation for the cross-Channel attack.

Regarding the Mediterranean, the planning exercises yielded little. The Combined Chiefs agreed that operations should continue, but with the transfer of the divisions mentioned above, and with no particular course of action specified by which Italy was to be taken out of the war. That would be determined after HUSKY. Now there was an upper limit on resources committed to this theater, or so the Americans believed.

As with any agreement, the actual phrasing mattered. The strategic concept regarding the reentry into the Continent was described as the concentration of "maximum resources in a selected area as early as practicable for the purpose of conducting a decisive invasion of the AXIS citadel." Under "Specific Operations . . . In Execution of Overall Strategic Concept," the Combined Bomber Offensive from the United Kingdom was identified with an approved plan of operation. As mentioned in chapter 3, there was also, under cross-Channel Operations, this statement: "The Combined Chiefs of Staff have resolved: That forces and equipment shall be established in the United Kingdom with the object of mounting an operation with target date 1 May 1944 to secure a lodgment on the Continent from which further offensive operations can be carried out."[16] This goes on to specify the number of divisions that COSSAC was given for planning purposes. Being resolved to locating troops in a specific area with the object of doing something is different than committing to a plan of action. Unlike the Combined Bomber Offensive, there was still no approved plan for securing the lodgment.

The COSSAC planners were intimately acquainted with the challenges of reentering the Continent by now. According to Brigadier McLean, COSSAC's senior British Army planner, the most important document they inherited was SKYSCRAPER, which formed the basis for their planning after double-checking the data and intelligence to satisfy themselves that the conclusions that Barker and Sinclair reached were correct. They apparently also received a plan prepared at some point by members of de Gaulle's staff that proposed the Pas-de-Calais first and Normandy second, which suggests that the likely alternatives for invasion were reasonably clear to anyone who examined the problem.[17] They didn't take anything for granted from any of the papers they received and made excellent use of the material that had been gathered by the Joint Intelligence Committee.

As they worked, it would be common for one of the planners to request that a paper be written to cover a specific problem (equipment "overheads," or how to bridge the gap between the ramp of LSTs or landing craft and the beach, or the need to use smoke with the first wave of the assault, for example). The head planners would then meet to decide, in general, what was needed. Then officers at the next level down would write a draft that would be circulated to all of the sections concerned. The senior officer (below the head planner) of the section most concerned would then write a summary of all the comments received and the initial draft would be rewritten. It would then be shown to McLean or Hughes-Hallett or Air Commodore Victor Groom (another old friend of Morgan's from India) or their American equivalents as required. If there were conflicts or disagreements, it went up to Maj. Gen. Charles West, as head of the Operations Branch. Drafts might be revised many times, and if conflicts could not be resolved, they landed on Morgan's and Barker's desks. They could, if necessary, be taken to the British COS—Morgan's May letter regarding landing craft being one example. Of course, there were many papers in various stages of revision circulating all the time. The process seemed cumbersome, but it worked, largely because the staff was comparatively small and there were no day-to-day operational issues to manage. It was also decided early on to keep the joint planners of the British COS in the loop along the way, avoiding as many surprises as possible.

As noted earlier, one of the challenges facing COSSAC involved personnel. McLean was chairman of the planning group and they worked hard at getting and keeping American officers for all the jobs. According to him, "all too often the Americans would take away their better material shortly after they gave them to us. The result was that we put our chief reliance on

British planners with the result that [later] Ike and others got the view that the British were undermining the American planning staff. If they had given us more [high-quality people] there would have been a great difference in the nature of the planning. All too often, the American members furnished us were good men who were not experienced in this type of work."[18]

In part, this was the result of a poor American command structure. There was no equivalent to 21st Army Group, 2nd British Army, or 1st Canadian Army, all of which were up and running by July 1943, let alone someone like Commander-in-Chief, Portsmouth. The American Army personnel working at COSSAC were, administratively, on temporary detached duty from ETOUSA. A similar relationship was held with U.S. Naval Forces in Europe, commanded by Adm. Harold Rainsford Stark. Officers from Stark's command were also assigned to COSSAC and Commander-in-Chief, Portsmouth, on a temporary basis. It wasn't until early October with the establishment of U.S. Twelfth Fleet that the U.S. Navy had something like an operational command in the United Kingdom. Even then, it wasn't until Adm. Sir Bertram Ramsay, RN, returned from the Mediterranean at about the same time in October to take up the post of Commander-in-Chief, Naval Forces for the invasion that the naval side of the operation, NEPTUNE, started to take shape in the form of task force commanders who reported to Ramsay.

General Devers and ETOUSA stepped into the breach during the period when the outline plan was created. But ETOUSA was a theater command, not an operational one. The absence of a senior operational command is understandable because at the end of June 1943 there was just one U.S. division in the United Kingdom, the 29th Infantry, which had arrived in October of 1942. The next division to arrive was the 3rd Armored, in late July 1943.[19] At the end of 1943 close to 40 percent of the U.S. troops in the United Kingdom belonged to the Army Air Forces, which had grown substantially.[20] Similarly, the U.S. Navy was otherwise engaged during 1943.

For most of 1943 V Corps Headquarters, which had arrived in May 1942, was as close as the U.S. Army got to a senior operational headquarters. Commanded by Maj. Gen. Leonard Gerow, Eisenhower's old boss at the War Plans Division, V Corps HQ took on the planning for the WADHAM portion of the COCKADE deception effort. The eventual commander of VII Corps (the other U.S. corps for the assault on 6 June), Maj. Gen. J. Lawton Collins, was still a divisional commander in the Pacific. His 25th Division relieved the 1st Marine Division on Guadalcanal in January 1943, and in August, the same time as the Quebec conference, he was leading the division on the island of New Georgia in the Solomon Islands. In January 1944 he took over VII Corps, which had arrived in the United Kingdom during October.[21]

Having a theater command substitute for the operational headquarters that will be directing an operation is less than ideal. This was particularly true given the importance of OVERLORD. There was a long discussion about how to resolve the issue, with Devers suggesting that ETOUSA become a general headquarters, essentially taking on both roles. Marshall didn't accept that recommendation.[22]

Finally, toward the end of October, Gen. Omar Bradley was transferred from the Mediterranean to the United Kingdom and First U.S. Army Group was created, somewhat late in the day. It was later renamed 12th U.S. Army Group so it wouldn't be confused with First U.S. Army, which was the American army whose units would be part of the initial assault, and First U.S. Army Group became a notional group used in the deception plan.

For most of the critical COSSAC period, the British and British Empire contingent represented the majority of the planners, and British operational commands were primarily the ones evaluating the plans, addressing tactical issues, and training their troops. It borders on irony that while it's generally accepted that senior British decision makers were less enthusiastic about the cross-Channel assault than their American allies, it was British officers from all three services who did the most to ensure there was a plan to execute.

As one might suspect by now, there were also some unconventional aspects to the planning process. On the COSSAC staff was Maj. Peter Wright of the Royal Canadian Engineers. Major Wright had been stationed in London for a while and had become a regular at the Black Horse Pub in Marylebone High Street (not far from the Regent's Park). Whatever the nature of pubs throughout the British Isles today, in 1943 the local pub was truly "the local," where one gathered for a pint and a discussion of the events of the day. The Black Horse's regulars, as Wright observed, were in the habit of debating what steps should be taken to bring about victory as well as engaging in a general railing against all obstacles, human or otherwise, to progress in the war.

Wright reported to Morgan that the "Black Horse Plan" for the invasion of Europe was well advanced, and when the two of them faced one of the many problems related to planning the real assault, Wright, who must have had an impish sense of humor, suggested it be referred to the team at the Black Horse. Morgan agreed. As Morgan told the story, while not every issue and problem could be brought forward for advice, when there was a suitable question, the crowd at the pub became unpaid and unknowing consultants. He noted, "Sound opinion is not the exclusive prerogative of those who are paid to give it. It [was] comforting . . . to record that our operation was not launched without some consultation with that cornerstone of Western democracy, the English pub."[23]

With the successful conclusion of RATTLE, the work on the outline plan accelerated. Not counting Morgan's cover letter, the digest of the plan was six pages and thirty-seven paragraphs long. The entire document was much longer, approaching the length of a book. According to McLean it took about six weeks, with West and McLean writing most of it.[24] (See appendix C for the cover letter and digest.) There were twenty-three appendices, many with annexes or sketch maps that covered everything from port capacities (over five sectors that examined every port from Saint-Nazaire to Antwerp and Rotterdam); the alternative advantages and disadvantages of conducting an assault in either the North or South Seine sectors (east of Normandy), the Pas-de-Calais, or just the Cotentin Peninsula; naval forces required; ships and landing craft available; provisional organization of naval assault forces; planning data for landing craft and shipping; rate of buildup; attainment of the necessary air situation; land, naval, and airborne forces available; resistance groups; enemy defense systems and flak defenses; beaches; topography of the Caen sector; administrative considerations (logistics); methods of improving discharge facilities on the French coast; and meteorological conditions.[25]

The Operations Branch was confident. They had conducted a series of war games for the period from D-Day to D+40, moving unit counters on maps and engaging in scenarios that tried to anticipate probable German responses to Allied actions and that clarified their proposed plan of action. West and

McLean thought that the Americans were convinced, that the British COS were stalling, and that the prime minister was not happy about the possibility.[26]

At the same time, COSSAC recognized that OVERLORD would only work under certain conditions. Unlike the central Pacific, it was not going to be possible to isolate the defenders, deprive them of reinforcement and resupply, and then conduct air and naval bombardment for an extended period. Achieving overwhelming force was never guaranteed. They were confident they could get ashore. Staying there and building up forces was another matter. Consequently, every effort to distract, delay, and mislead the enemy was desired to improve the odds. The artificial harbor concept, the only viable solution to the lack of port facilities and so enthusiastically welcomed at RATTLE, was still in a design phase and not yet approved by the Combined Chiefs, but everything depended on it. Every day the air was filled with "what ifs."

After more than a few sleepless nights Morgan had to decide if they were going to submit the plan or report that it couldn't be done. Looking again at the number of assault craft, amphibious assault ships, and transport aircraft he knew were going to be available, the plan seemed a great risk. The result of this plan—either success or failure—could change the outcome of the war in Europe. "Had we indeed been planning the assault there would have been nothing for it but to report failure. But we were not. We were required to say, whether, with a certain scale of provision, the adventure could be contemplated." He recalled the wisdom of one of his earlier commanders, Field Marshal Lord Archibald Wavell: "There comes a time in great affairs when one shuts the books, discards the papers . . . and then synthesizes the resultant general impression. . . . Is it 'on' or is it 'off'?" COSSAC said it was "on." It was going to be: go to Normandy or go home. The concept could be "safely remitted to those who would be charged with its execution."[27]

After a series of all-staff "all-nighters," the plan was submitted to the British COS on Thursday 15 July. The paper was in three parts. The first covered the strategic factors leading to the choice of the landing beaches and lodgment area, including options considered but not recommended. The second covered the tactical details of the assault phase and the final part covered the subsequent development of operations, including the capture of Cherbourg, up to D+40.[28]

The plan had four phases. The preliminary phase, which was to start as soon as possible, envisioned softening German resistance by "all possible means including air and sea action, propaganda, political and economic pressure, and sabotage" all integrated into a multilayered attack. The German Air Force and economic system were particular targets, and the plan relied heavily on the Combined Bomber Offensive. It was also intended that diversionary operations be conducted.[29] The preparatory phase was to be focused particularly against the Luftwaffe in northwest France and attacks on line-of-communications targets. At this point the three naval assault forces would begin assembling. The details of the assault phase included landing the three divisions simultaneously along with an airborne assault on Caen. The fourth phase, follow-up and buildup, would include the capture of Cherbourg and the creation of the lodgment area.

The principles embedded in the COSSAC plan were tactical surprise, speed, and concentration of force against German weakness. Notwithstanding the size of the invasion fleet, Morgan and his planners believed surprise was possible because the beaches were far from needed port facilities, not in a place where the Germans anticipated an assault, and, hence, at the time poorly defended. They also envisioned a relatively short preliminary bombardment but didn't specify any particular length. Nor did they specify a time for the assault. Choosing daylight or night was left to the supreme commander.[30]

Speed and concentration of forces were interrelated because it was necessary to get inland as quickly and as far as possible, and it was necessary to land divisions as quickly as possible to win the buildup race against the defenders. The beaches chosen for the initial assault were later code-named JUNO, GOLD, and OMAHA. The initial line was planned to run right to left from Grandcamp to Bayeux to Caen. If there were additional resources, a landing could take place north of the Vire River estuary on the east side of the Cotentin Peninsula at about the same time. The beach selected for that assault was ultimately called UTAH.[31]

This initial assault area would be expanded to gain room for a turning movement into the Cotentin Peninsula and for the capture of Cherbourg. Ideally the invaders would carve out an area on a line running from Granville on the west coast of the peninsula near the island of Jersey, through Vire to Falaise, and then back toward Caen more or less following the Dives River.

By D+14, it was expected that Cherbourg would be captured, eighteen divisions would have landed, with additional divisions landing at a pace of three to five divisions per month; fourteen airfields would be in operation with twenty-eight to thirty-three fighter squadrons flying out of them; and a defensive line would run roughly from Trouville on the Normandy coast opposite Le Havre, through Lisieux to Alençon and west beyond Avranches to Mont Saint-Michel.

From there, it was considered impractical to try to cross the Seine and head for Antwerp with the forces available at that point. Consequently, they planned a drive to the southwest, to seize Saint-Nazaire, cutting off Brittany and perhaps gaining the other Atlantic ports. The outer limits of the lodgment area would be "along the Loire from Nantes [thence to Angers and on to] Tours and Orleans, thence to Chartres, to Dreux, down the Eure to the Seine and so to the sea," around Honfleur.[32]

In his introduction, Morgan started by reviewing his directive and the information supplied to him by the CCS. That accounted for the first two paragraphs. Paragraph three reads: "I have the honour now to report that, in my opinion, it is possible to undertake the operation described, on or about the target date named, with the sea, land and air forces specified, given a certain set of circumstances in existence at that time."[33]

He went on to note that they would be required to support much if not most of the landing force over the beach for up to ninety days, which, taking Channel weather into account, led to the need for what he called improvised sheltered anchorages. Without those, he would recommend that the operation not be contemplated. Morgan also called the COS' attention to the fact that "as additional shipping, landing craft and transport aircraft can be made available, so the chances of success in the operation will be increased"—an excellent example of the British talent for understatement.

Morgan reiterated what he said to them when Ismay first asked for his opinion—namely, that if the plan is approved, everyone from every agency concerned must take the view that the operation is already in process and that all efforts need to be highly coordinated.

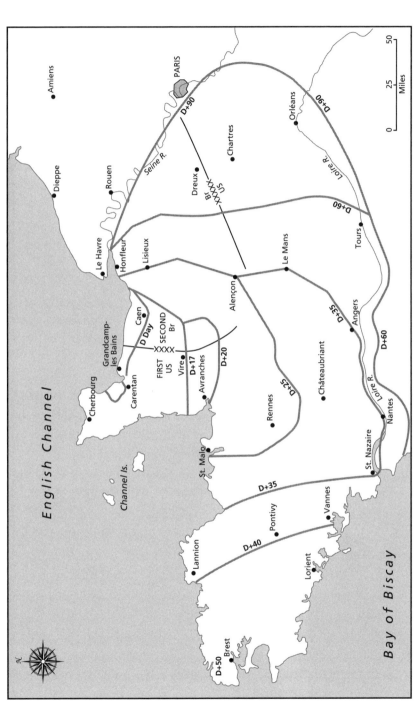

Map 1. Development of the Lodgment, 21st Army Group, February 1944. *Chris Robinson, based on Map IV, Gordon A. Harrison, U.S. Army in World War II, Cross Channel Attack (Washington, D.C.: Office of the Chief of Military History, 1951)*

Finally, because there was great enthusiasm about the success of the amphibious landings that had just occurred in Sicily, Morgan cautioned against seeing OVERLORD in the same light. As he pointed out, in HUSKY, "bases of an extended continental coastline were used for a converging assault against an island, whereas in OVERLORD it is necessary to launch an assault from an island against an extended continental mainland coastline." He added that the tidal range and weather in the Mediterranean had no resemblance to what was routinely experienced in the Channel.

Morgan was also explicit about what the major conditions affecting success would be. The first, already mentioned, was the need for "improvised sheltered waters" to unload troops and supplies. The second was the realization that naval assault forces would have to be trained to a much higher standard, which meant that the units would have to be formed in time to conduct the months of training required. Next was the need for "an over-all reduction in the German fighter force. . . . This condition, above all others, will dictate the date by which the amphibious assault can be launched." The last, and best known to later historians, was the requirement that German reserves on D-Day "not be more than twelve full-strength first-quality divisions. In addition, the Germans should not be able to transfer more than fifteen first-quality divisions from Russia during the first two months." He went on to specify that, in the Caen area, German mobile divisions that could join the battle should not exceed three divisions on D-Day, five divisions on D+2, and nine on D+8.[34]

The requirement regarding the number of German divisions that could be confronted was determined by a bit of backward planning. Rather than assigning particular values and crafting an algorithm to compute the effects of cover plans, air interdiction, or numbers of working locomotives, COSSAC sought to determine what was the maximum German resistance "against which we reckoned we should still be able to make headway to the extent and at the speed desired."[35] Morgan admitted that their estimate was good as far as it went, but it was far from a complete answer. "There could be fifteen German mobile field divisions in France on D-Day of which only half a dozen could ever arrive near Caen. There might be . . . ten such divisions . . . but five of these might be stationed within easy reach of our landing beaches."[36] One could easily come up with many variations and permutations, but some requirement had to be stated, and Morgan chose what he thought was a reasonable requirement. At the Quebec conference in August, Barker had to explain that it didn't mean that the operation would be cancelled if there were more German divisions but that more would have to be done by the Allies either by air attack or other means to mitigate the effect. As the plan stated, "The conditions under which the operation might be successful do not depend solely on the numerical strength of the reserves available to the Germans."[37]

The British COS met in London on Wednesday 4 August to review the plan with Morgan. For the past few weeks, their agenda had been filled with trying to forestall the movement of forces out of the Mediterranean in order to maximize the success of the upcoming amphibious landing at Salerno, south of Naples, considering the implications of Benito Mussolini's fall, debating possible Italian armistice terms, and trying to cope with manpower shortages. Brooke's diary entry is brief: "Morgan came to COS to discuss his plans for cross-Channel invasion—very over optimistic in places."[38]

Brooke, who was familiar with Normandy, brought up the issue of the hedgerows and their value for the defense. Morgan agreed, but according to his memoirs he pointed out that the proposed assault had what he called a defensive–offensive nature. If they could get inland, it would be the Allies who would be taking advantage of the hedgerows against German counterattacks.[39] There were other points that needed clarification, and eventually the chiefs accepted COSSAC's submission.

Morgan decided that, as his team had just successfully submitted what could become the plan for the reconquest of Europe, COSSAC should throw itself a party. By all accounts, it was as grand as wartime London could offer, notwithstanding the ongoing need for security and the requirement that everyone be at work the next day. Participation was almost completely limited by security requirements to those who were assigned to COSSAC (some invited guests also attended after proper vetting). On the top floor of Norfolk House was the former executive boardroom of Lloyd's Bank, now the COSSAC Club, which served as an excellent ballroom. The club pulled out all the stops. There were two dance bands, the first a very solid British one; the second, an American of the type so well known in the 1940s that could almost literally raise the roof. The staid and normally reserved atmosphere of St. James's Square was well and truly shattered for the evening. "By the time, in the early hours, that the troop-carrying lorries with their dimmed headlamps pushed their way . . . through the shades of sedan chairs, linkboys, hackney coaches and hansom cabs, one could say that the integration of the COSSAC staff was complete."[40]

As the British Chiefs of Staff prepared for the Quebec conference—a series of meetings that Brooke, for one, did not look forward to[41]—they gave Morgan orders that put him in a difficult position. They not only declined his recommendation that COSSAC brief the U.S. JCS ahead of the meeting, they also told him that, as they were one half of the Combined Chiefs, they would be the ones to brief their American counterparts, and it could be done in Quebec. They also instructed him to continue planning on the assumption that his proposal would be accepted.

His friends at ETOUSA let him know that not briefing the JCS ahead of time was a very bad idea. Morgan reported that they said it "with eloquence, emphasis and precision and they said it to us at COSSAC."[42] On the one hand, Morgan knew that if the JCS didn't have a chance to digest the plan, ask questions, and feel comfortable with the details, the opportunities for misunderstanding and unhelpful debate increased. On the other, the orders from his immediate superiors were unambiguous. Added to that was the fact that a group of British COSSACs, headed by McLean, would be on board the *Queen Mary*, with an opportunity to brief the prime minister and hold additional conversations with the British COS and their planners.

Morgan obeyed the orders of his British COS and he did not brief the Americans. As he later told the story, he also noted that Barker and a small team of American COSSACs were soon on the way to Washington to discuss many of the logistical and civil affairs related details that had not yet been addressed in the development of the outline plan. Consequently, on Morgan's order, with them went two complete copies of the plan with which Barker would be able to brief the necessary people in the newly completed Pentagon.[43]

Morgan also directed that both the British and American teams take with them a prioritized list of what they would do if resources could be increased. First would be an increase in the buildup rate of forces. Second would be adding the landing on the east coast of the Peninsula (Utah Beach), so long as the other assault forces were not reduced. Third, and only if the first two additions could be made, was the addition of diversionary attacks and feints in the Pas-de-Calais. He later recorded that there were differing opinions as to the need or even the possibility of creating a floating reserve. "In any ordinary land operation the smaller the forces [available], the more . . . essential it is to create and maintain a reserve in hand to be used as . . . the developing situation will indicate. But this operation was neither ordinary nor by land, and the theory seemed to break down."[44]

Barker's arrival in Washington was fortuitous. In July there emerged a serious debate within the ranks of American planners. One group within the OPD, headed by Brig. Gen. Albert Wedemeyer, took the view that the cross-Channel attack was the most important operation for 1944. Mediterranean operations could continue with the forces in theater, but if they interfered with or prevented the cross-Channel attack, then the United States should reevaluate the "Germany-first" policy in favor of the Pacific.

Maj. Gen. John Hull, on the other hand, was thinking that there were opportunities to be had in the Mediterranean, even if that meant not having a cross-Channel operation in 1944. This seemed to be the result of consideration of the logistical limitations that the Allies faced and not a rejection of the stated U.S. strategy position.

Rear Adm. Charles Cooke of the Joint Staff Planners felt that OVERLORD "was predicated on too many contingencies and might never be undertaken." Resources, in his opinion, ought not to be diverted to a *possible* operation from more certain operations in the Mediterranean and the Pacific. (On 6 June 1944, he ended the day on Omaha Beach and spent D+1 on Utah.[45])

Wedemeyer and others within OPD defended the TRIDENT decisions and argued that nothing had changed to warrant a shift away from a cross-Channel assault in 1944. Ultimately, the debate had to be resolved by Marshall and the American JCS.[46]

Barker's arrival with the outline plan on 5 August helped resolve the issue. Various OPD planners had known of the plan as it was being developed, including Col. Edward H. McDaniel, who visited COSSAC in July. Late in July Wedemeyer, who was visiting London as part of a European inspection tour that also saw him take temporary command of an infantry regiment in combat on Sicily, learned that the British COS were reviewing the plan.[47] Now Marshall and the OPD planners were able to examine the plan and the assumptions on which it was based.

When Marshall asked Wedemeyer for his evaluation of the plan in light of operations in Sicily, he replied that he was "very optimistic, especially in view of the U.S. Navy's efficient handling of its tasks in HUSKY."[48] Marshall also interrogated Barker. During the questioning, Marshall asked his opinion of British attitudes toward the operation. Barker replied that "soldiers of all ranks, up to and including General Morgan and General Sir Bernard Paget . . . were 100 percent favorable toward OVERLORD." He added that the COS were well aware of the prime minister's preferences and that Churchill was "always looking into the Mediterranean and especially into the Aegean."[49] The OPD, in its review of the plan, reached the conclusion that the limitations specified in the plan were capable of being overcome and that the plan was fundamentally sound. The JCS therefore decided to support OVERLORD without reservation.

On 9 August the American JCS submitted in advance of the conference its memorandum on the strategic concept for the defeat of the Axis in Europe.

> The present rapidly improving position of the United Nations in relation to the Axis in Europe demands an abrogation of opportunistic strategy and requires the adoption of and adherence to sound strategic plans which envisage decisive military operations conducted at times and places of our choosing—not the enemy's.
>
> . . . CONDITIONS HAVE NOT SO CHANGED AS TO JUSTIFY ON SOUND MILITARY GROUNDS THE RENUNCIATION OF THE TRIDENT CONCEPT. We must not jeopardize our sound over-all strategy simply to exploit local successes in a generally accepted secondary theater, the Mediterranean, where logistical and terrain difficulties preclude decisive and final operations designed to reach the heart of Germany.
>
> A careful evaluation of the march of events . . . indicates that the strategy enunciated in TRIDENT is sound—specifically:
>
> (a) That Operation OVERLORD, carefully synchronized with the Combined Bomber offensive, if given *whole-hearted* and *immediate support*, would result in an early and decisive victory in Europe.[50]

While Morgan, in his book *Overture to Overlord*, states that Barker also briefed FDR at Hyde Park before the conference, Barker doesn't mention what would have been a memorable meeting in his oral history. The more likely scenario is that when the JCS briefed the president in preparation for the conference, FDR was assured that they fully supported the plan and felt it was workable. It is clear the Americans were well prepared and in full agreement as to their positions for the upcoming series of meetings. It is also true that McLean briefed the president and the prime minister together at a special meeting in Quebec; Morgan may have conflated the two COSSACs and their performances.

On the morning of 5 August the British COS boarded the *Queen Mary* in Glasgow. The prime minister arrived after lunch. They headed out toward Canada that afternoon. The next day Brooke devoted a great deal of time to reading the COSSAC outline plan. He considered it "a good plan but too optimistic as to rate of advance to be expected."[51]

Over the next three days the British worked out how to best present their positions on the strategy to win the war. Brigadier McLean and the COSSAC team attended the third COS meeting on board and presented the plan. After answering the chiefs' questions in detail, they were told that the plan was satisfactory. The COS took Morgan's conditions to heart. In fact, they seized on them.

In their aide-mémoire, "Operations in the European Theatre of War," which was forwarded to the U.S. JCS ahead of the conference, the COS started by reviewing the key agreements reached at TRIDENT. They noted that the Combined Bomber Offensive, "though somewhat behind schedule, has otherwise fully justified our expectations. . . . It should be pressed forward with . . . vigour . . . because . . . it is one of the indispensable preliminaries to a successful invasion of the Continent."[52]

The COS then drew attention to Morgan's conditions for success of the OVERLORD plan and reshaped their desires for continued operations in the Mediterranean in terms of making the cross-Channel attack a success. They pointed out that much of German fighter production could be more easily attacked from bases in Northern Italy, compared with Great Britain. Hence, they argued, the Combined Bomber Offensive plus attacks launched from

Northern Italy would be the best way to achieve Morgan's requirement for reduction of German fighter strength.

If the Allies took Italy out of the war by invasion, the British argued, Germany could only reinforce the troops already in Italy with formations from France or the Low Countries. By placing the Germans in the dilemma mentioned earlier in the chapter, they would achieve the objective of maintaining maximum dispersion of German forces. The goal, therefore, should be to drive up the Italian boot until Allied forces reached a line that would run from Milan to Turin before attempting to cross the Channel. Naturally, the forces used would have to be of "sufficient strength to ensure that we achieve it."[53]

They ended by summarizing their position that OVERLORD should be carried out, on the basis of Morgan's outline plan, "as near the target date as possible." In order to do everything possible to ensure that OVERLORD would succeed, they believed it would be necessary to exploit Mediterranean successes by driving up to the Milan-Turin line. (Naples—just over four hundred mostly mountainous miles south of Milan—was taken in October 1943.) Their final point was that "the resources devoted to the campaign in the Mediterranean will be limited to those necessary to produce the conditions essential for the success of OVERLORD."[54] When Ismay forwarded a copy of the document to Churchill, he noted that it followed the lines of argument that the prime minister had approved.

An objective observer would note that the positions on both sides were familiar, with the Americans perhaps slightly more aggressive in approach and the British more nuanced. It was shaping up as a major decision point in the course of the war in Europe, and the cross-Channel attack might not survive the debate.

Two days later, as the *Queen Mary* steamed closer to Canada, McLean was summoned at short notice to Churchill's cabin to explain OVERLORD. With charts propped up on furniture the brigadier took the prime minister and other occupants of the suite through the plan. It's tempting to imagine that it was another one of Churchill's famous late-night meetings, but the time of day isn't specified in McLean's report.

While the prime minister liked the plan, he felt that the initial assault force was too small. "He produced, for McLean's inspection, his own plan which

relied on 'violence and simultaneity,' and visualized a series of simultaneous assaults by ten armoured brigades all along the coast" (revisiting his
concept from 1942). McLean, the practical Scot, pointed out some of the
limitations, such as number of landing craft, capacity of the beaches, and the
accommodation available in the assembly area. The prime minister replied
that if there were an insufficient number of landing craft, "more must be
produced."[55] Churchill agreed that the Caen area was the best choice for
a landing area, but he would have liked to see a landing on the east coast
of the Cotentin Peninsula as well. He also hoped there would be as many
diversions as possible.

The outlines of argument were drawn, and the British were briefed on the
likely American position by the Joint Staff Mission headed by Field Marshal
Dill upon arrival in Canada. The conference opened on 14 August at the
Château Frontenac, a magnificent hotel in the center of the old town of Quebec
overlooking the St. Lawrence River. From there it is an easy stroll via the
funicular railway to visit the small stone church, Notre-Dame-des-Victoires,
dating from 1723 and named to celebrate the French victory over the British
and colonials from New England in 1690. There is no record that either the
British or American conferees took the time for a visit.

The call and response of the two allies in their debate at the conference covered familiar ground. The Americans presented their case that OVERLORD
should be given overriding priority. The British responded that the best means
for meeting Morgan's preconditions for success was for additional action in
Italy. In particular, they pointed out that transfer of the seven veteran divisions
from the Mediterranean might create risks to Mediterranean operations
that could jeopardize OVERLORD. Brooke stated that the JCS position that
OVERLORD must have an overriding priority was too binding. Flexibility
was needed. If the Milan-Turin line was to be taken, all seven divisions might
be required. Afterward they could be transferred, with their replacements
coming from the United States or United Kingdom.

On Sunday 15 August, in the CCS meeting held after lunch, the discussion
became blunt. Admiral King, after observing that the British COS apparently
had serious doubts about accomplishing OVERLORD, stated that the "achieve-
ment of the necessary conditions was [not] dependent solely on operations

in Italy." Marshall then added that, in general, only by giving an operation overriding priority could success be ensured.[56]

> Unless a decision were taken to remove the seven divisions from the Mediterranean, and unless overriding priority was given to OVER-LORD, he believed that OVERLORD would become only a subsidiary operation. A delay in the decision would have serious repercussions on our ability to build up for OVERLORD and any exchange of troops, as had been suggested, would absorb shipping and complicate logistic considerations of supply as far back as the Mississippi River. . . .
>
> If OVERLORD was not given overriding priority, then in his [Marshall's] opinion the operation was doomed and our whole strategic concept would have to be re-cast and the United States forces in Great Britain might well be reduced to the reinforced army corps necessary for an opportunist cross-Channel operation [e.g., RANKIN].[57]

At this point Barker presented his paper explaining that COSSAC's view was that if the German forces were greater than the number specified, it was not the case that the operation became impractical but that "more extensive use would have to be made of available means to reduce the enemy's ability to concentrate his forces."[58]

The British and American chiefs agreed to continue the conversation. The next day the American JCS submitted a memo for consideration proposing that the Combined Chiefs reaffirm the May 1943 TRIDENT decisions and give overriding priority to OVERLORD. As for flexibility, they understood that "a grave emergency will always call for appropriate action to meet it. However, long range decision[s] for the conduct of the war must not be dominated by possible eventualities."[59]

The next agenda item on 15 August was the OVERLORD outline plan. Mountbatten outlined the artificial harbors concept, and then Barker and McLean presented the main features of the plan. "The Combined Chiefs of Staff approved the outline plan of General Morgan for Operation OVERLORD" without discussion and endorsed the British COS' action directing Morgan to proceed with detailed planning and "with full preparations."[60] In his presentation Barker made a strong pitch for more landing craft and troops "so we could extend the frontage and put another division ashore . . . on the UTAH beaches; But I didn't speak with any authority . . . we were just the planning group."[61] The next day, the minutes noted, "The Combined Chiefs of Staff discussed in closed session the strategic concept for the defeat of the Axis in Europe and . . . agreed to give further consideration to this subject at their next meeting."[62]

The final report to the president and prime minister, dated 24 August, made the following points regarding the war in Europe:

> The successful prosecution of the Combined Bomber Offensive from all convenient bases is a prerequisite to OVERLORD. . . . This operation must therefore continue to have highest strategic priority. . . . Operation OVERLORD will be the primary United States–British ground and air effort against the Axis of Europe. . . . As between Operation OVER-LORD and operations in the Mediterranean, where there is a shortage of resources, available resources will be distributed and employed with the main object of ensuring the success of OVERLORD. Operations in the Mediterranean Theatre will be carried out with the forces allotted at TRIDENT, except in so far as these may be varied by decision of the Combined Chiefs of Staff.[63]

The chiefs also agreed on the elimination of Italy as a belligerent, establishing air bases in the Rome area and, "if feasible, further north." At Churchill's insistence, a reference was made to a possible invasion of Norway, Operation JUPITER, "in case circumstances render the execution of OVERLORD impossible." It must be said that there were only two people who saw any value in an Allied invasion of Norway: Churchill and Hitler.

From the viewpoint of those who advocated an early cross-Channel attack, the JCS and COSSAC particularly, the results of the conference represented significant progress. The proverbial "can," however, was still kicked down the road in terms of a final decision. The agreements from May were reconfirmed, but there was enough ambiguity in the wording for multiple interpretations of the conclusions reached. From Brooke's point of view, "we have obtained quite fair results."[64]

It was also on 15 August that Brooke was told by Churchill that the Supreme Allied Commander for OVERLORD was going to be American and that

Marshall was being touted for the job by Harry Hopkins, among others. It is a mark of the man that, despite the huge personal disappointment Brooke felt (he described it as being "swamped by a dark cloud of despair"[65]), it did not interfere with his work. As the conference was considered to be on British soil, Brooke chaired the meetings, with all the extra work that entailed, and it ran extremely well. Nor did Brooke demonstrate any personal antipathy toward Marshall. The serious disagreements they had during 1943 were strictly of a professional nature.

COSSAC was also required to submit plans for RANKIN at the conference. It is to RANKIN that we turn in the next chapter.

—8—

"A PASSING PHASE"

The British hopes for RANKIN had a long genesis. For many reasons, mostly economic and political, Great Britain prepared in the late 1930s for a long war, while Germany hoped for a series of short, sharp campaigns. Germany got its campaigns but failed to compel Britain to end the war. Britain got its long war, but after Dunkirk Britain's prewar vision of how it was to be fought was out of date.

What Britain had left, in the absence of allies, was to attempt economic blockade; to search for tactical success on the periphery of German occupied territory; to develop and deploy strategic bombing; to generate propaganda directed at Germany, occupied Europe, and neutrals—most importantly the United States; and to encourage and support resistance groups if they emerged. Even after the Soviet Union and the United States became allies, the British still talked largely of bombing, support of partisan groups, and opportunism. Britain's focus was not on concentrating forces to overwhelm the Nazis but to disperse German forces and create vulnerabilities to be exploited. What Great Britain hoped was for Germany to collapse as it had in 1918. This hope evolved into the vision Britain had for reentering the Continent: Plan RANKIN.

The British wrongly believed that Germany was already fully mobilized for war in 1940 and would therefore be susceptible to air bombardment of industry and cities and to economic pressure. They also failed to consider the responses of Londoners and the citizens of the other British cities to German air bombardment as a guide to what German civilians could stand, either because of a belief that the German bombing wasn't heavy enough for long enough compared with what Bomber Command now proposed to do, or because they thought perhaps that Germans, living under a ruthless authoritarian regime, would be less resilient.

Based on an optimistic analysis of imperfect intelligence, "in September 1940, the Chiefs of Staff . . . predicted that the Wehrmacht, paralyzed by guerrilla attacks and shortages of essential supplies, would collapse under its own weight by 1942. The British Army would then be able to return to the Continent, not to fight expensive battles of attrition, but to accept the Germans' surrender."[1] As we've seen, this became an almost unshakeable, deeply held faith at the highest levels of British decision makers and commanders through 1943.

This also aligned with the British experience at the end of World War I when the so-called Hundred Days Offensive, directed by the French marshal Ferdinand Foch, broke the German will to resist. Food shortages at home, sudden reversals of fortunes on the battlefield, civil unrest, and ultimately a breakdown of civilian morale and loss of belief in the government led to Wilhelm II's abdication and the armistice. The speed with which the fighting ended in 1918 took the Allies by surprise. Consequently, the British COS always placed as much importance, or perhaps more, on the development of RANKIN as they did OVERLORD.

Hitler also remembered the way World War I ended, and he was determined to ensure that his domestic political situation remained secure. As a consequence, he sought by specific policy to guarantee that everything that could be done to feed Germany at the expense of the occupied territories would be done, including the acceleration of the Final Solution in Eastern Europe and the planned starvation of up to 30 million Russians.[2]

One of the three tasks COSSAC was assigned in April 1943 was the development of a plan to be employed in the event of German disintegration using whatever forces and transport could be found at the time. As there was little obvious indication that the Germans were near collapse, this was in some ways more challenging than working out the details of the cross-Channel attack. As Morgan later wrote, "It was difficult in the first place to know just how seriously the problem should be taken. It seemed to be one of those problems that could be dealt with quite superficially in a nice piece of circular writing. . . . It was a tough job to convince even the COSSAC staff that there might be something to this."[3] Still, it was what they were ordered to prepare. For Morgan, RANKIN became an intriguing challenge, in part because it was in his nature to consider the many facets of a particular problem and in part because of the issues that emerged from its examination.

What exactly would German disintegration look like? The direction from the Chiefs of Staff was lacking in detail on this point. Morgan started by developing three scenarios that, between them, seemed to cover the ground reasonably well. RANKIN Case A was based on the premise that German forces in the west had been reduced to a point where such British and American forces as were available prior to the OVERLORD target date could cross the Channel and successfully enter the Continent against weakened resistance, create the lodgment, and get on with the campaign. This was essentially the precondition described in the British "plans" for reentering the Continent that were crafted before SKYSCRAPER. While forces for this would not be available in the United Kingdom before January 1944, from then on Case A would begin to merge with OVERLORD.

Case B would cover the contingency of the Germans deciding to shorten their lines of defense in the west and withdraw from part or all of the occupied countries, most likely in a phased way. This was a bit trickier. On the one hand, the Allies would have a moral obligation to reenter those territories abandoned by the Germans, both to maintain contact with enemy forces and to feed and provide relief for the people who would look to the Allies for assistance after years of occupation. On the other hand, it would still be necessary to create the lodgment and build up forces for the final assault on Germany. If the Germans withdrew starting from western France and from Norway, the most likely scenario, forces sufficient for the repair and control of the French Atlantic ports and to create air bases and radar installations in Norway would be landed. There would also have to be humanitarian aid and the establishment of authority and security in the areas regained. However, the Allies had to guard against putting too much effort into relief and aid too soon. There was still the war to be fought. The main Allied forces wouldn't land until it was possible to seize Cherbourg, perhaps Le Havre as well, and move toward Antwerp, the assumption being that the enemy would hold on to the ports in the Pas-de-Calais for as long as possible.

RANKIN Case C addressed the possibility of a complete and sudden German collapse, in which case it would be necessary to get across the Channel as quickly as possible, liberate the countries that had been occupied, and enforce the terms of surrender in Germany. In addition to freeing the countries across the Channel, this would require seizing key German cities, transportation hubs, and the organs of power. It would also be necessary to round up and disarm the German military wherever they were found.[4] Particularly for this effort, it was important that rules and regulations not be a hindrance to getting the troops where they needed to be. The point of the exercise was "to transport the army to Europe rather than obey Board of Trade regulations. The forces would have to be crammed into whatever floated or flew."[5]

It wouldn't be as easy as it sounded, and the more Morgan looked at the problems, the more complex they appeared to be. A major problem was that to implement RANKIN, the Allies had to wait for the Germans to act and then react accordingly. That placed a premium on good intelligence about what was going to happen on the German side of the Channel as well as the ability to forecast with reasonable accuracy the flow of Allied troops and shipping to the British Isles. Neither was simple or easy. To the organs of Allied Intelligence, COSSAC was a customer, one whose appetite was going to grow. But the specifics of what intelligence and analysis COSSAC needed and how to provide it were still being worked out in May and June 1943. It also required coordination with AFHQ in the Mediterranean, as every possible source of troops and transport would have to be used. Finally, it meant that instead of combat troops, it would be a matter for civil affairs and military occupation, particularly for RANKIN Case C.

In May Morgan informed the COS of "an urgent requirement for a civil affairs headquarters and an operating organization equipped with a coherent body of policy procedure."[6] In the end, however, no such organization or direction was immediately forthcoming.[7]

In June COSSAC's principal staff officers were told to consider the concept of creating advance guards immediately so that German occupied territory could be entered as soon as needed, even if only in token strength. As the *History of COSSAC* from May of 1944 notes, "That some delay should elapse before the main forces could follow those advanced guards was inevitable, but it might not be a disadvantage. There was bound to be a certain amount of 'blood-letting' among the liberated peoples eager for revenge upon their quislings, and the delay in completing full occupation would both save the Anglo-American authorities from contamination and yet avoid the necessity of interfering and being compelled morally to save their enemies from very well-merited fates."[8]

RANKIN A and B were more or less straightforward problems that could be dealt with by variations on the plans for OVERLORD, with the addition of more reconnaissance, which was going to be necessary in any event. It was Case C that started to drive the planners to distraction. Some staff members apparently imagined with a twinge of envy what it would have been like to be on the staff of Genghis Khan, whose object "was to slaughter every living thing in his path and to raze to the ground everything that protruded above it, which must have simplified . . . both war and post war staff problems."[9] COSSAC planners weren't given quite that simple a task.

Case C was essentially victory without invasion. That meant, among other things, that everything that came with liberation and occupation arrived as well. To Morgan, the only source for the necessary postwar nation-building was through the military structure that had won the victory. No other agency had the power or could muster the resources needed. It wasn't simply a matter of food but of all the components of modern life. Grain and tractors, machinery for electrical substations, equipment to repair roads and railroads, fuel, oil, medicine, concrete—all the elements that would be required to get an economy moving again. In this he was, perhaps, ahead of the ministers and mandarins in trying to think through the postwar problems at a practical as opposed to a conceptual level.

The penalty for failing to provide the needed resources would be growing discontent and the increased likelihood of local political trouble and possible paramilitary action. Not all former resistance members could be expected to turn in their weapons and explosives. Some of them had spent years living outside the law or in double lives. As M. R. D. Foot, the excellent historian and author of *SOE: The Special Operations Executive, 1940–46*, noted, the one defining characteristic of those who went to the woods was "bloody-mindedness," not education, age, gender, or politics.[10] They could prove to be bloody-minded again if the Allies didn't get it right and quickly.

At the same time, there was the problem of establishing or reestablishing national governments in the liberated countries of France, Belgium, the Netherlands, Luxembourg, and Norway. The issues concerning Denmark, whose king remained monarch in the country during the occupation and whose government was still functioning up to August 1943, were initially deferred but ultimately included in the planning. Eastern Europe was outside the purview of COSSAC. Italy fell into a different category and was the concern of the Supreme Allied Commander in the Mediterranean. The answer to the question—What was the desired political goal of OVERLORD?—was not forthcoming. Clearly the objective was Berlin and the removal of the National Socialist government. But what was the object? For what positive purpose were the Nazis to be defeated? What would come afterward? Without clarification from the Combined Chiefs and their political masters, or direction from them to leave it to the diplomats, Morgan chose to assume an object—or, as he said—several.

In his original orders, Morgan was told to have no contact with any Allied government outside the British Empire or the United States. The time was rapidly approaching when those orders would have to be changed. Before he could address that issue, however, the RANKIN plans were due for presentation and approval in Quebec.

On Friday, 23 July, Morgan announced at the weekly staff meeting that planning for RANKIN must now be considered "the most urgent part of our business. We must take into account that there were already understandable signs that the highest authorities would be reluctant to undertake . . . OVERLORD if it could be avoided; the result of this trend of opinion was to bring . . . RANKIN into greater prominence."[11]

The following Tuesday, 27 July, a memorandum from COSSAC landed on the planners' desks.

Much has been written, more has been said, and there has been considerable discussion on the topic of Operation RANKIN since this staff was set up. But the fact remains that no progress whatever has, up to date, been made in the evolution of any sort of plan to cope with the state of affairs outlined in my directive. It has seemed . . . that the whole project is fraught with such difficulty that its solution defies our best endeavours. This cannot be so; the solution must be found.

. . . What it comes down to, I think, is this: There is an apprehension that the enemy, for a variety of reasons, may not be so obliging as to await our set-piece assault in the form of Operation OVERLORD. We have tended to divert far too much attention to the analysis of this variety of reasons, any one of which he might have for retiring before our blow should descend. Broadly speaking, these reasons may be divided under two main sub-heads:

(1) Either he may retire on account of his own internal weakness, or

(2) He may retire as a deliberate strategical move.

. . . I maintain that we derive no profit whatever from analyzing now the reason that may lie behind such a retirement should it in fact take place.[12]

Morgan then goes on to outline his ideas about what the plan should cover—namely, reconnaissance from Great Britain to detect any German retirement, followed by ground reconnaissance pushing inland on the far shore once the Germans moved. Planners were to consider the formation of task forces, drawing on lightly armored and fast-moving forces from various combat units plus engineers and other units that would meet specific needs. They were to consider the maximum use of both tactical air forces (an echo of the RAF in Iraq in the 1920s) and airborne troops, followed by amphibious landings at the most logical places.

I do not accept limitations imposed by the absence of craft and shipping. Should the enemy retire, we shall have to go after him even if we have to swim! I have dealt previously with the matter of taking risks, and in this critical situation, every remotely justifiable risk must be accepted and the cost must be paid . . .

In my contention it is not possible, however desirable it may seem, to indulge in any degree of detailed planning. I must emphasize that . . . RANKIN . . . must be designed to deal with a passing phase. By the time Operation OVERLORD is mounted and prepared, we shall be in a position to dictate to the enemy where and when he may retire. . . .

Again, I draw attention to the need for speed in producing a plan of some kind, and I suggest that we go to work without more ado on the lines indicated. I will discuss the matter with you at our next meeting, on Friday the 30th of July, by which time I shall be glad if the PSO's [principle staff officers] would have met and produced the outline of a project which is rather less discursive and more military in form.[13]

The minutes for the 30 July staff meeting note that a "thorough discussion" was held about RANKIN. The critical understanding was that, unlike OVERLORD, this was not a plan for a specific operation on a specific date. What they needed to produce was a "practical and flexible procedure which would be effective whatever the conditions in which RANKIN might be undertaken."[14] The procedures for Cases A and B were dealt with quickly. Case C took more time.

British forces were essentially located in the east of England; the Americans, arriving later, were quartered in the west as much for logistical reasons as anything else. The two supply systems were not compatible, and trying to mix them would have been a disaster. Port capacity was another factor. Working with the obvious assumption that the Russians would enter Germany from the east, the British and Americans, after crossing the Channel from their respective starting points, would wheel left and advance with the British brushing the Channel and North Sea with their left shoulder and with the Americans on their right. Everything was straightforward until the planners considered Germany.

Just how did one divide a country into three parts? Was it still to be one country or were there to be three separate political units? Was there to be a capital, and would it still be Berlin, with all the recent history associated with that city, on the one hand, but all the ministries, files, and bureaucratic details, on the other? A year later, in September 1944, Henry Morgenthau Jr., the U.S. Treasury secretary, put forth a plan that was briefly popular, envisioning a very different Germany: one that was divided into two and "deindustrialized," with an economy centered on agriculture and with the Rhineland, Ruhr, and other important centers of resources under international control. The plan was quickly withdrawn when it was realized it would make Germany reliant on foreign finance, and the United States wasn't interested in footing that bill.[15] Morgan, thankfully, didn't have to work with that guidance, but there was no other guidance forthcoming either. In the end, for planning purposes, COSSAC arbitrarily divided the country into thirds along existing provincial boundaries to provide "rough superficial equality."[16]

The actual decisions regarding the map of postwar Germany were made at the highest levels near the end of the war. Morgan, in the context of RANKIN, was trying to work out as many of the critical details as possible. In this, he engaged with issues and made recommendations that informed the decisions ultimately taken.

There was then the matter of those tasks that would immediately fall to the occupation forces upon their arrival in Germany. As mentioned earlier, forces would have to seize and hold the key components of the German war economy, at least until the end of the expected peace conference. They would have to disarm German troops around Europe and plan for the destruction or at least the control of what Morgan called German "war potential."

Not only would order have to be maintained and basic services made functional again, but some consideration had to be given regarding the sheltering and feeding of the tens of thousands of German civilians who had been "dehoused" by the Combined Bomber Offensive. This would be necessary for reasons of public health, security, and crime control, if for no other reason. In September Morgan noted that the Russians were considering the removal of heavy equipment from Germany to reconstitute their own industries. From an occupation standpoint, this led to the conclusion that higher than expected rates of German unemployment would also have to be coped with even beyond what would be contributed by the results of fighting in Germany to end the war and by Operation POINTBLANK.[17]

Next on the list was the issue of "displaced persons," both those forced to work in Germany who now wanted to go back to what was left of their homes and those Germans who had occupied other lands and now wanted to return to Germany before the Russians caught up with them. As many as 21 million people would be refugees of one sort or another, creating problems on an almost unimaginable scale.[18] Additionally, the return of prisoners of war had to be managed, with the medical and transport demands that came with them. The scope of the Holocaust may or may not have been suspected in mid-1943, but COSSAC did not have any orders to create specific plans to deal with those who had survived the camps. Related to that, there was no explicit Allied plan for the capture and trial of war criminals. The United States, Great Britain, and the Soviet Union issued a joint document on German atrocities on 30 October 1943, but that was not a matter for COSSAC planners.[19]

That seemed more than enough to take on for the submission and approval of RANKIN at the Quebec conference. Leaving the Russians to figure out their own plans, Morgan's team estimated that the American zone would run from the Swiss boarder to Dusseldorf; the British, from there to Lübeck. They estimated twenty-four divisions would be needed, which were more than could be found in the United Kingdom in 1943, but there were forces that might be spared from the Mediterranean as well as the possibility of shipping units from the United States that were not combat ready but could be put to work in a pinch. "This was an admittedly questionable expedient, since occupation duties call for as high a standard in many respects as any other form of military duty."[20]

COSSAC posited a Berlin that would be occupied by all three powers equally.[21] The boundary line between Russian forces and their Western Allies was not fixed, but if the British were to occupy the Rhine Valley, the Ruhr, Hanover, Hamburg, and thence to Lübeck, the line would be essentially along the banks of the Elbe River. (The Elbe flows from what is now the Czech Republic northwest into the North Sea at Hamburg.) Eisenhower's actions in April of 1945, stopping on the Elbe, directing 21st Army Group toward Lübeck, and waiting for the Red Army to meet British and American forces on the river's banks, may have had their genesis, at least in part, in RANKIN. Morgan, Barker, and many of the COSSAC planners were, at that point, part of Eisenhower's staff.

It was anticipated that the forces of the countries to be liberated on the way to Germany, and which were now in the United Kingdom, would not be able to establish security or order in their countries without the help of Great Britain and the United States. COSSAC's suggestion was that the British attend to Norway, Denmark, and Holland while the Americans take on

France, Belgium, and Luxembourg. The Channel Islands, of course, were to be retaken by the British.

All of this was drafted and redrafted, edited and re-edited. Finally COSSAC approved Plan RANKIN with variants and sent the plan, by teletype, to the Combined Chiefs in Quebec on Saturday 14 August, sometime after 2:30 p.m., the day before Barker would present the OVERLORD outline plan.[22] It was another near run thing. "Somewhat to the surprise of the COSSAC staff, these plans received a general blessing, with the rider that the forces projected for . . . Case 'C' were excessive."[23]

The British COS directed Morgan to continue preparing contingency plans for Case A. This put COSSAC on the horns of yet another dilemma. If they moved forward with the plans for a return to the continent against weakened opposition, they would now have to start issuing orders to the units that would be used in the event. Setting aside for the moment the absence of a Supreme Allied Commander who could give the orders, the event in question didn't seem likely, and there was the business of the next phase of planning for OVERLORD to get on with, not to mention that STARKY was a live operation that was just about to be mounted.

RANKIN C, on the other hand, fit in nicely with OVERLORD. Once the campaign had been successfully concluded, the occupation of Germany would begin. The work on Case C would be of use in either situation. As Morgan said, the problems that would come with the end of the war would come in any event. The only question was the cost to get there—it would either take the efforts and sacrifice of OVERLORD and the campaign that followed, or it might be gotten "for free," with a German collapse. Consequently, Morgan directed his planners to work on C and ignore the other two.

There Is So Much More to War Than Fighting Battles

Working on RANKIN C brought Morgan deeply into the realm of civil affairs, the active-duty forerunner of military government and postwar commissions. He found himself and COSSAC with the possibility of being responsible for a great and complex operation but without a civil affairs staff of any kind, without clear direction, and with the final authority in this arena, "to the extent that it existed . . . vested in and divided between the Civil Affairs Section, ETOUSA and the Civil Affairs Directorate of the British War Office."[24]

Morgan noted that if the intelligence estimates were close to accurate, the collapse of Germany could occur at any moment. He gave his opinion to the COS that what would be needed in that event were not large numbers of combat units but the ability to manage civil affairs. He requested that a policy be created covering military government in enemy territory and civil affairs in countries liberated as a result of war's end or the withdrawal of German forces. That policy took more time to emerge than it should have, and Morgan pressed on, rather than waiting for guidance, despite having "no staff to do the detailed planning, no organization to execute any plans that might be made, and no policy direction on which to base plans in the first place."[25]

The idea of a military government of occupation was hardly new. The American general Winfield Scott ran an excellent administration in Mexico City toward the end of the Mexican War in 1847–48. The American administration in the Philippines after the Spanish-American War, and the insurrection that followed, had mixed results. The Allies had occupied parts of Germany after World War I. The British Empire certainly had both direct and indirect means of governance or administration over local populations. Come to that, Rome had administered an empire for centuries based on the legion as much as anything else. The question now was how to apply the principles to a continent that had been destroyed as a result of a comprehensively total war waged with all the tools that could be provided by modern industrial societies. In all of the countries, people would have to be fed, clothed, and housed while the systems of modern life were rebuilt. In some liberated countries, the governments that were there before the war would return; in others, new governments would replace those that had been found wanting. To what degree were American and British civil affairs officers in western European countries to include or exclude groups, such as the Communist Party, from participation in politics and labor issues? In Germany, as in Italy and Japan, liberal democracy was to be intentionally substituted for prior forms of government, which meant, among other things, new constitutions, new civic societies, and new political forms as well as teaching the citizens of those countries what all that would mean, what rights and responsibilities they now had, and making sure that the new institutions took root and were survivable.

In all this, Morgan could not look on civil affairs as they were being carried out in Italy as a guide. Nor was the Allied experience in North Africa of much use except as a negative example. In North Africa there was a government of sorts with which AFHQ worked, eliminating the need for formal civil affairs activities, although *l'affaire* Darlan left a bitter taste in everyone's mouth.[26] Morgan certainly didn't want to see a repetition of that opera. If, for example, Vichy prime minister Pierre Laval were to welcome the Allies after the invasion, it would be helpful to have a policy in place that had been agreed by the political leaders of the Western Powers. That way, the Allies would know "whether we were to kiss him on both cheeks or only one, or alternatively, to shoot him in the stomach."[27]

Italy was enemy territory that later moved to cobelligerent status, and the organization and conduct of civil affairs there left much to be desired. Civil affairs in Italy ran through what was called AMGOT—Allied Military Government for Occupied Territories, which had a parallel command structure that eventually went up to the Supreme Allied Commander and his chief of staff. In other words, there were essentially two independent commands in the same theater. Morgan and the civil affairs personnel that became part of COSSAC took the view, ultimately accepted for western Europe, that everything had to run through one command structure to the Supreme Allied Commander. As he said, "Civil affairs was a function of command."[28] What COSSAC ultimately created was the concept of mobile civil affairs teams that were fully integrated with combat units and would be part of operations, not just rear area and postwar concerns. As such, they were part of one integrated military command, reaching down as far as the division level.[29]

This structure did not come at once. Like much of COSSAC's formation and work, the civil affairs section evolved through a period of trial and error. There were a series of debates between the Americans of the Combined Civil Affairs Committee in Washington, ETOUSA, the European Advisory Commission in London, and COSSAC as to which was the preferable system and who was to be in charge, with Barker representing COSSAC's views. Ultimately, in spring

of 1944 COSSAC's recommendations, although modified by Walter Bedell
Smith, were generally accepted, and civil affairs became part of SHAEF's G-5
section, with a Combined Civil Affairs Committee (Liaison) based in London
representing the views of the CCS.

An additional challenge that Morgan faced was in the quality of many of
the civil affairs officers that were, at least initially, identified for OVERLORD.
They were too often "people no one else wanted."[30] This mirrored the experience of at least one officer in Italy, who expressed the opinion that the senior
officers in the Allied Control Commission Headquarters (the parallel command to the army command structure) were, "for the most part, made up of
military failures. This was true on both the British and American side."[31] On
the American side, this is certainly not surprising as there was no civil affairs
school before 1942, when one was established on the University of Virginia
campus. Nor was civil affairs considered a career path that led anywhere. It
would take time for the joint military–civilian faculty to develop a syllabus
that was relevant to the needs of the commanders in operational theaters and
to find ways to recruit at least a cross-section of officers that could be relied
on. There were similar problems on the British side.

For Morgan, this was a great deficiency that he felt should be addressed on
an ongoing basis. There is a period at the end of any conflict during which a
country must be rebuilt, and some form of administration established. "For a
period, at any rate, [this] must be the responsibility of military commanders.
It seems thus unavoidable that military officers must be trained to this end.
There is so much more to war than fighting battles."[32]

Ultimately, they got enough of what was needed, but the challenges faced by
civil affairs officers in the liberation, occupation, and reconstruction of Europe in
the immediate aftermath of the war is a story well worth a detailed examination.

Western Europe held the possibility of providing material support in an
attack on Germany and was of substantial political importance both during the
war and for any vision of a postwar environment. French-controlled colonies
in the Mediterranean, Caribbean, and Africa were also beneficial to the Allies
in the prosecution of the war against Germany. Consequently, it would be
helpful to the Allied cause if the governments of the countries being liberated
were active political supporters of the Allies, not just grateful recipients of aid.

The British, having been at the war for longer, had spent some time considering some of the aspects of the problem at the political level. They had established relations with the various governments-in-exile as well as housing many of them in London. As part of the attempt to get organized for ROUNDUP, there was a cabinet-level committee, Administration of Territories (Europe), set up in June of 1942. Its task was to plan, in general terms, for the administration of liberated countries. Under their guidance, and except for France and Denmark, agreements with the governments of each of the western European countries occupied by the Germans were reached that addressed issues relating to Allied military presence in their countries. It made sense to make it explicit that this was not going to be the replacement of one German-style occupation with another. "These agreements, which contained the basic policy guidance for all planning and civil affairs operations, originated in considerations of policy rather than legality."[33]

This meant that, although the Allies could have invoked military necessity and invaded the occupied countries, they chose to gain the agreement of the various governments and enter with their consent. That is, unlike Italy and the territories of the Mediterranean, these countries were to be liberated, not occupied. This was possible because Norway, the Netherlands, and Belgium had recognized de jure governments-in-exile located in London. (The prewar Belgian government had fled to London while the king remained behind, ultimately being imprisoned by the Germans.) It was believed that having specific understandings with these governments would make it easier for troops to operate in each of the countries and would set up a positive environment for postwar cooperation. The agreements had to be tailored for each country. There was, for example, a state-of-siege law in the Netherlands that was applicable, requiring that the agreement be crafted respecting that law but not restricting the options available to the Allied forces. Similar considerations were made for each country. After some discussion, the United States agreed with the British approach.

France was a different and larger problem. The search for a solution extended beyond the time frame of COSSAC's existence—indeed, there was not a resolution of the situation until mid-August 1944. The Vichy regime could make an argument that they were born out of the embers of the Third

Republic and that the National Assembly had granted them the power to form a government and to write a constitution, which they managed to avoid doing. Perhaps not very creditable, but de Gaulle was also making claims about his authority and support that didn't always hold up to close examination.

The French Committee of National Liberation (FCNL), headquartered in Algiers, was as close to a government that the Allies could find to work with. However, President Roosevelt in particular had a certain antipathy for de Gaulle and did not want to create a situation where the FCNL (or CFLN, in French) was given formal political recognition in advance of elections that could be portrayed as representing the will of the French people. While conversations could occur on a military operational level, he wanted to avoid what would be seen as government-level negotiations. The British were more pragmatic. The American president's eventual acceptance of the FCNL as the governmental agency for France was encouraged by the formal recognition of de Gaulle's organization by the governments of Belgium, Luxembourg, and Czechoslovakia on 13 June 1944 and by Poland a day later. Churchill also played a key role as mediator and supportive interlocutor between the president and the general.

In the end, the FCNL was treated as the de facto authority for the liberated areas of France, but along the way there were disputes about almost everything, including the normally obscure question of printing currency and setting rates of exchange. Morgan recalled a conversation with John McCloy, U.S. assistant secretary of war, "on the subject of currency adjustments between ourselves and the liberated countries—of which [Morgan] understood not a single word."[34]

The failure to reach an understanding regarding France created a last-minute crisis with de Gaulle over his public support for the Normandy assault. It was only on Sunday 4 June 1944 that de Gaulle arrived in England from Algiers. Eisenhower briefed the French general about OVERLORD and then presented him with the script of speech that he hoped de Gaulle would make. Eisenhower let him know that the speech had been approved by the U.S. government, and it couldn't be altered. Not surprisingly, de Gaulle found the script unacceptable and refused to make the speech. Just before the scheduled broadcast time of 6:00 p.m. on 6 June, and after the intercession of Charles Peake of the British Foreign Office, whom Morgan had brought into COSSAC and who was an old friend of the French general, de Gaulle agreed to speak on the BBC. He delivered "a brief but artfully crafted speech that managed to override what Eisenhower had previously said in his," telling the French people to obey the officials of the FCNL.[35] Eisenhower had asked the French to follow the instructions given by the Allies. Morgan commented, "When the political history of this period comes to be published no doubt it will be proved that we pursued our relentless aim under the inspiration of the highest motives. But at the time, it did not seem like that."[36]

Morgan had already moved on his own authority to begin the process of creating a civil affairs section within COSSAC. There simply wasn't time to wait for the issues to reach the top of the pile of concerns that the Combined Chiefs were dealing with, if RANKIN C was going to have any viability. As well as all the high-level negotiations, there was the basic but urgent question of staffing, organizing, and training the civil affairs staff that would be deployed. To Morgan, that meant finding someone to head up the new civil affairs section at COSSAC.

Who was that person, and where could they be found? Should it be a military officer with an understanding of civil affairs or a civil administrator comfortable operating in a military environment? Morgan raised the issue with his aide, Capt. Robert Jenkinson, who was a most remarkable resource and someone who had an amazingly broad network that reached from wine stewards (and their cellars) at the best hotels in London, to the upper reaches of Whitehall ministries, to the denizens of Broadway theater in New York City, and heaven knows who else in between.

A few days after their initial conversation, Bobbie, as Morgan called him, invited COSSAC to a meeting at the Cavalry Club in Mayfair to meet a friend. The friend turned out to be Sir Roger Lumley, 11th Earl of Scarborough, K. G., of Eton, Sandhurst, the 11th Hussars, and Magdalen College, Oxford. He had served in Parliament for fourteen years and had been parliamentary private secretary to Sir Austen Chamberlain and later private secretary to Anthony Eden. He had just returned to London, his term as the governor of Bombay for the past six years having ended. As governor, in the course of a generally much-admired administration, he had ordered the imprisonment of Gandhi and the other leaders of the All India Congress in 1942. He was now looking for employment.

After a brief discussion, Morgan suggested that Sir Roger apply via the appropriate channels for the position at COSSAC. "In due course he became our first Chief Staff Officer, Civil Affairs at COSSAC [with an American deputy, Col. Karl Bendetsen], and under his able guidance there took shape the embryo of the network that eventually served General Eisenhower in his campaign."[37] Morgan also got "bawled out" for offering Lumley the job but survived.[38] Sir Roger was given the temporary rank of major general.

Without much guidance, Morgan managed to give COSSAC and the Supreme Allied Commander the foundations of a civil affairs function for northwest Europe and for military government in Germany. For Germany, the initial purpose of any military government that would be established was to assist the Supreme Allied Commander in imposing his will on the defeated enemy. "Relief, an important function in liberated Allied territory, would be restricted in Germany 'to those measures which the Supreme Allied Commander may specifically direct to prevent a general breakdown of civil life and the spread of disease.'"[39]

The last great action of COSSAC for civil affairs was to establish a written policy and procedures manual. While a routine document, and one of many similar manuals produced to cover various topics, it unambiguously assigned command and control of civil affairs to the military commanders. In Germany or other enemy territory, the Supreme Commander would be the military governor, and he could delegate such authority as necessary to subordinate commanders in various geographical areas. "The tasks of the civil affairs staffs and detachments would be to relieve the combat troops of civil commitments."[40]

Some modifications were made to the structure created by COSSAC, based on the experiences of those who took over civil affairs at SHAEF later in the spring of 1944. The handbook was amended, but the basic principle of a civil affairs headquarters as part of a unified military command and civil affairs staffs that were to be closely integrated with the other staff functions was maintained.[41]

COSSAC was growing in other related departments as well. It was essential that the planners and later the operational headquarters would have ongoing access to the best political advice and guidance without delays or filters between the diplomats and the generals. In response to another of Morgan's requests, William Phillips from the U.S. State Department and the previously mentioned Charles Peake of the British Foreign Office were assigned to COSSAC by early October. They were welcome additions, and the political advisors section added substantially to the shaping of plans and policy. They continued in their roles after SHAEF was created.

COSSAC also created something called the European Allied Contact Section in the immediate aftermath of the Quebec conference. This was separate from the General Staff sections and, while related to civil affairs, functioned as a connection point to external organizations, particularly governments-in-exile.

As Morgan explained at the weekly staff conference on 20 August, "signs and portents were not wanting that the time had now come when it was no longer possible to dispense with such contacts" between COSSAC and the staffs of the Allied European nations.[42] One example given at the meeting was that the implementation of RANKIN contemplated the use of forces controlled by the FCNL in southern France. At the same time, the entire operation was to be commanded by the Supreme Allied Commander. It followed that the French would have to be contacted to work out the details and gain agreement. This was exactly the sort of conversation that the representatives of the Supreme Allied Commander would need to have with governments-in-exile or their military staffs.

At the same meeting, Peake recommended that COSSAC claim the right to supervise the security arrangements of any Allied officers who might be admitted to Norfolk House, and Sir Harold Wernher added that "Combined Operations Headquarters had had painful experiences as a result of the indifferent security of the Allied staffs."[43] As part of the security considerations, the European Allied Contact Section would be the only point of contact with COSSAC, and the representatives of the other governments were not allowed to meet principal staff officers or anyone else in other parts of the building. Indeed, as part of a general review of security procedures on 8 October, Peake warned the principal staff officers that the French were particularly skillful in pretending "that they were fully informed on matters of which they only possessed fragmentary information."[44] This may have been an indication that certain national stereotypes were widely accepted.

In another meeting, Sir Roger Lumley noted that, when dealing with foreign officers, operational matters would not be discussed at this stage, nor would specifics of civil affairs plans be revealed. For now, the object was "to obtain information from them without disclosing any in return." There was also to be specific guidance as to what subjects were not to be discussed. It may be proper to discuss relief operations, public health, or technical services issues, but, as a specific example, the subject of military government "was better avoided."[45]

At the end of the 20 August meeting, Morgan directed the principal staff officers to draft a paper to the COS that would explain why contacts were now necessary and would also contain practical and specific proposals explaining how the system would be securely established and functional. By 1 October the chiefs had approved COSSAC's plans. What Morgan needed now was someone to head up this new section. It would have to be a person who understood how to work with politicians and diplomats as well as was able to function in a military environment. How Morgan found that person is part of the story in chapter 10.

RANKIN and the Joint Chiefs of Staff

The U.S. Joint Chiefs also had strategic interests regarding Europe that RANKIN both informed and supported. Sir Halford Mackinder, a British geopolitician and strategist, had put forward a theory that the Eurasian landmass was the key geographical consideration for security and power. In an article for *Foreign Affairs* in 1941 he pointed out that, in 1938, Russia had produced "more wheat, barley, oats, rye, sugar beets and manganese than any other country, ranked second in oil production, was tied with the United States for first in iron production, possessed enough coal to supply the entire world for three hundred years and was virtually self-sufficient." He also predicted that a victorious Russia would be the "greatest land Power on the globe . . . in the strategically strongest defensive position."[46] By 1943 the Americans, mindful of their own growing presence on the world's stage, could hardly ignore those facts.

The American political commentator Walter Lippmann wrote a best-selling book in 1943 in which he argued that the security interests of the United States required that America be engaged with western Europe. The Atlantic Ocean was not a border, he declared, but "the inland sea of a community of nations allied with one another by geography, history and vital necessity." Given the potential military and economic power of Eurasia, "the New World cannot afford to be isolated against the combined forces of the Old World"—that is, against a Soviet Union that could also draw on the resources of western Europe.[47]

The U.S. government also heard the concerns of the Czech and the Polish governments-in-exile located in London. They warned U.S. ambassador Anthony J. Biddle Jr. that the Western Allies would have to race toward Berlin in case of a German collapse or Soviet breakthrough, otherwise there would not be an Allied victory in Europe but a Russian one.[48] Various intelligence appreciations that were generated over the spring of 1943 suggested to the Americans that the possibility of a German collapse and Russian domination of western Europe could happen, and it also appeared that there was a start of a Soviet diplomatic effort in Europe to prepare the ground for Russian expansion.

U.S. planners, aware of the political implications of a sudden German collapse, thus rejected the British Mediterranean approach both on the military grounds that it was a secondary theater where it would take too long to get results and on the political grounds that it would suit British political interests in the Mediterranean but not U.S. postwar interests as they would relate to western Europe. Nor would the Mediterranean provide the most effective way to confront emerging Soviet power, if that became necessary. RANKIN did provide such a way, if Germany collapsed before Allied forces landed on the Continent.

In this way RANKIN became the natural complement to OVERLORD. Both would allow the forces of the Western Allies to meet the Russians as far east as possible and, ideally, to get to Berlin at the same time as the Russians. The contingency plans that the U.S. developed for the postwar period considered the possibilities of either confrontation or collaboration with the Russians. But in either event, it was recognized that western Europe was essential to U.S. national security interests and was not truly defensible against Russian influence or invasion without a U.S. commitment and U.S. forces in theater. RANKIN and the concept of the cross-Channel assault show, as Mark Stoler points out, that there was a "definite American appreciation . . . of the relationship between strategy and politics and the necessity for specific military action to prevent Soviet domination of Europe."[49]

American interest in RANKIN continued throughout 1943. On the way to the Cairo and Tehran (SEXTANT and EUREKA, respectively) conferences, Roosevelt spent a great deal of time considering what the map of postwar Europe might look like. On board the new U.S. battleship *Iowa*, the president and his advisors prepared for the meetings, discussing both their plans to resolve the issues around the strategy for winning the war and what to do after the war was won.

In the meetings, FDR made it clear that he did not like RANKIN. He started by finding the American zone of occupation in Germany in the southwest objectionable. He much preferred that the British should have the southwestern zone and be responsible for France and the Low Countries while the United States occupied northwest Germany, Norway, and Denmark. He felt that it was evident that "British political considerations were in the back of the proposals . . . and that the British would 'undercut us in every move we make' in the southwestern zone." He also didn't like the fact that French lines of communication would be behind the American zone. Additionally, he wanted U.S. troops out of France and Italy as soon as possible, "though some might have to be kept in France to help create a buffer state from Calais, Lille, and the Ardennes through Alsace and Lorraine."[50]

While it is true that Morgan could have received input from the Foreign Office and other ministries, Barker and the other Americans at COSSAC were full participants in the RANKIN process. It seems clear that the explanation that Morgan put forward was genuine. COSSAC drew the occupation lines according to how forces were deployed in the United Kingdom and how they would land and fight the battle. It didn't make sense for the Americans to move from west to east while the British and Canadians were moving east to west in the middle of the Channel so their landing would facilitate the eventual occupation of liberated countries and Germany. It would only be slightly less complicated to move the forces after the German surrender, taking time and complicating issues while the Russians would be pressing ahead. It is also true that the Americans in Washington didn't really start studying the issues around postwar occupation of Germany in a serious fashion until December 1943, and even then the Civil Affairs Division of the War Department was not particularly helpful in moving the discussion forward.

Lt. Gen. Sir Frederick Morgan. The photo was probably taken after D-Day. Note the SHAEF shoulder patch and the expeditionary setting. His deputy at COSSAC, Maj. Gen. Ray Barker, USA, said of Morgan, "Here was a man who above everything else was honest and straightforward." *Imperial War Museum (EA33078)*

Topographical map of part of North Africa, Sicily, Italy, Western Europe, the Balkans, and Turkey. The mountainous terrain of Italy and the Balkans is clearly shown, as is the Lombardy Plain in northern Italy, just south of the Alps. The proximity of the Pas-de-Calais to Dover is easy to see, as well as the greater distance to Normandy and the Cherbourg Peninsula to the west. To defend against invasion and in the absence of definitive intelligence, the Germans took the position that landings could occur anywhere from Norway to Denmark, across the North Sea toward the Dutch and Belgian coast, or along the coast of France from the Channel down to the Spanish border or to Mediterranean France. *Imperial War Museum (TR991)*

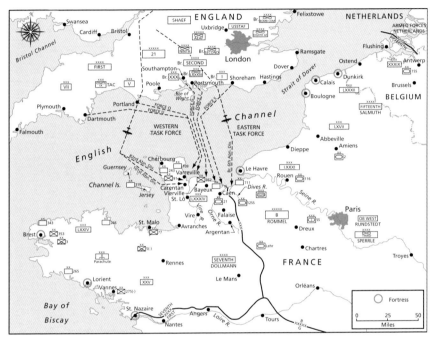

Northwest France, final OVERLORD invasion beaches and positions of German forces on 6 June 1944. Antwerp is in the upper right-hand corner of the map; Saint-Nazaire, Nantes, and Angers are at the bottom right/center. *U.S. Military Academy, West Point, History Department*

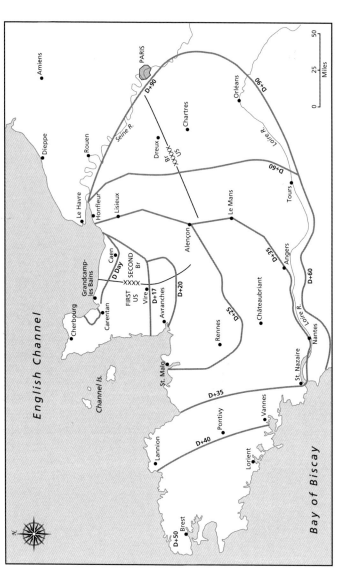

Map created by the 21st Army Group in February 1944 showing their estimate of how the OVERLORD lodgment would develop. It is very close to the outline OVERLORD plan that COSSAC developed in July 1943. In the COSSAC plan, the initial area to be seized was bounded by a line from Grandcamp (toward the Channel from Carentan), through Bayeux to Caen and Ouistreham (on the coast just east of Cabourg). The ultimate outer perimeter of the lodgment would be from Nantes to Angers to Tours and Orleans, thence to Chartres, Dreux, down the Eure River to the Seine and to the Channel at Honfleur, across the estuary from Le Havre.

U.S. Army in World War II, Cross-Channel Attack. Office of the Chief of Military History, U.S. Army, 1951

Contemporary photo of Norfolk House, St. James's Square, London. It was the location of Eisenhower's initial headquarters for Operation TORCH as well as the home of the COSSAC staff. Ideally situated, it was a five-minute walk to Trafalgar Square and less than ten minutes on foot to the War Office. *Alamy Ltd*

HOLLYWOOD HOME, LARGS

Postcard from 1930. HMS Warren, also known as the Hollywood Hotel, Largs, Scotland. Site of the RATTLE conference that broke the logjam in the debate about the feasibility of and the location for OVERLORD. *Author's collection*

The Combined Chiefs of Staff in Washington, D.C., May 1943. Behind Prime Minister Churchill and President Roosevelt (*left to right*): Field Marshall Dill, General Lord Ismay, Air Marshal Portal, General Brooke, Admiral Pound, Admiral Leahy, General Marshall, Admiral King, and General Arnold. *Imperial War Museum (A17106)*

Lord Louis Mountbatten as a captain in the Royal Navy, 1939. After Mountbatten became chief of Combined Operations, Churchill promoted him from captain, acting commodore to the acting ranks of vice admiral, lieutenant general, and air marshal. Morgan wrote in his memoir that he felt that Mountbatten didn't get all the credit he deserved for his role in the early development of the OVERLORD plan.

National Portrait Gallery, London (NPG x9452); photo by Walter Stoneman

John Hughes-Hallett, RN. He was an amphibious war expert and the senior British naval planner on the COSSAC staff through the summer of 1943. "An exceedingly capable man who was able to get everyone's back up" Hughes-Hallet was also the holder of many motorcycle speed records on the Portsmouth to London road. He later commanded the cruiser HMS *Jamaica* and participated in the pursuit and sinking of the *Scharnhorst*. The photo dates from 1952. *Getty Archives*

The two teams of COSSAC planners, one British and one American, who briefed the American and British Chiefs of Staff ahead of the Quebec (QUADRANT) conference in August 1943, shown here meeting at the Château Frontenac Hotel in Quebec City. *Left to right*: Captain Mansergh, RN; Captain Hutchins, USN; Brigadier McLean; Major General Barker; Air Commodore Groom; and Colonel Albrecht, USA. *U.S. Signal Corps Photo, U.S. National Archives (SC 439154)*

Maj. Gen. Ray Barker being congratulated by Lt. Gen. Sir Frederick Morgan after Morgan presented him with the Order of the British Empire, June 1945. Morgan was the senior British officer at SHAEF and was awarded the U.S. Army's Distinguished Service Medal and the U.S. Legion of Merit. *U.S. Signal Corps Photo, U.S. National Archives (SC 439154)*

Maj. Gen. Sir John "Sinbad" Sinclair, coauthor with Brig. Gen. Ray Barker of the SKYSCRAPER plan that was a key source for the COSSAC planners. After the war Sinclair became head of the British Secret Intelligence Service (MI6). *National Portrait Gallery London (NPG x96656); photo by Walter Stoneman*

Gen. Sir Bernard Paget, Commander-in-Chief, Home Forces in conversation with unidentified American officers during a training exercise, fall 1942. He was a highly regarded professional soldier who was given great credit for the training of the British troops of 21st Army Group, which he commanded until being replaced by Gen. Sir Bernard Montgomery in December 1943. *Imperial War Museum (TR143)*

Multiple types of landing craft approaching Omaha Beach, 6 June 1944. Visible are LCM, LCI, and LCT. Specialized craft were first used in large numbers for operation HUSKY, the invasion of Sicily, which had occurred eleven months earlier. *Naval History and Heritage Command (SC 189988)*

Early wave of assault troops landing on Omaha Beach, 6 June 1944. Note the depth of water the troops have to wade through and the numerous beach obstacles. The German defenses were the most formidable the Allies faced for any amphibious assault in Europe. *Naval History and Heritage Command (26-G-2337)*

Members of Lord Lovat's 1st Special Service Brigade getting ready to land on Sword Beach, 6 June 1944. Morgan interceded with Mountbatten to have the brigade stay in the United Kingdom for OVERLORD and not to be transferred with Mountbatten to India. *Imperial War Museum (MH33547)*

LCI(I) at Omaha Beach. The forward 20-mm mount is engaging a target inland, and there are half-tracks at the water's edge firing their weapons inland. *Naval History and Heritage Command (80-G-421289)*

U.S. Coast Guard–manned LST approaching Normandy. Some of the vehicles have the large star roundel to help Allied tactical aircraft identify friend from foe, one solution to a problem brought forward at RATTLE. *Naval History and Heritage Command (26-G-2358)*

Troops go ashore on Omaha Beach late on 6 June 1944. Note the half-tracks and
DUKWs in the background and the line of troops heading inland in a single file.
Naval History and Heritage Command (SC 320902)

FDR continued to object to the zones of occupation proposed in RANKIN, and in September of 1944 the issue came up at the second Quebec conference (OCTAGON). There the CCS asked for direction on the issue from the prime minister and president. Roosevelt suddenly reversed course and accepted what had been COSSAC's proposal. A similar agreement regarding the division of Berlin into sectors of occupation was reached at Yalta (ARGONAUT) in February 1945.

Planning for RANKIN continued through the fall. On 19 October Barker reported to the COS in Morgan's absence that work on RANKIN continued "and is ranked as of highest priority."[51] This was at the same time that all energies were being strained to convert the OVERLORD outline plan into something with which an operational commander could work, and every idea for strengthening the assault was being considered. As we've seen, RANKIN continued to occupy the minds of senior politicians and generals throughout 1943, and the broader issues became real with the end of the war in Europe.

The intelligence estimates on which RANKIN was based took time to evolve toward something more accurate. As late as the day of the invasion at Salerno, 9 September 1943, the joint intelligence subcommittee of the British War Cabinet issued a report stating that an analysis of the broad situation "leads us inevitably to the conclusion that Germany is, if anything, in a worse condition today than she was at the same period in 1918." In an interview two years after the war ended, Hughes-Hallett dismissed this as "our annual collapse of Germany prediction."[52] That may have been a case of being wise after the fact. It is difficult to judge what factors, either emotional or rational, may influence an enemy to continue to fight or to quit. This is particularly true when confronting a totalitarian state with an effective domestic security force.

Estimates are just that and are only as good as the intelligence that is gathered and analyzed. It took months for the Western Allies to appreciate that, despite the battlefield losses of 1943, Germany still had manpower reserves and was just converting to a total war economy. This allowed Germany to both reequip and reestablish divisions lost in the east, albeit at lower manning levels and with fewer armored vehicles, and to expand the Waffen SS and add panzer and panzer grenadier divisions. By late November 1943 these refined intelligence appreciations dispelled the more optimistic views of what might be possible, which had influenced many of the concepts regarding OVERLORD and RANKIN.[53]

For the British, RANKIN represented a hoped-for end-of-war scenario that also reflected the only successful outcome for the war against Germany they could imagine that didn't require taking the considerable risks of an amphibious assault and that would permit them to play a significant role on the continent. For the Americans, RANKIN was a contingency plan that also met political concerns regarding the potential for Russian dominance in western Europe. There was nothing that could be done on the ground to influence the postwar situation in the Baltics or Poland. Western Europe, however, particularly if it also contained at least part of Germany, would serve as an effective counterweight to anticipated Russian expansionist desires.

It was reasonably clear by early 1944 that RANKIN was not likely to happen. In November 1943 it was handed off to 21st Army Group, as McLean said, "so they could have something to do."[54] This was a bit unfair given all the OVERLORD planning that 21st Army Group was involved in, but it was reflective of how one senior planner felt about RANKIN by then.

Still, when Eisenhower was given his directive as Supreme Commander by the Combined Chiefs, paragraph three read: "Notwithstanding the target date [the month of May, 1944] you will be prepared at any time to take immediate advantage of favorable circumstances, such as the withdrawal by the enemy on your front, to effect a reentry into the Continent with such forces as you have available at the time; a general plan for this operation when approved will be furnished for your assistance."[55] Regarding the relationships with Allied governments, the reestablishment of civil governments in liberated Allied territories, or the administration of enemy territories, he was told: "Further instructions will be issued to you on these subjects at a later date."[56]

— 9 —

THE FAR SHORE

Germany's problems in 1943 were not just confined to the battle fronts. They were also occupiers of countries that had been defeated but not, perhaps, conquered. As the situations on the battlefields were going from good to manageable to problematic, the Germans continued to seek ways to regain the initiative in the East, defend territory in the Mediterranean, and prepare their forces in northwest Europe to repel the anticipated invasion there while continuing to administer and exploit their captured territories. They were starting to feel the stretch.

Military occupation of a country is never easy. Germany's need to take as much as possible from France and the other areas it occupied to feed both the German war machine and its civilian population made it worse. Food, clothing, raw materials, money, motor vehicles, armaments, finished goods, and manpower all started heading east across the Rhine shortly after the fall of France. "French consumption fell accordingly, especially . . . when deliveries from North Africa ceased and German demand grew dramatically in all areas after the defeat at Stalingrad."[1]

In all this, the Vichy government severely overestimated its ability to function independently of the Nazis. In 1943 Hitler repeatedly informed the head of the government, Pierre Laval, and the head of State, Philippe Pétain, that the first priority was to deal with the threats from the East and West; after that, France's future would be clear. What exactly that might mean remained to be seen, but it was evident to the French that "concessions could be wrested from Germany only when they were in the occupying power's interest or cost it nothing."[2] Nevertheless, the Vichy government was a great aid to the Nazis. Because it existed, the Germans, with a relatively small administrative staff, "directly or indirectly controlled an administrative and police apparatus of Frenchmen which functioned for them with a diligence and thoroughness they could never have provided themselves during wartime."[3] The Vichy civil administration eliminated the need for a German civil affairs administration and allowed the Nazis to deploy only 2,000 to 3,000 police and roughly 60,000 dedicated occupation troops to France (over and above the units deployed to defend against Allied attack or to refit after fighting on the Eastern Front).[4]

While it took time, with the survival of the Allies and increasing German oppression, the attitude of the French population grew increasingly negative toward Germany. There were some who would take direct action against the occupier and others who would inform and collaborate. For many, occasional passive resistance was a small act of disobedience to the occupation. For most it was about finding ways to make daily life work. The key question asked about officials by de Gaulle's forces after the liberation was: Did they collaborate more than was strictly necessary? There is still a great debate about the range of support for and passive and active resistance to Vichy and Germany.[5] The essential point is that German troops were working and living in an increasingly hostile environment, although one that still could be compared favorably by the Germans with the outright partisan war that was being waged in Yugoslavia. For the occupiers, Paris was still Paris.[6]

On 23 March 1942 Hitler issued Directive No. 40, prompted by the realization that Allied troops could—and, at some point, probably would—attempt a landing on the Continent. That realization was the result of the U.S. entry into the war and the situation on the Eastern Front, both of which led to the conclusion that the war was going to last longer than Hitler hoped. As a consequence, serious defensive measures now needed to be taken in occupied Europe.

Hitler noted that "the enemy's choice of time and place for landing operations will not be based solely on strategic considerations. Reverses in other theaters of operations, obligations toward his allies, and political motives may prompt the enemy to arrive at decisions that would be unlikely to result from purely military deliberations."[7] In other words, they should prepare for either ROUNDUP or SLEDGEHAMMER. Implied in his statement was the expectation of the buildup of forces in the United Kingdom as well. Three days later the commando raid on St. Nazaire underlined this newfound concern.

The general idea as outlined in Directive No. 40 was that the defense would be based on "close and complete co-operation between all the services"; intelligence and reconnaissance would be thorough and timely; the invasion force would be attacked by air and sea at their embarkation points and from there to the location of the landings; and the invasion must be stopped no later than as the Allied troops landed on the beaches. "An immediate counterattack must annihilate landed enemy forces, or throw them back into the sea." And, of course, "fortified areas and strongpoints are to be held to the last."[8]

Recognizing the need for a single commander to be responsible, the defense of western Europe was given to Field Marshal von Rundstedt, Commander-in-Chief, West. He reported directly to the Armed Forces High Command (OKW). This was a result of splitting the management of the war between OKW and OKH (the Army High Command), with OKH having the burden of the fight on the Eastern Front while OKW essentially took on everything else in terms of land warfare. OKW was not a real joint staff; the air force and navy functioned outside its control. "The only unity of command in Germany rested in the person of Hitler, who no longer had adequate machinery through which to exercise it."[9] This made close and complete cooperation between the services challenging.

Since 1941 the construction of the U-boat pens in the French Atlantic ports had taken the efforts of tens of thousands of laborers as well as almost all of the concrete poured in France. Now the concept of a west wall for the Atlantic coast began to take shape. On 29 September 1942 Hitler held a three-hour conference in Berlin. Present were Hermann Goering, Albert Speer, Rundstedt, representatives from the Organisation Todt, and other staff officers. In his presentation to the gathered audience, Hitler expressed confidence that they would defeat Russia the next year but expressed concern over the possibility of the Western Allies establishing themselves on the Continent. While the Dieppe Raid the month before had been a complete disaster, Hitler warned his audience not to reach the conclusion that the raid's failure meant amphibious operations against the French coast were impossible. He added that "the British cannot arrive at a similar conclusion simply because they have no alternative but to try again."[10]

Hitler called for the construction of 15,000 concrete strong points and emplacements that would be manned by 300,000 troops. He was convinced that, with enough concrete, it would be possible to create a defensive line that would stop any invasion attempt. The first construction priority was protection of the U-boats (these were becoming the main offensive weapon in the West and the best way to delay and disrupt any Allied buildup in Britain). Next, reflecting his threat assessments, was the reinforcement of Norwegian coastal defenses. Then work was to focus on the Pas-de-Calais area of northern France and Belgium, between the Seine and the Dutch border. Work on the Normandy, Brittany, Dutch, and German coasts was to begin after that. Early in 1943, as a result of TORCH, the coast of southern France was added as well.[11]

Knowing that the Allies would need port facilities to supply their armies, the emphasis was to be the fortification of harbors, ports, and landing areas near them. Open beaches and coastline would be the lowest priority. The completion date was to be 1 May 1943. The experts thought they would be lucky to finish 40 percent of it by then—and the defensive measures for the coastline might not be completed before it didn't matter anymore.

For his part, Rundstedt concentrated on the Pas-de-Calais. In the absence of any intelligence to suggest other areas of the coast, he reasoned that it was the best location for an Allied assault as Allied air cover would be strongest over Calais. It was also the shortest crossing, which meant less shipping would be needed, and it was closer to Antwerp and the Ruhr than the other possibilities. Normandy and other sites were also on his list but with a lower priority.

To accelerate construction, Rundstedt suggested to the high command that Russian prisoners of war be used on the project. In his mind, there were many advantages. He believed that the Russians would be "content with little," and being, in his view, simpleminded, they would be "only marginally susceptible to enemy propaganda. Disciplinary problems would also be easier to deal with than in the case of western European workers, since 'if [Soviet prisoners] didn't jump to it, they could simply be shot).'"[12]

As anticipated, the program fell behind schedule, and at the end of February 1943 only six thousand of the emplacements had been built. As there wasn't yet a fully thought-out plan for the defense of the Continent, this didn't matter as much as it might have. Commander-in-Chief, West thought if the fixed defenses could disrupt and delay the landing forces and canalize their attacks so that high rates of casualties could be inflicted, that would set the stage for an effective German counterattack. Somehow the German navy and air force would also be active in major ways in defending the beaches. It's not clear how that was to be or what they would do, as Rundstedt, even though he was commander in chief, West, had no direct control of the air force and navy. They were merely ordered to cooperate with him. "There was consequently no lack of friction."[13]

By 1943 France had become the rear area for the Eastern Front. Divisions that were worn out from the fighting in Russia were routinely transferred to France for replacements and re-equipment. Units and individuals were transferred from the West in answer to the incessant demands of commanders in the East for reinforcements and replacements. From October 1942 through August 1943, twenty-two infantry and six panzer or panzer grenadier divisions were transferred east. In a report in fall of 1943 the chief of staff at Rundstedt's headquarters noted that in 1942 there had been in France a garrison of twenty-two divisions, mostly of the older, larger three-regiment type. There had been a reserve of six infantry divisions and seven, fully mobile, first-class panzer or panzer grenadier divisions. That had now become twenty-seven divisions, but most of them were the new, smaller, two-regiment type, and of the thirteen divisions in reserve, three were new formations that were still in the process of forming up. In other words, as the likelihood of active operations on the Western Front had increased, the quality, mobility, and offensive power of the German forces had decreased.[14]

The war in the East and in the Mediterranean both contributed to the inability of the Germans to properly reinforce the French coast. They were active fronts that were using aircraft, armor, and men as well as supplies and other matériel. Indeed, the Eastern Front always held at least two-thirds of German ground forces. There they were engaged in a massive attritional struggle.[15]

The failure of German intelligence—or, if you prefer, the success of Allied intelligence, deception efforts, and counterintelligence—also contributed to Germany's failure to achieve its goals for the defense of the West. Being unable to discern with confidence where the Allies might land, the Germans were forced to spread their forces to cover all the possibilities.

In February 1943 Rundstedt issued a basic order to his troops. In it he announced that there were "increasing indications that we shall soon be facing the long-expected Anglo-American offensive. The main landing would 'definitely' take place [somewhere] on the coast from Holland [the North Sea] to Nantes [on the French Atlantic coast] . . . followed by a landing in the Bay of Biscay, and a secondary offensive in the Mediterranean."[16] While perhaps encouraging everyone to be vigilant, this was of little help in forming a plan of action or concentrating forces where they would be needed most.

In November 1943 Rundstedt's authority was blurred even further with the arrival of Field Marshal Erwin Rommel. Initially Rommel's command was Army Group for Special Employment with orders both to make plans for defeating the Allied invasion and to direct the fighting. Within a few months of arriving, his command was retitled Army Group B and placed into Rundstedt's chain of command. But Rommel also retained his position as inspector of all coastal defenses and had direct access to Hitler, skipping over both Rundstedt and OKW. (As a field marshal, Rundstedt also had the privilege of direct access.) Given Rommel's reputation and prestige position in the hierarchy of German generals, he had influence beyond what his place in the chain of command would otherwise suggest.

There was, famously, a great debate about how to defeat the invasion. Rommel argued for attacking the invasion on the landing beaches, believing that German reserves placed too far behind the front lines would be interdicted by tactical airpower and naval gunfire and would not be deployable. The German experience in Sicily and at Salerno demonstrated that it was difficult to attack across open terrain in the face of Allied naval gunfire support and fighter-bombers.

Rundstedt took a somewhat different approach. While accepting the idea of fighting at the water's edge, he believed that if the enemy somehow made it ashore and got through the first line of defense, then the attack should be slowed up by a defense in depth and then counterattacked by corps and army reserves. The German armored expert in the West, Gen. Leo Geyr von Schweppenburg, went even further, arguing that the armor could only be successful outside the range of naval gunfire support and therefore should be held away from the coast, and the counterattack by massed armor should occur inland—using the successful experience of German forces in the East as a model.[17] That, of course, required the armor to be placed in the right location, which meant that someone would have to decide where the battle was to be fought. The static defense versus mobile or maneuver warfare debate was never fully resolved. (There were three first-class panzer divisions that could have responded to the invasion on 6 June. Two of them, however, were under the direct control of Hitler—the result of another compromise—and stayed where they were. The third entered the fight late in the day.)

Rundstedt tried to get Hitler's attention about the many deficiencies in France and the gap between concept and reality, finally writing a detailed report in October 1943. In response to that report and in response to German defeats on the battlefields of the East and South, Hitler issued the well-known Directive No. 51 on 3 November 1943. In the directive, Hitler acknowledged that the Eastern Front had consumed "the bulk of our military resources and energies." Now, the growing power of the Western Allies was to be considered a greater threat. Unlike in the East, there would be no ability to trade space for time.

All signs point to an offensive against the Western Front of Europe no later than spring, and perhaps earlier.

For that reason, I can no longer justify the further weakening of the West in favor of other theaters of war. I have therefore decided to strengthen the defenses in the West, particularly at places from which we shall launch our long-range war against England. For those are the very points at which the enemy must and will attack: there—unless all indications are misleading—will be fought the decisive invasion battle.

. . . Should the enemy nevertheless force a landing by concentrating his armed might, he must be hit by the full fury of our counterattack. . . . The counterattack . . . will prevent the enlargement of the beachhead, and throw the enemy back into the sea.[18]

Hitler reached the rational if simplistic conclusion that with the placement of the V-1s in the Pas-de-Calais, the Allies would be forced to attack there. He apparently discounted the possibility of a more robust and layered Allied response to his terror weapons. He also got the timing more or less right, May 1944 being the end of spring.

With Rommel's arrival, more was done to build fortifications, lay mine-fields, and create underwater obstacles, with the scope of work expanding to include Normandy. While they were the most formidable the Allies would face in Europe, the obstacles to invasion never reached the scale that was envisioned, perhaps because it was an unobtainable goal. What was achieved in the first half of 1944 was enough to require the Allies to land just after low tide, so they could see as many obstacles as possible, and not high tide, which would have reduced the amount of open beach that the assault troops had to cross.[19] The assault was made more difficult and bloody, but the preparations were not enough to prevent the attempt being successful, however thin the margin may have been.

The Eastern Front continued to draw manpower and resources away from the West regardless of Hitler's edict, and manpower shortages were now such that a range of expediencies were used to find enough troops to at least man the front line. In addition to recruiting units made up of former prisoners of war and of ethnicities formerly excluded from German military service, we can read in Directive No. 51 that "all school, training and other shore-based personnel fit for ground combat must be prepared for commitment." Even the SS (Schutzstaffel) was not immune. "The *Reichsfuehrer-SS* will determine what *Waffen-SS* and police forces he can release for combat, security and guard duty. He is to prepare to organize effective combat and security forces from training, replacement and convalescent units, as well as schools and other home-front establishments."[20] Some of the units were equipped with weapons captured from the French and Czechs. Thus, the Atlantic Wall can be seen as a response to the shortages in manpower and matériel that were starting to take away Germany's options for fighting the war at an operational or even tactical level.

Notwithstanding their manpower limitations, the difficulties the German army faced on 6 June and over which they (at least in theory) had some influence were primarily ones of command and control, combined with an intelligence failure, not a shortage of formations. Elements like loss of initiative and Allied control of the airspace over northwest Europe were beyond their control.

For Germany, the long-range trend of the war didn't look good at the end of 1943. But they felt it wasn't irretrievable. If the German army could fight one of their famous short, sharp campaigns and defeat the Western Allies' attempted invasion, they could then turn East with new weapons and confidence and regain the initiative against the Russians. It would take a dose of good fortune, but they were confident that a land battle was winnable. In truth, Hitler and his generals may have been working toward a concept for defeating the invasion they knew was coming, but as 1943 slogged its way into 1944, the ways and means for them to implement any plan successfully were slipping away.

They could, however, still defend themselves effectively and take offensive action of a sort in the West.

POINTBLANK

The Casablanca conference in January 1943 directed the launching of the Combined Bomber Offensive. That led to the POINTBLANK directive, which was given to the U.S. Eighth Air Force and RAF Bomber Command on 10 June 1943. The goal was the "progressive destruction of sources of German power and the sapping of the will to resist"[21]—in other words, the creation of RANKIN-like circumstances. The destruction of German fighter aircraft was placed at the top of the list of objectives, ahead of the U-Boats and oil, and with all the specific objectives assigned to the Americans. Bomber Command was given a separate task described as the "general destruction of German industry."[22]

What was not decided were the specifics of how the campaign was to be carried out or what, specifically, would be the chain of command. It was a combined offensive in that two heavy bomber forces were deployed, but each went their own way, with their own target sets and methods of operation. Rarely was there any coordination between the two.

For Bomber Command during 1943 there was the Battle of the Ruhr (March to July 1943), the Battle of Hamburg (July to November 1943), and the Battle of

Berlin (November 1943 to March 1944). Other cities were also attacked, but this was a planned sequence of campaigns designed to end with the destruction of the German capital.

By the end of July Harris believed he had achieved his goals in the Ruhr. He was wrong. Forty-three major raids had reduced industrial output for four to six weeks, at an average loss per raid of 5 percent of the aircraft that reached the target area. There is speculation that continuing against the Ruhr would have led to greater results, but it was not to be.

Beginning 24 July, the campaign against Hamburg, Operation GOMORRAH, featured the first use of "Window," the metal strips that jammed German radars. By the end of the operation, it was evident that "Window" had, at least initially, been beneficial in keeping bomber losses to 2.8 percent over the four major raids, which saw some participation from the Eighth Air Force as well. More than 35,000 buildings in Hamburg were destroyed, with 43 percent of all dwellings destroyed or made uninhabitable. While there is no agreed-on figure for the dead, the generally used figure is 42,600, with other estimates ranging from 30,000 to 50,000. "In all, the casualties in Hamburg over this period were equivalent to around 80 percent of the number of British civilians killed by the German air offensive [in the 9 months] from August 1940 to May 1941."[23] Economically, Hamburg remained at roughly 85 percent of its prewar level from then to the end of the war. However, the armaments factories on the outskirts of the city were back at full capacity by the end of 1943. Overall, about two months' production was lost.

Notwithstanding the fact that German forces had been able to defend Berlin successfully against Bomber Command raids in the summer of 1943, Harris ordered the start of a series of raids against Berlin on 18 November. There were to be sixteen large raids in the Battle of Berlin plus smaller nuisance raids. The city was not only a political target and a symbol of Nazi Germany; it was a vital industrial center. It was also the best-defended German city.

Going into the Battle of Berlin, Harris believed—and presented the argument to Churchill—that "Germany must collapse before this programme, which is more than half complete already, has proceeded much further."[24] British intelligence, on the other hand, was never able to find any evidence of a weakening of German civilian morale. There were a mix of decrypts and assessments of various types from various sources. Reports intercepted and decrypted from the Japanese ambassador to Germany noted that the raids were violent, but since the targets were primarily towns and dwellings, the "resultant reduction of production potential amounted to not more than 10 percent, and that the government would quickly redistribute work to other factories."[25] (The British didn't put much faith in the analytical abilities of the Japanese ambassador and, consequently, didn't rate his observations very highly.) As to when the cumulative effect of the bombing and dehousing of Germany might reach the tipping point, intelligence couldn't say. Consequently, they reported to the War Cabinet that it "might happen at any time, and must happen in the long run, if the Allies kept up the pressure."[26]

In addition to the raids on Berlin, the British bombed Frankfurt, Stuttgart, Leipzig, Nuremberg, and other cities in another nineteen large raids from November to March. Bomber Command's loss rate was over 5 percent, increasing to 6.5 percent over Berlin with the last raid on Nuremberg on 30 March 1944 suffering 9 percent losses. In all, Bomber Command lost more than 1,000 bombers in these Berlin raids. To that we can add 923 in the Battle of the Ruhr and 813 over Hamburg.[27] For all of 1943, Bomber Command wrote off 2,751 aircraft, more than three times the number equipping frontline squadrons as of January of that year.[28]

By the end of the operation, Harris admitted that German defenses would soon be of a strength and type that "night-bombing attacks by existing methods and types of heavy bomber would involve casualty rates that could not be sustained. . . . We have not yet reached that point, but [the] tactical innovations which have so far postponed it are now practically exhausted."[29]

The Allies ultimately gained control of the air over Germany and northwest Europe. However, as General Eisenhower was taking charge of SHAEF and considering the reentry of the Continent in early 1944, the Luftwaffe was handing Bomber Command a significant defeat in the Battle of Berlin.

The Eighth Air Force in 1943 conducted what could be called proof-of-concept operations. Delays caused by the demands of operations in the Mediterranean meant that it wasn't until May 1943 that the Americans were able to launch raids from England that averaged two hundred aircraft. Additional bomber groups started to arrive, and by early summer the Americans were launching three hundred bombers on a strike. American fighters still did not have the range to escort the bombers all the way to targets deep in Germany, but this was the opportunity to prove "that 300 bombers can attack any target in Germany with less than 4% losses."[30]

In August, the Eighth attacked Schweinfurt and Regensburg. The two raids lost a total of sixty aircraft, which was more than 10 percent of the U.S. Air Force's operational strength and more than 17 percent of their crews at the time. After that blow, the Americans didn't return to raids beyond fighter cover until October. Between 8 October and 14 October, they bombed Danzig and Marienburg, suffering light losses, and bombed Münster, losing 24 percent of the attacking aircraft including all but one B-17 of the 100th Bombardment Group. They ended the week by going back to Schweinfurt, where 21 percent of the bombers were shot down and 47 percent were damaged.[31]

In November improved versions of the P-51 began to arrive on English airfields. "The autumn disasters finally brought an end to the theory of the self-defending bomber."[32] In addition, it was becoming clear that POINT-BLANK was not going to create or accelerate the conditions for any version of RANKIN.

Air Marshal Portal, head of the RAF, was obliged to report to the CCS on 3 December that the Combined Bomber Offensive, the essential prerequisite to OVERLORD, on which so much importance was placed, was three months behind schedule.[33] Neither the American nor British heavy bombers had achieved their goals. German fighter strength had not yet been neutralized and was, in fact, increasing. Churchill's Mediterranean inclinations were not without reason.

While the Germans successfully defended the airspace over their homeland in 1943, it was a classic pyrrhic victory. For example, they had been obliged to use night fighters as part of the interception force against daylight raids, and in October they lost 42 percent of their fighter force. The German defenses had been stretched to the breaking point by the attacks. As one historian wrote, "The situation had not yet reached the point it did in 1944 when half of Germany's artillery was at home pointing skyward, but the omens were there."[34] In early 1944, renewed attacks by the Eighth Air Force—joined by the newly formed U.S. Fifteenth Air Force in the Mediterranean and combined with efforts by the RAF—essentially destroyed the threat posed by German day fighters over northwest Europe.

The Germans had launched only a few raids against the United Kingdom in 1943, and Hitler was more than eager to retaliate for the raids over Germany, both to meet domestic political needs and for ideological and emotional reasons. On 21 January 1944 the Luftwaffe launched what the British called the "Baby Blitz," with more than two hundred bombers heading toward London and with 60 percent of the bomb loads being incendiaries. "About half the bombs hit the British mainland."[35] All of the deficiencies of the German Air Force were now exposed.

By the end of the "campaign" on 29 May 1944, there had been twenty-nine raids, each with between 160 and 240 attacking aircraft. London had been bombed fourteen times, with the port cities of Hull, Bristol, Plymouth, Portsmouth, Falmouth, and Torquay also being attacked.[36] The Germans had unintentionally contributed to the success of the Combined Bomber Offensive as the raids failed to have a meaningful effect on the preparations for invasion, did little damage other than inflict casualties, and so wore themselves out in the effort that they were not able to respond to the invasion when it came. Still, for Morgan, Barker, and those who were planning OVERLORD, it was not only an ongoing reminder of what was at stake and why it had to happen; it was a demonstration that the Germans were not close to collapse or voluntary withdrawal in the West.

Intelligence

As noted earlier, German intelligence did not correctly determine where or when the cross-Channel assault would take place, but this was not for want of agencies involved in the task. OKW had the Foreign Intelligence Department, headed by Adm. Wilhelm Canaris. The staffs of the army, navy, and air force all had intelligence divisions, as did their various subordinate departments and operational commands. OKH had a Foreign Armies West section, and the Foreign Ministry was also collecting intelligence. They were "in constant competition with Department VI of the Reich security main office [RSHA]."[37] There was no central clearinghouse or method of independent analysis for all the data gathered, and each organization interpreted the information through the lens of their own needs and the political environment within which they each worked. The task was further complicated by the successful Allied deception operations and other efforts to add "noise to the channels," in Roberta Wohlstetter's wonderful phrase.[38]

German intelligence was far from being totally deaf and blind, however. The amount of Allied shipping in the Mediterranean, divisions in that theater in excess of estimated requirements, and the forming of new French divisions in North Africa all suggested to Foreign Armies West that the south of France could be a likely invasion site.

Their estimates of the buildup of forces in southern England suggested to army intelligence that the main Allied operations would be in the Channel area, and other attempts would be diversionary. Notwithstanding the fact that Hitler was still concerned about Norway, by the end of 1943, the Germans were convinced that the main landings would be somewhere between Boulogne and Cherbourg—not the most helpful analysis but an improvement on somewhere between the North Sea and the Loire River estuary.

Naval Group West estimated in May 1944 that the Allies had shipping available to land between seven and thirteen divisions, and they noted that the bulk of the Allied fleet was concentrated in the west of England, suggesting a landing somewhere between the Somme estuary and the Cotentin peninsula. From their partial observation of Allied training exercises and their experience in the Mediterranean, the Germans guessed that the invasion would occur at dawn, two hours after low tide. At the beginning of May 1944 Naval Group West noted that if the invasion did not occur that month, the only period in June "that was similar to the Allies trial maneuvers was the 5th through the 7th." If not then, the next period would start on 20 June.[39]

Also in May 1944, Luftwaffe intelligence officers interpreted the bombing of the Seine bridges as suggesting an invasion attempt somewhere between Le Havre and Cherbourg. Foreign Armies West dismissed the report and saw the bombings as just part of an overall campaign against transport and communications targets in northern France.

The overriding inclination of those responsible for German preparations for invasion was to decide what they believed the Allies would do and then bend and fit the facts to conform to their beliefs while dismissing those bits of data that might be inconveniently inconsistent. This was a systems failure aided and abetted by Allied deception and the BODYGUARD cover plan. This in turn was assisted by the German expectation that diversionary attacks would be part of the assault.

COSSAC had specified that for OVERLORD to succeed, the Allies would need to have air superiority on D-day, and the Germans would need to have not more than twelve full-strength, first-quality divisions in northern France and the Low Countries. He further specified that there should not be more than three full-strength, first-quality divisions available in the target area on D-day, growing to not more than five on D+2 and nine on D+8. As planning progressed in the spring of 1944, Morgan's criteria from July 1943 remained unmodified by Eisenhower and Montgomery.

In May 1944 Allied intelligence revised the methodology by which they classified German Divisions and put them into four categories:[40]

1. Panzer and panzer grenadier divisions
2. Field divisions, capable of mobile operation and including paratroop and mountain divisions
3. Limited employment divisions, including line of communication divisions, training divisions and the Luftwaffe infantry divisions as well as those made up of foreign troops
4. Static divisions, capable only of defensive fighting in the sectors which they were formed to hold

The first two categories met the criteria of first-quality divisions for Allied planning purposes, and they were the ones most likely to be at or near full strength.

On 23 May 1944 the COS reported to Churchill:

Although the first-line strength of the GAF [German Air Force] has increased, this increase has been achieved in part at the expense of reserves and the GAF is today severely handicapped by its lack of depth and reduced production. This, together with its qualitative decline, renders the GAF incapable of sustaining a scale of effort such as would normally be expected of an air force with a first-line strength of this size.

We estimate that, on the target date of OVERLORD, the Germans will have six to seven full-strength, first-quality divisions in reserve in France and the Low Countries. They will also have in reserve some eleven to fourteen offensive divisions of rather lower quality.... There will thus be a total of seventeen to twenty-one offensive divisions which will be the equivalent of some twelve to sixteen full-strength first-quality divisions.

During the first two months it is unlikely that the Germans will be able to transfer any divisions from the Russian front . . . but they may make available from elsewhere . . . some five to seven divisions of varying strength and quality. Dependent on the course of events [in other theaters] a further six divisions, at the most, might be brought against OVERLORD. This represents a maximum of thirteen divisions . . . as compared with the maximum of fifteen which COSSAC considered acceptable.

In the following table we compare the build-up in equivalent full-strength, first-quality divisions . . . Our estimate makes no allowance for interference by air or airborne attacks or by sabotage.

Date	Maximum build-up acceptable to COSSAC	Present estimate
By D-Day	3	3
D+2	5	6–7
D+8	9	11–14

It should be noted . . . [that] the OVERLORD plan has been revised with the object of increasing the breadth and weight of the initial assault, ensuring the earlier capture of a deep-water port, and improving the rate of our build-up. These factors, together with the reduction in the likely rate of German reinforcements against OVERLORD in the first two months of operation, should in some measure compensate for the present increase in German opposition during the initial stages of the operation.[41]

At the end of May, then, Churchill was reassured by his Chiefs of Staff that, while OVERLORD still had a narrow margin for success, it could be launched with confidence.

The Germans could sense what was going to happen and made attempts to prepare their defense against the amphibious assault. Systemic weaknesses, the accumulated losses of more than four years of war, ideological blindness, responses to domestic political needs, the growing impact of strategic bombing, the ability of the Allies to organize and direct their war production with greater confidence and understanding, and all the other factors great and small were now pushing Germany to the brink. The enemy on the far shore was a veteran force. It would fight hard, inflict casualties, and give ground only grudgingly. Their defensive preparations would be the most challenging and formidable the Allies faced in their European amphibious assaults. Their ability to dictate where and when the fight would occur, however, was limited. Superb Allied intelligence gave the Allies the information they needed to make key decisions. COSSAC's criteria were essentially being met, and the invasion would go forward.

This was all of vital interest to COSSAC, but how it would play out was beyond their control. What Morgan and his staff desperately needed was a Supreme Allied Commander, agreement on an operational command structure that reflected the nature of the coalition forces going ashore, and more landing craft. Morgan also hoped that when the grand strategical and political spins of the wheel stopped, it would be at a place that was in COSSAC's favor. To facilitate this process, and at the invitation of General Marshall, General Morgan went to Washington.

— **10** —

"YOUR ARMY, YOUR GENERAL MARSHALL AND YOUR AMBASSADOR BIDDLE"

In late summer of 1943 there was speculation in the press and in various circles in Washington as well as concern in the Pentagon that General Marshall was going to move from being the U.S. Army's chief of staff to assume the top command of the European theater. Nothing, however, had been decided.

There were two parts to the problem surrounding the selection of a Supreme Allied Commander. First, there was not yet an agreed-on structure and organization for the command. COSSAC was developing a framework for the operational headquarters, but it was not yet decided what the headquarters commanded. It could be the army groups that would conduct the cross-Channel attack and the subsequent drive into Germany. It might just as well represent a larger unified European command that would place overall control of both the European theater of operations and the Mediterranean under one supreme commander with two operational commanders reporting to him. The latter was preferred by Morgan and by many Americans as that would ensure that northwest Europe would be "top of the bill" and stay there. To Morgan, it made sense to view operations in Europe as one theater and not divided between north and south.

Second, and not withstanding agreements reached in Quebec and in Washington before that, there was a general feeling in Washington that the Western Allies' strategy for Europe and the relative relationship between operations in northwest Europe and the Mediterranean was not yet firmly agreed on. The Americans would need help from the Russians to resolve that issue.

Both Secretary of War Henry Stimson and presidential advisor Harry Hopkins were strong supporters of Marshall for Supreme Allied Commander, particularly if it became the larger command. FDR, as was so often the case, was not yet taking a firm, public stand. However, in a response to a letter sent to him by retired general John Pershing, arguing that it would be unwise to remove Marshall as chief of staff, Roosevelt advised the general that the operations being considered would be the "biggest that we will conduct in this war. And when the time comes, it will not be a mere limited area proposition, but I think the command will include the whole European theater. . . . I want George to be the Pershing of the second World War—and he cannot be that if we keep him here."[1]

It was in this context that Barker and Marshall had a conversation in Washington after the end of the Quebec conference in mid-August. Marshall was famous for keeping note of officers who impressed him and appointing them to positions when the need arose.[2] The most well-known example was his advancement of Eisenhower. Marshall wanted to be ready in case he became the Supreme Allied Commander. Consequently, he approached Barker and asked if he would be interested in serving as his (Marshall's) chief operations officer for the campaign. It would be a key job to have in the most important operation in Europe, perhaps in the war. Barker later recalled that Marshall also said that he was considering Morgan for his chief of staff.[3]

Barker replied that if Morgan was going to be Marshall's chief of staff, then he'd rather stay as deputy chief of staff. He let Marshall know that he considered Morgan and himself a team, and they had come to work well together. To get to know Morgan better, Marshall thought it would be a good idea for him to come to Washington for a week. Barker endorsed the idea, and Marshall sent the invitation to London, even personally arranging Morgan's visit.[4] From that point until the decision for Eisenhower was made at the end of the year, Morgan and Barker worked under the assumption that they would carry on as a team under Marshall.[5]

When the invitation arrived in early October 1943, Morgan was more than pleased. Not only would this be a first opportunity to see at least part of the United States, he would also have the chance to make his arguments in person to those who could make the decisions regarding the need for the appointment of a supreme commander and for more landing craft.

There was a great deal of practical detail that COSSAC could not address without a decision about the commander. They could, of course, take as a working hypothesis that the commander would be American. Consequently, while Morgan spent what was initially planned to be five days but turned into six weeks in the United States, Barker, working with Morgan's approval, completed the transformation of COSSAC into an American-style structured headquarters of staff sections (G-2 for intelligence, G-3 for operations and plans, etc.). The expectation was there would be one commander at the top of a unified command and not the British-style three-service committee at the top of the pyramid. (During this period, British theater commands would typically have a naval commander, military commander, and air force commander who functioned as a committee for command decisions.)

In the Mediterranean, Eisenhower was the supreme commander, but Alexander, as his British deputy, was the ground commander in chief for the invasion of Sicily, directing their single army group made up of George Patton's Seventh Army and Bernard Montgomery's Eighth Army. (After Patton was relieved of command, it was Mark Clark's Fifth Army for the invasion of Italy.) Naval forces were under the command of Adm. Sir Andrew Cunningham, and Air Chief Marshal Sir Arthur Tedder commanded the Allied air forces.[6] Eisenhower "behaved more like a CEO in charge of external relations than an operational commander."[7] It wasn't clear to Morgan whether the Mediterranean arrangement was by choice or by necessity.

The commander for the European theater of operations would not be hundreds of miles away from the centers of politics and diplomacy. He would be in proximity to the pressures emanating from Downing Street, the War Office, and all the other British ministries, so one couldn't take the structure from a relatively distant theater of operations and graft it onto OVERLORD without some modification. There also was the consideration of personalities—the supreme commander would have his preferences both in terms of personnel and his approach to command.

COSSAC also needed to know what the command structure would be for the assault. The planning for HUSKY (Sicily) was, in Montgomery's opinion, "a dog's breakfast," with none of the proposed plans being found acceptable to all the members of the commanders, committee and with Eisenhower unable or unwilling to resolve disputes and put his stamp on the plan or the process. It is not surprising the planning process was confused as inputs flowed in to the planners from London, Algiers, Malta, and Tunisia, with no truly unified command or combined operations headquarters. Added to that, the commanders were also busy finishing operations in North Africa, which, being more immediate, gathered more of their attention. Montgomery eventually forced a compromise plan but made no friends doing so.[8]

The 9 September 1943 amphibious landing at Salerno (AVALANCHE) by Clark's Fifth Army was one of two widely separated landings on the Italian mainland. Montgomery's Eighth Army went ashore on 3 September at the "toe" of the Italian "boot" as Operation BAYTOWN. Montgomery had argued for a two-army assault, side by side at Salerno, but Eisenhower opted for the two assaults, along with a secondary landing, Operation SLAPSTICK at Taranto. This approach meant that neither force could support the other, which violated the fundamental principle of concentration of forces. The attack was provided with fewer landing craft than at Sicily, was based on faulty assumptions about likely Italian and German reactions, and was not grounded in the execution of any particular strategic goals.[9] Morgan was well aware that the systems and process for OVERLORD had to be better. There would be little margin for error in France.

As Morgan considered the command situation, OVERLORD's initial assault was a three-division attack across the beach, plus an airborne landing, which sounded like a force that could be directed by a corps commander. Adding the other components involved in the assault—air forces, naval vessels, special units such as commandos and engineers, independent tank brigades, and the rest—made it appear that an army headquarters or similar organizational structure would be needed.

Another complication stemmed from the realization that the forces going ashore would be the advance elements of what would ultimately become two army groups, one American and one British/Canadian, that needed, for political considerations, to land at the same time. (A third army group was added after the successful landings by American and French forces in the south of

France.) The structure needed to be flexible enough to adjust to what would become army groups made up from units of seven countries and with both American and British army group commanders.[10] All these questions needed to be resolved soon, and answers were not forthcoming from higher authority.

What Morgan did receive was permission from the COS to visit Washington, although according to Morgan it felt like it was given "with a certain froideur in contrast with American enthusiasm for the proposition."[11] He was also warned at every turn to be careful in his dealings with the Americans lest he get sold a bill of goods by the crafty Yanks.

Before he left London, Morgan had two more immediate concerns. The first was how he would be received and where he and his small team would live and eat. He knew from firsthand experience that British officers were often selected for duty overseas by virtue of their private incomes, of which Morgan had none. He had to hope for American generosity. The second concern was on whose behalf was he making the journey. It was not exactly a British effort, but it didn't seem to Morgan that it could be called American business either. He concluded that it didn't really matter—the Combined Chiefs of Staff had approved the outline plan, and Morgan had always insisted that his was an Allied organization, neither British nor American. COSSAC had pressed the limits of what authority they had to keep things moving. "What was needed was more means and more authority. The place to get them was . . . the States."[12]

At 10:40 p.m. on 6 October 1943, Morgan; Major General Brownjohn, head of logistics for COSSAC; and Captain Jenkinson, the remarkable Bobbie; left Addison Road Station in London on board General Dever's private train, headed for Prestwick airfield in Scotland. Maj. Gen. John C. H. Lee, USA, the head of the Service of Supply in the United Kingdom, escorted them as far as Scotland.[13] The U.S. Army was certainly doing its utmost to get the trip off to a good start.

Their dedicated C-54, after having some mechanical issues fixed, took off on the afternoon of 7 October at 5:00 p.m. Taking both the headwinds and the icing level into consideration, they crossed the Atlantic at between four thousand and five thousand bumpy feet, landing at 5:30 a.m. local time on Friday 8 October at Stephenville, on the west coast of Newfoundland. Morgan noted in his diary that this meant they were too early for breakfast.

From there, it was a three-hour flight to cover the 725 miles to Presque Isle, Maine, the location of the headquarters of the Army Air Force Wing that flew ferry missions across the North Atlantic. It was here that they got another indication that their journey might be considered an important event, at least by the Americans. They were met by a welcoming committee consisting of most of the officers who could be rounded up from the area, and there were two large automobiles, one adorned with a three-star flag and the other with a two-star flag. In these the group was driven approximately four hundred feet to the local hotel, "where a breakfast was served which alone was well worth a double Atlantic crossing in war time."[14]

From there it was a flight of just under three hours to reach LaGuardia Field in New York for another refueling stop, then on to Washington, D.C., landing just before 3:00 p.m. local time on 8 October, having spent the better part of twenty-three hours in the air. Here the COSSAC group was received by a delegation headed by Lt. Gen. Joseph McNarney, the Army's deputy chief of staff. McNarney had spent time in 1941 in London as a member of the Special Observers Group, and after the war he would replace Eisenhower as commander of U.S. forces in Europe.[15] They were assigned Lieutenant Colonel Morgan (USA) as general guide and escort, a Women's Army Corps corporal as secretary, a car, and a driver.[16]

From there they were transported to what Morgan described as the lavish General Officers' Quarters at Fort Myer, their rooms having been especially redecorated for their visit under the personal supervision of Mrs. Marshall. They were attended to by three senior African American noncommissioned officers. Morgan commented that there wasn't much about soldiering that they didn't know.

Before Morgan had a chance to settle in, he was summoned to meet Marshall. When they met, Marshall started by saying, "I have heard the most unsatisfactory reports about you." A brief pause. "I hear you have taken no rest whatever for a long time and that won't do. While you are over here I intend to see that you take leave, and the longer the better."[17] With that, they spent an hour together, with Morgan discovering that there was no certainty about Marshall's appointment as supreme commander, but they agreed for the purposes of the trip to act as if it were to be the case. Before leaving the

Pentagon around 6:00 p.m. on 8 October, he also spent the better part of an hour in an initial discussion with Lt. Gen. Thomas T. Handy, head of the Operations Division (OPD). This finally marked the end of Morgan's long first day in the United States.

The next morning was Saturday, and while Morgan had wanted to sleep in, he was unable to resist "the temptation of American breakfast" and was up, dressed, and ready for the day by 8:30. Which was fortunate, because at 9:00 a.m. he was summoned to the Pentagon to join Marshall's regular, six-days-a-week morning conference, starting a routine that continued throughout his stay.[18] From then on the British general was included in the American chief of staff's briefing, usually conducted by General Handy with additional comments made as needed by officers such as Gen. Henry "Hap" Arnold, chief of the U.S. Army Air Forces, or Maj. Gen. George Strong, the War Department's G-2. The briefing reviewed activities in each theater at the strategic level, allowing Marshall to review, comment, and ask questions while avoiding micromanagement. It was probably at this meeting that one of the Americans in the room referred to the "bloody British," which was followed by an awkward pause. Morgan quickly spoke up and asked if he "could be treated as a 'bloody Yank.'" After that, they "all made use of the vernacular with equal fluency."[19]

Morgan had become aware of the remarkable activities of George Kenny's Fifth Air Force in the southwest Pacific; their transportation and supply of elements of an Australian division solely by air in New Guinea (a unit commanded by a Quetta classmate of Morgan's—Major General Alan Vasey); and, as already noted, the effective use of air power alone in their destruction of Japanese shipping in the Battle of the Bismarck Sea, to cite two examples. He took the opportunity, with General Arnold in the room after the briefing, to raise the issue of the possible expanded role of aircraft for OVERLORD.

Having studied the problems surrounding the lack of landing craft and the uncertainties about obtaining enough of them, Morgan posed a hypothetical concept to Arnold: What if OVERLORD could be made primarily an airborne assault with amphibious support instead of the other way around? In other words, what if COSSAC could build on the remarkable achievements of Fifth Air Force and do something really creative? This was typical Morgan-style, out-of-the-box thinking. Marshall, Arnold, and Morgan discussed aspects of the question, and Arnold sent a query to General Kenny asking if the New Guinea techniques could be applied under the conditions that would exist in northwest Europe. This became a concept that was explored in depth while Morgan was in Washington.

The rest of Saturday was spent in meetings at the Pentagon, including his first with senior members of the British Joint Service Mission and another with General Handy that included a happy reunion with Walter Bedell Smith, who had just arrived from Eisenhower's headquarters. Handy and Smith helped Morgan develop a plan of action concerning who to see regarding various topics and agreed that Field Marshal John Dill should be included in any discussion about the appointment of a commander.

Field Marshal Dill was one of the most important figures in the Anglo-American alliance. He had a great appreciation for the American viewpoint as well as that of the British, and time after time his was the voice of reason and compromise during the great strategic debates in 1943. He died on 4 November 1944, while still serving as head of the mission. In a gesture of friendship, he was buried with full honors in Arlington Cemetery. FDR said of him, "Not only . . . a great soldier and a great friend but . . . the most important figure in the remarkable accord which has developed in the combined operations of our two countries."[20]

Smith also gave Morgan good news about staffing. Eisenhower's AFHQ in Algiers was reducing its establishment and would be able to make available to COSSAC several British-American teams of officers from various staff sections who would be available for transfer to London where they could get to work at COSSAC without much of a break-in period.[21]

Morgan's somewhat hectic introduction to wartime Washington ended on Sunday. It being a nonworking day at the Pentagon, the impulse to be a tourist got the better of this first-time visitor, and he went to Arlington National Cemetery, including Arlington House, also known as the Custis-Lee Mansion, parts of the cemetery, and the Memorial Amphitheater. They were an easy walk from his quarters.

He then went out to Mt. Vernon. Here the romantic part of his character caused Morgan, as it has others, to mischaracterize the United States "as the development of the British characteristics unhampered by tradition as has been the case in Europe."[22] This is an understandable observation from an Englishman, but one that missed the influence on the nature of the United States by multiple waves of immigrants from the rest of Europe and the rest of the world. Nor did he comment on or seem to notice being in a segregated society. He was very much a man of his time.

That night the three visitors were guests of honor at a reception at the Alibi Club. Located at 1801 I Street NW, Alibi was a very private men's club founded in 1884, allegedly with membership limited to fifty. General Marshall was a member and used it to meet informally with congress members to lobby them to support the Army. Other members have included George H. W. Bush; Allen Dulles, of Office of Strategic Services and Central Intelligence Agency fame; and his brother, John Foster Dulles, who was President Eisenhower's secretary of state.[23]

Welcoming COSSAC were Adm. William D. Leahy, chief of staff to FDR; Admiral King; Adm. Sir Percy Noble from the Joint Service Mission representing Field Marshal Dill, who was in Montreal; Hap Arnold; General McNarney; Lt. Gen. Carl Spaatz; General Handy; and most of the relevant staff from the OPD and the Joint Planners. It was an impressive welcome for a serving member of a foreign army who was the chief of staff for an operation that, while increasingly likely to happen, was not yet assured, and who was still reporting to an empty desk.

The next week started with discussions about civil affairs, proposed modifications to RANKIN Case C, and meetings with Secretary of War Stimson, who was an early and enthusiastic supporter of the cross-Channel attack and whom Morgan had met the previous summer in London. Morgan also continued to pursue the topic of transporting troops and all their equipment by air. Marshall approved Morgan's decision to focus on RANKIN C and to ignore the other variants.

He had his first meeting with Admiral King on the topic of personnel for Admiral Stark's 12th Fleet. King promised that both Rear Adm. Alan G. Kirk and Rear Adm. John Leslie Hall Jr. would be assigned, a great relief to Morgan as they were the most capable U.S. Naval officers available who had experience with amphibious operations in Europe. Hall and Morgan were, of course, Southern Democrats together, going back to their time in Algiers.[24]

Initial conversations Morgan had with various officers regarding landing craft did not advance the cause particularly well. The bottleneck was the LST. COSSAC's plan called for 250 LCI(I)s, 900 LCTs, 480 LCMs, over 1,000 LCA types, and 230 LSTs.[25] The smaller craft could be built in a variety of locations, but the LST, at just over four thousand tons, needed a more properly organized space that had some of the attributes of a shipyard, even if most LSTs were built on inland waterways and then sailed down to the Gulf Coast or Atlantic seaboard.

The challenge of producing enough landing craft and ships can be traced back to the inability of the Western Allies to balance strategy, production, and manpower. As Hap Arnold had said at Casablanca, it was necessary to decide then what the plan was not only for 1943 but also 1944, otherwise "our priorities in production might be wrongly decided."[26] The consequences for a coalition that needed time to agree on a strategy included shortages and delays in what had become critical tools of war. Those in charge of production, like Donald Nelson, chairman of the (U.S.) War Production Board, and William Knudsen of the (U.S.) Supply Priorities and Allocations Board were trying to hit a target that was not only moving but changing shape as it went. U.S. industry was powerful, and amazing efforts were being made to harness that power, but its capacity, while large, had limits. In mid-1943 it was still getting organized.

Production is a complex process, especially so when attempted on the vast scale seen in World War II. Contracts had to be let to each firm or factory for each item needed, whether rifles or aircraft carriers. If strategy or circumstances changed, then those contracts might have to be cancelled and new ones issued.[27] Raw materials had to be allocated and delivered in the right sequence to the proper factories at the right time. Then the intermediate materials—rolls of steel, for example—had to be transported to where the finished goods, like ships, tanks, and artillery pieces, were to be built. Then the subcomponents, like radios and machine guns, made in yet other factories and delivered to the final assembly plants or field depots had to be added. The finished weapons—in the case of ships, a system of systems—had to be tested, delivered to the appropriate service, shipped to a unit or station, and manned. Again in the case of ships, the crews had to complete their training with the ship before joining the fleet in combat. All of which had to be managed both vertically and horizontally to create and maintain a balanced force. There was also competition between companies and industries for skilled workers.

Every time a change was agreed on at a conference, tens of thousands of workers and managers had to shift their plans. To minimize these effects, production plans were not linked to specific operations but rather to overall targets within a system of priorities and "must haves" versus "like to haves." In 1943 this was still tied to conservative estimates of the capacity of U.S. factories, although some thought setting aspirational goals that were unlikely to be met would be a way to inspire people.

When Marshall went to London to present the BOLERO/ROUNDUP plan in 1942, Hughes-Hallett, who was part of the conversation, noted that many of the craft the Americans were starting to build were too small for Channel operations. Added to that was the problem that the U.S. Army's cross-Channel needs were for craft and ships that could carry tanks and vehicles while the Navy, which was building the craft and had the Pacific in mind, emphasized craft that could carry assault troops.[28] As a consequence of this newly realized need for different types of vessels, landing craft went to the top of the priority list for a short period of time. That caused delays in the construction of warships. Admiral King told the Combined Chiefs in June 1942 that the construction of two fleet carriers and several cruisers were being delayed, as was the construction of escorts and antisubmarine warfare vessels as a result of the reprioritization of landing craft.[29]

In another example from the ROUNDUP period, the combined planners initially estimated the shipping requirements for a cross-Channel assault at approximately 1,950 ships, including 200 of what would come to be known as LSTs and 570 LCTs. Less than a month later that list more than doubled and then increased again to about 4,100 craft. A month after that, Major General Eisenhower, as commander of ETOUSA, added another 100 LSTs and 200 large troop lighters to the list of initial requirements and asked that 30 additional ships of each of those two types be added to the pool each month after the assault.[30] Having never attempted an amphibious assault on this scale, no one had a clear idea of what exactly it would take.

Of course, the Mediterranean and Channel were not the only places where amphibious assault forces were to be employed. By late 1943 there were two offensive drives in the Pacific, and the possibility of another centered around Burma. Ships and craft used in the Pacific generally could not be transferred to the Atlantic or Mediterranean and vice versa.

Great Britain was a powerful, industrialized nation that was almost fully mobilized for war. However, the demands of global war on Britain and the British Empire meant that Britain could not pay the "bill" for OVERLORD. "Britain lacked both the money and the shipyard resources to expand the Royal Navy as the United States Navy was expanding."[31] Thus, any resolution of the LST crisis that required the building of ships would have to come from U.S. construction sites. The alternative meant reallocating forces and that meant taking shipping from the Mediterranean.

Try as he might, Morgan could not get definitive answers to his landing craft problem. General Handy became interested, and Morgan wished him the best of luck. Assistant Secretary of War John J. McCloy, a high-energy personality if there ever was one, committed himself to addressing the issue. Admiral King was not unmoved by Morgan's request, but there was no immediate solution.

Most of Morgan's days were long and challenging. Ten- to twelve-hour days, six days a week were not uncommon for everyone at the Pentagon and Navy Department. There were, however, more enjoyable moments that occurred along the way. Amid his first week in Washington, Morgan had lunch with General and Mrs. Marshall in their quarters at Fort Myer. There Marshall asked Morgan if there was any particular place in the United States that he would like to visit. Morgan and Brownjohn were both students of the U.S. Civil War, so Morgan responded by naming the Shenandoah Valley, with all its history. This was taken as quite a complement by the Marshalls as they made their home in Leesburg, Virginia, at the north end of the valley. Consequently, Marshall arranged for the COSSAC group to take an extended tour of the eastern United States, starting with the Shenandoah Valley (with a private dinner at the Marshalls' home) and ending at an Air Corps pilot training base in Miami Beach, visiting as many military bases and training facilities as possible along the way. This included part of a day inspecting the 4th Infantry Division, which was undergoing amphibious training in Florida. Barker considered this division the best trained in the United States, and he had recommended back in August that it be the initial U.S. assault division.[32]

The group traveled for a week, visiting Ft. Bragg and Ft. Benning as well. Full use was made of Marshall's private aircraft and his car and driver. For the tour of the Shenandoah, Marshall arranged for the military historian of the Library of Congress to go along as guide as well as Marshall's aide, Lt. Col. Frank McCarthy. Morgan noted that when he arrived back in Washington, he felt "a sensation of homecoming."

There were also shopping excursions in Washington and later in New York City, as Morgan, with help from Bobbie, found items to bring back for his wife and daughters. Given the number of times he mentions exploring U.S. department stores in his diary, it may well have been that Morgan returned to Britain with quite a bit more luggage than when he left.

The group also found time for dinners at a series of the better restaurants. In Washington this meant, among others, the newly built Statler Hotel (now the Capital Hilton), which advertised the relatively new feature of central air conditioning; the Salle Du Bois on the corner of 18th and M Streets; and, thanks to Bobbie's effective reconnaissance of metropolitan D.C., a memorable meal at a "joint" called the Troika Club, located on Connecticut Avenue NW at the corner of K Street, so named because back in the 1880s the building housed the Russian legation. Before that it was the home of Alexander "Boss" Shepard, a corrupt minor government official. It was considered one of the most elegant supper clubs in the city.[33] Morgan was impressed. He wrote, "I know a whole lot more about the U.S.A. than I did before I went to the Troika."[34]

The number of meals that Morgan records in his diary suggests that wartime rationing in Great Britain had taken a toll, and the relative abundance found in the United States—even with the rationing that existed—was nearly overwhelming. While at the Pentagon one afternoon, Morgan was taken to lunch at a cafeteria, his first such experience. The place was called the Allies Inn. His comment to his diary: "What an experience!—What a lunch."[35] Morgan admitted that they were "living American" courtesy of the JCS, and after their years of austerity in the United Kingdom, their new—albeit temporary—standard of living seemed to be "slightly higher than that portrayed by Hollywood as benefiting a multi-millionaire."[36]

Morgan and Brownjohn continued to meet and discuss almost every aspect of OVERLORD with their American counterparts. Morgan's first meeting with the planners from the OPD lasted three hours, and they went over the plan in remarkable detail. Unlike similar meetings with British planners, which were at least superficially casual and were likely as not continued in the bar next door after the meeting, Morgan was "confronted by a mass convention of War Department officials, each one of whom knew their stuff, and ours, by heart and had searching enquiry to make."[37] This particular meeting was witnessed by Walter Bedell Smith and Carl Spaatz, deputy commander of the Mediterranean Allied Air Forces. As a lieutenant, Spaatz had flown one of the aircraft used in Pershing's pursuit of Pancho Villa, the same operation in which then-lieutenant Ray Barker participated.[38]

In a later meeting with the CCS, Morgan, frustrated at not getting an answer regarding a commander, came out and asked that he be given the full powers of the supreme commander until such time as one was appointed. Admiral King responded that if he were in Morgan's position, he would interpret the orders already received as more than enough authority to issue whatever commands would be necessary. At this point, Morgan reflected on the difference between an American four-star admiral who had fought in the Spanish-American War while still a midshipman, was awarded a Navy Cross in World War I, and was now both Chief of Naval Operations and Commander-in-Chief, U.S. Fleet, on the one hand, and a British temporary three-star general serving as chief of staff to no one in particular while heading up an ad hoc staff, on the other. Morgan was doing everything he could think of to keep the process moving, but it didn't seem like much progress was being made in terms of finding a commander.

One of Morgan's more interesting meetings was with the Joint Strategic Survey Committee, or, as King called them, the "elder statesmen." The committee was set up in November of 1942 with the brief to make independent recommendations to the JCS on global and theater strategy—in other words, to advise on "the soundness of (the United States') basic strategic policy in light of the developing situation and on the strategy which should be adopted with respect to future operations."[39]

It was a three-member committee of senior or retired officers headed by Lt. Gen. Stanley Embick, formerly head of the War Plans Division during Douglas MacArthur's time as Army chief of staff. Embick was Albert Wedemeyer's father-in-law, was distrustful and disdainful of the British, and had been strongly opposed to Secretary Stimson's hardline approach to Japan before the war. Notwithstanding his views, his professionalism and willingness to act as a "devil's advocate" led to him being called out of retirement to act as a senior advisor at a most critical time. The Air Corps was represented by Maj. Gen. Muir Fairchild, a distinguished and thoughtful officer who had entered the military as an enlisted man in the Washington State National Guard in 1916. He learned to fly, was commissioned in January 1918, and flew combat missions from then until the end of World War I. He had a distinguished interwar career and by 1942 was director of military requirements and then served most recently as assistant chief of the Air Staff. Vice Adm. Russell Willson was the Navy's representative. Admiral Wilson had a long career at sea; was the inventor of the Navy Cipher Box, which provided secure communications for the Navy at the end of World War I; and capped a forty-year career with key service at the Dumbarton Oaks conference in 1944.[40] The committee pressed Morgan hard but came away satisfied and renewed their endorsement of OVERLORD to the JCS.

Tuesday, 26 October, undoubtedly marked the high point of Morgan's trip. He was summoned by Admiral Leahy to the White House for an hour-long, one-on-one meeting with FDR. Lieutenant Colonel McCarthy took him to the White House. Harry Hopkins escorted him into Roosevelt's study. Grinning broadly, FDR started by saying, "You realize, General, that I have risen from my bed of sickness on purpose to see you, so what you have to say had better be important." Morgan responded, "Mr. President, I don't want to overtax you in your delicate health and will be brief. All I need of you is your Army, your General Marshall and your Ambassador Biddle." Roosevelt agreed to the Army, "if the reasons are good," doubted whether Marshall could be spared (an early indication perhaps that he was having second thoughts about losing his chief of staff), and he said no to Ambassador Anthony Biddle, U.S. representative to the European governments-in-exile located in London and former U.S. ambassador to Poland.

Their conversation then ranged from stories that FDR told about his dealings with Churchill, to asking Morgan's opinions about what he had seen in his U.S. travels, to a discussion about the desirability of invading Europe from the southeast rather than the northwest. The last, while Morgan strongly suspected the source of the idea, didn't seem to be too strongly held a position by Roosevelt, who admitted he was completely unaware of the topography of the area.

Near the end of the hour, Morgan tried again to get a commitment regarding Marshall and tried again to gain Ambassador Biddle for COSSAC's Allied Contacts Office. The president deftly deflected both requests but did agree to send a cable to Churchill regarding the appointment of a British deputy supreme Allied commander, if Morgan would draft it. Morgan's idea was that a deputy commander would be better able to speak for the unnamed commander and he, Morgan, could then get out from under the increasingly awkward set of situations in which he found himself. Even though the president did not provide the answers to his problems, Morgan wrote that he left "feeling all the better for having met him and, moreover, with a sensation that all would yet be well."[41] Such was the charm and skill of Roosevelt's personality.

Morgan worked on the text of the cable overnight and the next morning had it reviewed by Marshall and Dill. He then sent the draft to Admiral Leahy for the president's review. He had taken the extra step of also having it reviewed by McCarthy, who, as Morgan said, "was bilingual in American and British." Morgan was pleased to discover that his studies of American English had progressed to a point where only one word of the text was altered. It was sent to London and didn't get a response.

Roosevelt did change his mind on one issue. Later that fall Ambassador Biddle became Lt. Col. Tony Biddle, USA, who joined COSSAC to head the section tasked with liaison with the appropriate governments-in-exile.

Morgan had numerous meetings with Ernest King, both formally and socially. They found themselves agreeing on many subjects, not the usual outcome for British officers dealing with the Chief of Naval Operations. At one of their last meetings, Morgan made his case once again for more LSTs. King understood the problem but was adamant that the Pacific was not going to be raided for the benefit of OVERLORD. As King shook his hand and wished him well at the end of the meeting, a colleague waiting for Morgan in the hallway remarked that if a British admiral or an American general had made the same request, no one would have ever seen him again.[42]

A sense of success and resolution may not have been immediately obvious, but before Morgan left Washington, King announced on 5 November that increased numbers of landing craft, particularly LSTs, LCI(L)s, and LCTs, beyond amounts already designated for OVERLORD, would be sent to the United Kingdom in the next few months. The British general and American admiral seemed to have reached an understanding.[43]

Another individual for whom Morgan had great respect was Secretary Stimson. Stimson led a remarkable life. A Theodore Roosevelt–inspired progressive Republican, he had been an effective U.S. attorney in New York. William Howard Taft appointed him secretary of war in 1911, where he continued the Army reforms initiated by his friend Elihu Root, which paid dividends in the development of the generation of leaders that emerged in World War II.

When World War I broke out Stimson, a strong advocate of preparedness, called for a system of universal military training. He believed in leading from the front and, despite being forty-nine years old and nearly blind in one eye, he enrolled in an officer's training camp. He did so well that he was pronounced fit for service.[44] When the United States entered the war, Stimson managed to get commissioned as a lieutenant colonel and became the executive officer of a field artillery regiment. He went to France ahead of his regiment to train with the 51st Highland Division of the British Army. He was then ordered home to assume command of a newly forming artillery regiment. After the war he returned to Washington and public service. For the rest of his life he enjoyed being called "Colonel Stimson."

Stimson served as Herbert Hoover's secretary of state during his four-year term of office (1929–32). He became frustrated by what he saw as "foolish nations and inadequate statesmen" failing to respond adequately to the growing crises in Europe and Asia.[45] He became a passionate advocate for collective security, if for no other reason than he knew that the belief that the "United States could save itself 'by isolation is today an economic fantasy—worthy of the ostrich.'"[46]

Stimson's public stands on foreign policy, counter to the isolationist inclinations of his fellow Republicans, led FDR to ask him in July 1940 to become secretary of war for a second time. Putting country ahead of party, he agreed and served throughout the war, leaving public service on his seventy-eighth birthday in September of 1945, having served every president from Theodore Roosevelt to Harry Truman, with the exception of Warren Harding.

Stimson never wavered in his belief in and support of the cross-Channel assault and gave Morgan great encouragement throughout the COSSAC period. One measure of the degree of that support and high regard in which he was held was the invitation to Morgan and Brownjohn to dine at the Stimson home on Cathedral Avenue. They were joined by Edward Stettinius (then undersecretary of state and later secretary of state) and Harvey Bundy (special assistant to Stimson and the father of McGeorge and William Bundy), along with their wives. Occasions such as these were often used to get beyond the public personality and to get a sense of the human being behind the position. In this period, the connections between professional and personal relationships, particularly among those with long records of public service, were important factors in making programs or campaigns a success.

While he was unsuccessful in advancing the appointment of a commander, Morgan did make a small but important contribution to the general subject while in Washington. Working with the planners and the JCS, Morgan produced the draft directive that was to be issued to the Supreme Allied Commander as soon as they knew who he was to be. It was, with but little amendment, the document that was issued to Eisenhower after the Tehran conference. Thus, he managed to craft the orders that gave his eventual commanding officer the authority to direct the invasion that Morgan had done so much to make possible.[47]

Morgan's ongoing discussions regarding the employment of aircraft for OVERLORD reached a point where it was felt that more expertise was needed than Morgan could provide. As a result, Leigh-Mallory was summoned at short notice to participate in the discussions as well as to engage in more general conversations about command and control of the air forces for the operation. He arrived on 3 November and brought with him news from London that clearly staggered Morgan.

On 19 October, Churchill submitted a minute to the COS, "Relation of OVERLORD to Mediterranean":

I should be glad if the Chiefs of Staff would carry out a staff study of the situation in the Mediterranean with particular reference to the growing resistance to Germany, both active *and potential*, which is developing in varying degrees in all the Balkan countries.

I am fully aware of the engagements in which we have entered with the Americans at QUADRANT with particular reference to OVERLORD and South East Asia. Nevertheless, we must not shrink from taking a stern view of the policy we ought to adopt as opportunities open themselves to us for exploiting successes in any theatre of war. . . .

Pray let this enquiry be conducted in a most secret manner and on the assumption that commitments into which we have already entered with the Americans particularly as regards OVERLORD could be modified by agreement to meet the exigencies of a changing situation. . . . It may be that we need not recant on OVERLORD except as regards emphasis and the balance of our effort.[48]

After all the long hours at Norfolk House that culminated in the acceptance of the outline plan in Quebec; the reorganization of the staff into the start of an operational headquarters; and meetings in Washington with officials at the highest levels, including the president, receiving this news from Leigh-Mallory was an emotional low point for Morgan. He wondered what point there was, if any, in all his efforts and those of everyone at COSSAC. He was beginning to wonder whether he had "completely wasted my time by coming over here. If indeed I have, I should have probably wasted my time even more by staying in London."[49] He also pondered the "Churchillian theory of trying everything else first" rather than a Channel assault.[50]

At the same time, news was starting to arrive at the Pentagon from the foreign ministers' conference that was held in Moscow from 19 to 30 October. Anthony Eden, Cordell Hull, and Vyacheslav Molotov met, along with their delegations, both to prepare the ground for the upcoming meeting in Tehran and to discuss various other issues related to occupation of liberated countries (including Italy), the war in the Pacific, the end of the war, and the postwar order, including the establishment of a postwar international organization.[51]

There was one topic on the Russians' agenda: What can be done to end the war against Germany as quickly as possible? They received the news about OVERLORD with pleasure but also indicated that they might be as interested in immediate action in the Mediterranean, "for example, increased pressure in Italy and some operation in the Balkans for the purpose of drawing off German strength from the Eastern Front."[52] Both Brig. Gen. John Deane, head of the new American military mission in the Soviet Union, and U.S. Ambassador Averell Harriman, who had also been at the Quebec conference, reported back to Washington that it wasn't clear that the Russians would prefer OVERLORD versus more immediate action in the Mediterranean. They were unsure whether the Russians would take on the British view at the expense of the cross-Channel assault.

Back in the Pentagon, the planners worked out that the most attractive Mediterranean choices would inevitably delay OVERLORD, and while those choices might prevent the Germans from using units in the Balkans or in Italy to reinforce the Eastern Front, stopping or delaying the buildup for the cross-Channel assault would allow the Germans to pull troops from northwest Europe. Thus, actions in the eastern Mediterranean might not help the Russians all that much but could, possibly, make a cross-Channel assault easier, albeit a year later than desired.

The planners could see that, for the British, the opportunity for increased operations in the Mediterranean was "becoming hard to resist. Should the British receive Soviet support for their projects, it would probably be most difficult not to yield [to their point of view]."[53] They suspected that the British hoped that a combination of more pressure in the Mediterranean, combined with additional Russian successes, and POINTBLANK would create the RANKIN C circumstances they so hoped for. They also rightly suspected that the British would argue in favor of keeping those seven veteran divisions in the Mediterranean for as long as possible.

It was clear that the upcoming conferences at Cairo and Tehran were going to be a showdown. It appeared to Morgan as he prepared to leave Washington that even Marshall had, "at the back of his mind, the same doubts about the wisdom of the unswerving pursuit of OVERLORD that have assailed many of us for so long." He indicated to Morgan that it might be necessary to accept "the logic of the situation that has been created in southeastern Europe, irrespective of how this situation has come about."[54] In other words, the demands of coalition warfare might require the Americans to agree to continued effort in the Mediterranean at the expense of OVERLORD.

There were more meetings. Morgan attended at least three of the CCS meetings in Washington and had numerous meetings with the British Joint Service Mission and with Field Marshal Dill. There were more meetings about civil affairs and postwar Europe as well as many meetings with General Handy and the planners at the Pentagon. He met numerous times with General Arnold about the role of aircraft, a topic that was pursued with vigor but without result. In the end the planners realized that the only way the buildup of forces against German reinforcements, particularly panzer divisions, was going to be successful was by using LSTs and other landing craft.[55]

Morgan was also able to host a return dinner reception as he prepared to leave, as an acknowledgement and thank-you to his hosts. Among the attendees at the cocktail and buffet supper were all three of the American JCS; General McNarney, General Handy, and most of the OPD; John McCloy on behalf of Secretary Stimson, the British ambassador to the United States, Lord Halifax; and most of the Joint Service Mission.

The COSSAC group also managed one more field trip, this one to Gettysburg, which was by all accounts considered to be the best visit of them all, enhanced by the skillful presentations made by their National Park Service guide.

Before they left for New York City on 11 November, Morgan had one last meeting with John McCloy. He expressed his fears to McCloy regarding what he saw as Stimson's "obsession in relation to Operation OVERLORD" and asked McCloy to look after the secretary of war. Morgan had developed a great respect and affection for Stimson and was concerned that the colonel would not tolerate alternatives to the cross-Channel attack and that he seemed willing to go to the wall over the issue. Morgan hoped that, if the British, with Russian support, delayed the cross-Channel assault in favor of operations in the eastern Mediterranean, Secretary Stimson would find a way to yield graciously. McCloy "promised to take care of the old man if anything should happen, as well it may, to interfere with the progress and eventual consummation of Operation OVERLORD."[56]

Arriving at LaGuardia Field in New York, they were piled into a convoy of automobiles and driven to the Waldorf Astoria on Park Avenue, where they were ensconced in a set of rooms on the tenth floor. That night dinner was at the 21 Club, about six blocks away. The next day was filled with a guided tour of the New York Port of Embarkation, their cars being escorted along the way by a fleet of New York motorcycle police "at top priority, disregarding all traffic signals, stop lights and what-have-you. The only disappointment was [they] did not use their sirens."[57]

The scale of effort at the port was staggering to their eyes. Morgan wrote of the American spirit of buoyant optimism that he encountered at every turn. That was underlined for him that night, when they somehow managed to receive tickets to *Oklahoma!*, which was in the middle of its successful premier run on Broadway. The generous and enthusiastic spirit of the musical had a great effect on the Englishman. This was after yet another grand dinner as guests of the U.S. Army, this one at Le Pavillon, across the street from the St. Regis Hotel and long considered to be the best French restaurant in New York.

The next morning was their last in New York. Morgan was up early. His companions, clearly weary from work, did not respond to the room service delivery of their breakfasts. This allowed Morgan to enjoy his breakfast as well as theirs in peace.

The flight back to the United Kingdom on 13 November retraced their steps. This C-54 was apparently a regular shuttle flight. It was a full aircraft, and other occupants included MacArthur's chief of staff, Gen. Richard K. Sutherland. The aircraft needed repairs in Stephenville and took off from there around 3:00 a.m. Thunderstorms and heavy clouds forced the aircraft to climb to 22,000 feet over the Atlantic. No oxygen was distributed because the steward in charge of the unpressurized cabin had already passed out as the plane climbed to altitude. Fortunately, they didn't need to stay at altitude for long and otherwise had an uneventful flight back to Prestwick, landing at about 9:00 p.m. local time. Morgan recorded in his diary that he "never hated leaving a place or a country quite so much."[58]

Met by Ray Barker, the party was told there was less than ten minutes to make the train for London. Thanks again to the U.S. Army Air Corps, they managed to bypass customs and emigration entirely, and everyone and everything got on the train amid the blackout. Upon arrival in London, Barker, perhaps understanding the transition from wartime Washington to wartime

London, treated Morgan to breakfast at the American Mess at Stanhope Gate. Morgan was grateful. He noted, "I do not think I could have stood an English war-time breakfast after what has just gone [on]."[59]

Morgan's reception in Washington was as if he were a victorious supreme commander and not just the chief of staff to someone to be named later. In part this was because OVERLORD was seen by the Americans as the critical operation of the European war, and COSSAC was a primary reason there was a practical, concrete plan that could go forward within a workable organizational structure. It was also because of who Morgan was as a person. The respect he received reflected the respect he gave to others as well as his professionalism.

He had traveled to Washington to seek a commander. He did not succeed. He also sought more landing craft. In this he may have been partially successful, although he also came to suspect that not every request for more craft and more support was truly essential. The thoroughness with which he discussed the plan and the breadth of issues that he was addressing in preparation for the assault must have been of assistance to the Americans as they prepared for another round of debates with their British counterparts in Cairo and Tehran. His conversations with Marshall, Stimson, and others likely strengthened their views about the operation.

Morgan came back to London with a better understanding of America and of the approach the Americans were taking to the war in Europe. He also brought with him the full confidence of General Marshall as well as an understanding of what Marshall wanted in terms of a command structure. As Marshall wrote Devers in a letter asking him to fully cooperate with Morgan and COSSAC, "He knows exactly what I want."[60] That resulted in COSSAC issuing a directive on 29 November 1943 to Paget as commander in chief of 21st Army Group spelling out the command structure for the detailed planning and execution of OVERLORD. In the directive, issued on the letterhead of Supreme Allied Headquarters, Morgan made clear that 21st Army Group, Admiral Ramsay, and Air Marshal Leigh-Mallory would be "jointly responsible for the planning of the operation, and, when so ordered, for its execution."[61] The directive made the commander of 21st Army Group the ground commander for the initial phases of the assault but put a time limit on the position. When there were enough divisions ashore to form a second army group, the supreme commander would take direct control. There would be no duplication of the structure found in the Mediterranean, where Brooke and the British COS maneuvered to have Eisenhower pushed "up into the stratosphere" to cope with coalition politics and brought in British general Harold Alexander as deputy supreme commander to fight the campaign.[62]

OVERLORD now depended on the outcome of the next major conference of the CCS. Confiding to his diary, Brooke admitted that he shuddered "at the thought of another meeting with the American Chiefs of Staff and wonder whether I can face up to the strain of it." A few days later: "How I hate those meetings and how weary I am of them. . . . To satisfy American shortsightedness we have been led into agreeing to the withdrawal of forces from the Mediterranean for a nebulous 2nd Front, and have emasculated our offensive strategy."[63] Brooke believed that the best, most sure way to defeat Germany was to create circumstances favorable to RANKIN, and he believed the Mediterranean provided the opportunities to achieve that goal (along with POINTBLANK and the Russians). To him, Europe was one large strategic front, and continued offensives in southern Europe would draw German divisions away from France.[64] He became increasingly frustrated that the Americans would not yield to reason, as he saw it. Unfortunately for Brooke there was little evidence that significant numbers of German formations were heading south in late 1943 or in the spring of 1944.

While Morgan was in Washington, he could watch at close range as the Americans prepared for the next conference. He had seen them "muttering imprecations about the adjectival British and their perfidy." Back in London, he watched the British chiefs set off, "equally pugnacious and determined to put the Americans straight once and for all over this strategy business."[65] He was well aware what the American planners had written in a briefing memo for FDR, which the president took to Tehran and which attempted to draw a line in the sand. "The time has now arrived when further indecision, evasion and undermining of agreements cannot be borne."[66] What the Russians thought, no one really knew. How it was all going to turn out was anyone's guess. The meeting of "the Big Three" at Tehran would determine if Morgan had indeed been wasting his time.

—11—

"THE SUPREME OPERATIONS FOR 1944"

Working on an "Acting, Unpaid" Basis

When COSSAC's outline plan for OVERLORD was approved at the QUAD-RANT conference in Quebec in August 1943, Morgan reasonably expected that "the great man," the supreme commander, would be appointed. Instead, the CCS ordered Morgan to continue with detailed planning and to issue the orders needed to ensure the assault would be ready to launch in May 1944. Morgan later recalled, "It was obvious that I was expected to function as Supreme Commander on, what the British Army would have it, an 'Acting, Unpaid' basis."[1]

The first problem Morgan needed to address was his lack of command authority. It was one thing to be tasked with formulating a concept. It was quite another to now both make operational decisions regarding the campaign and issue orders on behalf of a nonexistent commander to officers-in-command like Leigh-Mallory for creation of the air plan for the invasion, to Paget for detailed assault planning to start, and to the at-this-point unnamed naval commander for the creation of the plans to move the invasion force and naval task forces to the assault beaches and conduct the initial assault. This was not a situation covered in Morgan's directive. He had no legal authorization to issue orders. To Morgan, either a commander would have to be produced or the British would have to accept that orders issued by COSSAC were the same as orders issued by a supreme commander, even an unnamed one. (As noted earlier, the Americans were accustomed to receiving orders from a chief of staff "by direction" of the commander.)

After the Quebec conference a compromise was reached. By the time Morgan visited Washington in October, the compromise was wearing thin, and some needed decisions were deferred longer than they should have been, but, with the understanding and support of a variety of senior officers, it was made to work well enough for long enough.

The first attempt at giving Morgan something that looked like executive authority took the form of drafting a paper that would cover, in detail, exactly what decisions and orders Morgan could make and issue on his own, what needed the approval of the CCS before action could be taken, and what was still reserved for a future commander. The British COS decided that it was Morgan's problem, and he was ordered to draft the document in question and submit to them for approval. Somewhere around the tenth page of qualifying conditions, Morgan gave up. "What we were essentially trying to do was make an impossible situation reasonably possible for practical purposes."[2]

For his second attempt, COSSAC proposed that they use the smallest piece of paper they could find on which would be written the absolute minimum of words they could come up with and then trust to everyone's common sense. Surprisingly, that worked. As issued after QUADRANT, the new amendment to his directive read: "Pending the appointment of the Supreme Commander or his Deputy, you will be responsible for carrying out the planning duties of the Supreme Commander and for taking the necessary executive action to implement those plans approved by the Combined Chiefs of Staff."[3]

It turned out that Morgan not only wrote what became Eisenhower's directive but part of his own as well. He was now able to issue orders to Paget at 21st Army Group and to Leigh-Mallory as OVERLORD's Tactical Air Commander (designate) to move planning along. Before similar orders could be issued to the naval forces, more structure needed to be created and a decision made regarding a naval commander, which didn't occur until mid-October.

Morgan also had to wait for the establishment of what became the 12th U.S. Army Group in October. There weren't many U.S. combat formations in the United Kingdom yet, although COSSAC was aware of units training in the United States (like the 4th Infantry Division), which were going to be part of the operation. From mid-October, when Gen. Omar Bradley took command of what was becoming First U.S. Army and First U.S. Army Group (later renamed 12th U.S. Army Group to avoid the obvious confusion), the Americans had to scramble to catch up with the planning that the British had already undertaken.

Everyone accepted that this was a less-than-perfect stopgap measure, with Morgan being perhaps the most frustrated of them all. He wrote to General Devers, "While I hate the sight of this whole business, I am completely at a loss to suggest anything better, short, of course, of appointing the great man himself which appears to be quite impossible."[4] He never stopped trying to get a commander appointed, knowing how much more needed to be done and how fast the clock was ticking.

The second thing to do, in Morgan's opinion, was to make sure that everyone at COSSAC, down to the cooks, knew where they stood after the Quebec conference. In early September, Morgan assembled everyone in the ground-floor café, run by the British catering services. He noted that the first time he called a meeting like this, there was plenty of room for everyone, but now it took skillful commando technique for the latecomers to get in. He gave the gathering an abbreviated version of the report from Quebec and ended by repeating what he had said at the most recent weekly staff conferences: "Effective immediately, the Supreme Allied Commander's Staff [has] ceased to be a planning organization and assumed its proper role as an executive headquarters. This having been done, we are off and nothing shall stop us."[5]

While it may seem a commonplace action today, at the time, during what had become total war, it was remarkable that Morgan, with all the security concerns surrounding OVERLORD, would take this step. On both occasions he was explicit about what the circumstances were that brought them together, what was happening now, their roles in the great affair, and what their next steps were to be. Morgan was of the view that this was a situation in which blind obedience would be a hindrance. Indeed, his approach was as far away from one of having to control and approve each detail as could be found. "We badly needed all the intelligence assistance we could get, and intelligent assistance cannot be got from those ignorant of the object they are trying to gain." To achieve this, he decided "to tell the whole outfit just exactly what we were setting out to do instead of keeping the main secret to a small inner circle, while the pick-and-shovel boys . . . worked in darkness."[6] It's difficult to imagine a diverse staff, thrown into a newly created and constantly evolving structure, producing a series of high-quality plans in such a short time using any other technique. It was a risk well worth taking.

COSSAC continued to grow, getting far away from Morgan's original vision of a small coordinating body. Before they evolved into Eisenhower's headquarters, COSSAC had drafted into their ranks "ambassadors, microfilm operators, bankers, agriculturists, newspapermen, lawyers, foresters, and a host of others, each master of some technique that was needed."[7] Indeed, it expanded to such an extent that COSSAC outgrew Norfolk House and had to move some staff around the corner to 80 Pall Mall, an impressive block of offices near the Army and Navy Club.

At least one of the new additions to COSSAC was the result of Barker's conversations with Marshall in Washington. When Barker suggested that he stay as Morgan's deputy, Marshall asked for a recommendation as to who should be the operations officer (G-3) for the Supreme Headquarters. Barker suggested Maj. Gen. H. R. Bull who was the G-3 for the War Department at the time.[8] On 8 October, while Morgan was flying across the Atlantic, General Bull arrived as the new senior U.S. Army member of COSSAC's Ops Division. Marshall's preparations for the command reached beyond consideration of Morgan, and he indicated a willingness to transfer other talented officers from the Pentagon to OVERLORD if he became the supreme commander.

COSSAC was evolving in terms of structure as well. It did not have an administrative section (G-1). That was still handled by the two national authorities and would only change when there was a supreme commander and the requirement to handle personnel issues had been clearly established. It did have the other usual general staff sections, plus an air and a naval staff as well as special staff sections for engineers, signals, and the adjutant.

Morgan's initial intent to keep his staff small and utilize existing sources of knowledge evolved into something a bit different particularly as regards intelligence. British major general Philip Geoffrey Whitefoord, COSSAC's G-2, didn't want to duplicate the efforts of existing intelligence bodies, at least during the planning stages. He hoped to collect from existing departments the data needed and to use the intelligence appreciations prepared by the Joint Intelligence Committee for the British COS.

Even so, and notwithstanding the fact the detailed planning for OVER-LORD was assigned to the force commanders of the Allied Expeditionary Force once they were established, the intelligence organization grew from around 35 officers in late 1943 to 209 in April 1945. "It developed from January 1944 alongside the Whitehall machinery into 'a rival intelligence system' supplying the Supreme Allied Commander with appreciations of current intelligence and with notes and studies bearing on future operations and preparing for the procurement of intelligence on its own account once operations had begun."[9]

With the acceptance of the outline plan, COSSAC, as the supreme commander's representatives, would now supervise, control, or monitor almost every offensive oriented action that emanated from the United Kingdom and that had an affect on northwest Europe—and some of the defensive ones as well (air defense, for example). While this did not mean supervising POINTBLANK, the actions of the Royal Navy or U.S. Navy, COSSAC did need to be briefed on the progress and activities of these services on a regular basis, particularly that of the air forces, along with their success or lack thereof.

Closer supervision was required of all agencies involved in reconnaissance and raiding, including the work of the office of the Special Operations Executive and the Office of Strategic Services in occupied France. The Admiralty and Air Ministry were directed to coordinate their activities with COSSAC in terms of reconnaissance, much of which was being done at Morgan's request anyway. Special Operations were given general direction by COSSAC, which had no desire to interfere with or inhibit their work. The goal was merely to ensure that no operations were undertaken that would unintentionally provide useful information to the Germans about the location or timing of the invasion.

Many of the operations that COSSAC now found itself involved with or that needed supervising were at the opposite end of the scale to which they were accustomed to dealing. They had no means of dealing with both the planning of assault divisions storming across the beach, on one hand, and controlling the activities of patrols or excursions of one or two individuals or of a small specialist party as they examined Norman beaches or German defense preparations, on the other. Consequently, COHQ lent them support from their own planning and intelligence sections, a most welcomed supplement.

Morgan also set up a committee to ensure there was proper coordination of all these efforts. The committee included representatives of COSSAC's three sections and was chaired by the Army representative. Other members included representatives of the commanding general of the U.S. Ninth Air Force (which had just been established and was the equivalent of the British Second Tactical Air Force), the air officer commanding the Second British Tactical Air Force, the commanders in chief of 21st Army Group and 12th U.S. Army Group (once it was established), the chief of Combined Operations, and the commander in chief of Scottish Command. Morgan admitted that this was an unwieldy body but felt that its "principal virtue was that it was possible by means of it to prevent activities inimical to our design."[10] By November 1943, this group was functioning smoothly in coordination with COSSAC's G-3 section.

Morgan also tried to tackle issues around the security of the operational areas where troops were going to be located and where they would be staged for embarkation. Findlater Stewart helped draft the security proposal. While the COS agreed with his proposed restrictions on civilian movement and access, the British War Cabinet did not, and final decisions in this area had to wait for the supreme commander's arrival.

While COSSAC was not responsible for the training of assault troops, it needed to oversee the training process and keep track of which units had received training after arriving in the United Kingdom and balance that with the training they had received either in the United States before deployment or in the Mediterranean, in the case of units transferred from that theater. They also coordinated with 21st Army Group for the training of British and Canadian units. While not every unit needed to be trained in the techniques of amphibious assault, getting some exposure to battle school—type exercises, practice in combat in built up areas, and general field training—would benefit every unit.

Morgan was not above using personal relationships to get or keep units that were needed for the assault. On 3 September 1943, he wrote a letter of congratulations to Mountbatten on the latter's appointment as Supreme Allied

Commander for Southeast Asia. Over the course of a brief, five-paragraph "Dear Dickie" letter, he mentions four times the desirability of leaving Lord Lovat (Brig. Simon Fraser) and his "gang of cut-throats" (First Special Service Brigade) in the United Kingdom for OVERLORD as opposed to taking them along to Asia. "The progress they have made towards solution of the particular problem that we have hitherto had in view for them has been most remarkable, and one had looked forward to having in them an invaluable spearhead for the operations that we have in prospect here." Morgan ended by saying, "I hope you realize that, in memory of the recent past, you may call on me for anything or everything (with the possible exception of Lovat and his gang)."[11]

On 6 June Lovat's command, which included the French No. 10 Inter-Allied Commando; No. 45 Royal Marine Commando; and No. 3, No. 4, and No. 6 Commandos, would knock out the artillery batteries and the garrison at Ouistreham on the extreme left flank of the British landings as well as linking up with the 6th Airborne Division.[12] Churchill described Lovat in a letter to Stalin as "the mildest-mannered man that ever scuttled a ship or cut a throat."[13]

Immediately after the Quebec conference, in September 1943, was the deception Operation STARKY and its aftermath. While it did not achieve the desired results, it took time, energy, and resources from COSSAC to execute at a time when both OVERLORD and RANKIN were clamoring for attention. STARKY also marked the end of Hughes-Hallett's association with the planners, being replaced at COSSAC by Rear Adm. George Creasy, RN.

We've seen how Morgan devoted a great deal of time to civil affairs and to setting up liaison procedures with allied governments. He also worked effectively with Maj. Gen. John C. H. Lee, USA, commander of Services of Supply for the European Theater of Operations. General Lee joined many of the weekly COSSAC staff conferences throughout the summer of 1943, and Morgan encouraged him to modify his perspective from one of gathering supplies and troops in the United Kingdom to a view of supplying forces engaged in combat on the continent.[14]

COSSAC staff also addressed technical problems related to the assault— for example, finding ways to bridge the water gap (the distance between the lowered ramp of a landing craft and dry land) and, related to that, the waterproofing of vehicles. The challenge of waterproofing vehicles was that it was going to be done at the unit level, and therefore they had to create a process that was simple and quick. Fitting extension pipes for exhausts was easy enough, but the protection of electrical components and other vitals required something that could insulate, be shaped into various forms, and resist heat. The solution, literally, was a mix of heavy grease and asbestos, with the asbestos having been baked beforehand to remove moisture.[15] Discovered through yet another sequence of trial and error, the mixture addressed just one of many problems that needed to be solved before D-Day.

There were, of course, larger issues. As a result of another decision taken in Quebec, COSSAC was now also tasked with planning Operation JUPITER, an invasion of Norway in the event that the Germans somehow put Normandy out of reach. There also was the discussion about the command and control of the Normandy assault and, related to that, the creation of and coordination between the Supreme Headquarters, the commander of the Tactical Air Forces for the invasion, and the commander of Naval Forces for the Expeditionary Force.

Operation JUPITER was one of Churchill's pet projects. That did not endear it to others, however. McLean knew the idea "was nonsense."[16] Troops gathered in the south of England to cross the Channel would be in exactly the wrong place to mount an assault on Norway. Many of the craft that could be combat loaded in England and land in Normandy could not cross the North Sea to Norway under similar circumstances. Air cover could only be provided by aircraft carriers that were not available, and it would not be possible for COSSAC to plan OVERLORD and JUPITER simultaneously (without consideration of the additional challenges that came from RANKIN).

It was a moment when Leigh-Mallory's presence at COSSAC's weekly staff meetings and his ongoing support of the planners was a great benefit. At the 17 September meeting, Morgan, Leigh-Mallory, and the principal staff officers all agreed that the planning for JUPITER "would have a most disadvantageous effect on the planning for OVERLORD." Leigh-Mallory added his authority to Morgan's recommendation to the COS for the creation of another planning staff to take on Norway. With that, Morgan "quietly let it die."[17]

As noted in the last chapter, the commander of 21st Army Group became the overall tactical commander for the assault, with Bradley serving as the commander of First U.S. Army and Lt. Gen. Miles Dempsey coming from a corps command in the Mediterranean to lead Second British Army in the assault. When the assault was enlarged from three divisions to five, the concept of the command structure that Morgan brought back from Washington, D.C., remained unchanged.

After the cross-Channel assault, in September 1944 Eisenhower, as Supreme Allied Commander, took direct command of what had become, by then, two army groups. There were the U.S. First and Third Armies formed into the 12th U.S. Army Group under Bradley and the British Second Army and Canadian First Army as the 21st Army Group.[18] The commander of the 21st Army Group, who had been the tactical commander until September, was, of course, Montgomery and not Paget.

At Quebec, when Churchill told Brooke that an American would command OVERLORD, the prime minister also mentioned that Montgomery would replace Paget as commander of 21st Army Group. While Brooke and the prime minister knew of the proposed change, it wasn't announced until December. In his diary, Brooke notes that Paget "had done a marvelous job in training up these forces [for D-day]" and that he had "a great personal admiration and affection for him," but that he (Paget) "had no experience in this war of commanding a large formation in action [and] his abilities in my mind suited him better for the duties of a Chief of Staff than for a Commander."[19] Brooke also noted that the general selected should have already proved himself in battle and be one in whom everyone could have confidence and advocated in favor of Montgomery. Morgan had reached a similar conclusion.

Morgan pressed the edges of his newly found authority by approaching the prime minister regarding the command of 21st Army Group. COSSAC had sensed an attitude developing in at least some of the public's mind that could be described as a type of war weariness. A sense of "we've done our bit; let the Americans and Russians carry it from here." One step in combating this feeling, in Morgan's view, was to put an inspirational character in charge of 21st Army Group so that the public and the soldiers who were to do the fighting would see how important the campaign was. Acting on behalf of his commander, as would any good chief of staff, he went to Churchill and suggested that Montgomery replace Paget.[20] The fact that he was granted time with the prime minister suggests that COSSAC had gained some amount of stature in a short period of time. Morgan clearly did not present new information to Churchill, nor did he cause the command change at 21st Army Group. At best, his was one additional voice that reaffirmed what had already been decided. It was, however, also an indication of how seriously Morgan was taking on his responsibilities as the representative of the Supreme Allied Commander.

For his part, Paget took the news, which was not entirely unexpected, with typical professionalism. On 24 December 1943 Paget was notified that he would become Commander-in-Chief, Middle East, replacing Gen. Henry Maitland Wilson, who was to replace Eisenhower as supreme commander in the Mediterranean. To make these "musical chairs" a bit more complicated, General Devers moved from ETOUSA and replaced Eisenhower as commander of U.S. troops in the Mediterranean and later was the 6th Army Group commander for the invasion of Southern France (ANVIL/DRAGOON), with Eisenhower becoming both the Supreme Allied Commander for northwest Europe and the commanding general of ETOUSA.

Deception planning was another requirement that was central to the OVERLORD plan. The deception plan needed to be created and integrated with the ongoing efforts of the London Controlling Section and the XX Committee. Development of the plan began in the summer of 1943. Colonel Bevan's London Controlling Section produced a paper, reasonably titled "First Thoughts," which sketched out the basic structure of the approach. In broad terms, the deception planning took the strands of real situations or plausible interpretations of real situations and then added a bit of a twist.

For example, some of the stories that were suggested include explaining that STARKY and WADHAM had been canceled when the Allies realized the strength of German defenses, combined with an ongoing shortage of landing craft. The alternative that the Allies were embracing was a reliance on Operation POINTBLANK, along with a series of diversionary attacks on the South of France from Italy and in the eastern Mediterranean as well as raids on Norway and Denmark.

As plans for the cross-Channel attack grew and preparations became noticeable, it was to be suggested that the Allies were waiting for RANKIN-like circumstances before launching the attack. According to one member of the London Controlling Section, COSSAC's reaction to these ideas was "more despairing than unfavorable," and Morgan suggested that it might be possible to exaggerate Allied strength to a point where the Germans would decide to withdraw. Bevan pointed out the danger that, in those circumstances, the Germans might also decide to reinforce to a point where OVERLORD would not be possible.[21]

These initial rough outlines were developed into a proposal called JAEL (named after a Hebrew heroine from the Old Testament who deceived the enemy king and then killed him with a tent peg and hammer as he slept), which was further developed after the Quebec conference and was based on the decisions taken there. The essential goal of the plan was to keep German forces below the threshold COSSAC had specified in the outline plan. JAEL was the work of the London Controlling Section and dealt only at the strategic level. Operational-level deception planning was left to COSSAC.

JAEL's story was that, despite the presence in the United Kingdom of a growing number of Allied divisions (many of which were notional and found their way onto the Germans' Allied Order of Battle), few divisions were trained for amphibious operations. There were some experienced divisions that could be transferred from the Mediterranean, but personnel from those divisions would be used to train the new divisions. Landing craft that would be transferred from the Mediterranean would also be used for training. While there was a great increase in Americans arriving in the United Kingdom, these were mostly bomber crews or ground personnel to be used for POINTBLANK.

The story continued that the Allies had great faith in POINTBLANK and hoped that it, plus a Russian offensive in the spring plus their own continued operations in the Mediterranean, would stretch the Germans to a point where a late-summer cross-Channel landing could be conducted against weakened opposition. Additionally, Allied forces would seek to establish bomber bases in Northern Italy. Amphibious attacks from Turkey toward the Balkans were also to be considered. This would require a diplomatic offensive to convince Turkey to enter the war.

The plan's first draft was completed on 22 September. Review and revisions by COSSAC took another month, and a final draft was agreed to by COSSAC on 23 October. On 26 October the British COS deferred any decision on the plan because "of the prevailing situation in the Mediterranean."[22] They would not address the plan until after the Cairo and Tehran conferences that were to occur in about a month's time, where they hoped the Russians would agree with them about the value of additional operations in the Mediterranean, thereby making much of the deception plan irrelevant. After the Tehran conference the plan evolved into BODYGUARD. Deception planning for BODYGUARD began in early December 1943, and it and the story of FOR-TITUDE are properly part of the SHAEF story rather than that of COSSAC.

At the same time, COSSAC was working on its operational-level deception plan, ultimately called Appendix Y to the OVERLORD plan. After seven revisions it was presented to the British COS on 20 November. Basically, the plan was about concealing as much as possible of what was going on in the west of England while selectively revealing by radio traffic, by incomplete attempts at camouflage (including life-sized rubber models of tanks and trucks), and by troop movements the existence of notional divisions in the east of England, which could threaten the Pas-de-Calais.[23] Knowing that the Germans had radio monitoring posts throughout occupied Europe, small units were established to generate scripted message traffic from various locations, mimicking what real units would produce. They also introduced periods of radio silence to reduce the attention that the final period of radio silence would attract just before the invasion was launched.

The plan was accepted and put into operation although it also had to be modified in the spring of 1944 as preparations for the invasion grew to a point where it was no longer possible to conveniently conceal and reveal as one wished.

As noted in the story of STARKY, the role of the XX Committee and the Double-Cross System was vital to the deception campaign's success. Agent Garbo's story is well known. Other important agents included Brutus, a Polish agent sent over by the Germans who had immediately turned himself in upon arrival in England. Tricycle was a Yugoslav native who had been recruited by the Germans in Belgrade and who then told the British Embassy of his recruitment. He was later able to make his way to the United Kingdom and work from there. Agents Tate and Treasure were other agents who had wireless sets and who were important to the OVERLORD deception plans.[24] It was largely through them that the cover story was told and sold to the Germans.

While COSSAC was aware of and signed off on the progress of the plans and the deception efforts, it was not an operation that was run by COSSAC, and the XX Committee story is interwoven with the other aspects of BODYGUARD.

Not least on Morgan's list was the development and construction of the artificial harbors. The MULBERRY project was part of the engineers' section, headed up since August by Maj. Gen. Sir Harold Wernher, who had a special knack for managing a project that was needed by the military but that was being created and built largely by civilians. It was, in some ways, a mini Manhattan Project. Progress on the development of the artificial harbors was reported weekly at the COSSAC staff conferences from the end of August onward. It wasn't until January 1944 that they were sure the harbor system, arguably the single most critical project that COSSAC developed, would be ready in time.

A lesser-known but significant issue that COSSAC confronted was the threat to the invasion buildup by German V weapons and the need to decide what preparations, if any, should be taken to mitigate any potential damage or disruption they might cause. By the end of August 1943 British intelligence had evaluated enough information and data from various sources to assess that the Germans were developing two weapons, one a pilotless aircraft and the other a rocket. Less was known about the first, but of the rocket, officially known as the A-4, they had reasonably good knowledge of range, method of launch, and certain flight characteristics. They lacked good information about the warhead size and propellent.[25]

By early November more was known about both weapons, and many of the "ski-jump" launch sites for the V-1 were being discovered by aerial reconnaissance and plotted on maps, showing their locations from roughly Dieppe to Calais and showing that they were oriented toward London.[26] COSSAC was told of the potential threat, and they worked out what a possible "fall of shot" would be and how intense, in theory, a bombardment might be on areas of importance to OVERLORD, particularly London and the British Channel ports.

Morgan felt that "intelligence officers are paid to be pessimistic" and "the worst might not happen." He recommended that, unless circumstances required it, preparations and staging for the invasion remain as they were.[27] The alternative would have included using the Thames, the Clyde, and northern ports instead of the Channel ports—but so much concrete had already been poured in the south for the loading of troops and supplies that it was hard to see how such last-minute shifts would have been effective.

There were tentative plans, "in case of emergency," for COSSAC's key personnel to relocate from Norfolk House to "the Rotundas" in Westminster, where some space had been allocated for them and where the COS and various service ministries would also relocate. The rest of COSSAC would, in those circumstances, head for the country.[28] The Rotundas were two giant bomb shelters, capable of handling up to three thousand people for ninety days, created from abandoned underground gas storage facilities, located in the center of London at the corner of Marsham Street and Great Peter Street.[29] By the time the V-weapon attacks started, the invasion had begun and Supreme Allied Headquarters was no longer in London. COSSAC's signals department did have offices in the shelters until Eisenhower's headquarters moved south, out of London.[30]

In October 1943 Adm. Sir Bertram Ramsay left Eisenhower's staff in the Mediterranean and returned to England to assume command as Allied Naval Commander, Expeditionary Force. With his arrival, COSSAC now had a full complement of senior commanders with whom to work. Ramsay had been chosen by Churchill for the position, and it was an inspired choice. The First Sea Lord, Adm. Dudley Pound, had, before his illness and death, suggested that Adm. Charles Little be formally confirmed as naval commander for the assault. He had held the position as "designate" during the spring and summer. While Pound's point of view is understandable, Churchill's decision was unquestionably the better one. Not only had Ramsay conducted the evacuation from Dunkirk, he had been the naval chief of staff for TORCH and naval commander for HUSKY. Consequently, his understanding of relevant amphibious operations and his demonstrated success in working with the Americans would be essential to the success of NEPTUNE, as the operation of transporting the whole of the Allied Expeditionary Force across the Channel and the initial assault came to be named.

As a result of these new circumstances, yet more changes were put into effect that affected COSSAC's organization. On 22 November Morgan announced at the weekly staff conference that, with the formal appointments of Ramsay and Leigh-Mallory, the naval and air staffs at COSSAC, which had been considered as branches of the headquarters, were now exclusively the domain of their respective commanders. While "an intimacy of thought and liaison must be maintained at all levels," Morgan emphasized that "opinions expressed in such contacts must [now] be those of the commanders."[31] In practice, this meant that COSSAC's naval and air staffs ceased to exist, being transferred from what was to become the Supreme Headquarters to the headquarters of the air and of the naval commanders. He went on to note that in the absence of the supreme commander, all other staff (other than naval and air force) were to consider him as their commander. If anyone was in doubt or confused by this, Morgan suggested that the appropriate division heads consult him.

At the same meeting, Morgan announced that an "inner cabinet" had been formed, consisting of the naval commander, the tactical air force commander, their chiefs of staff, Morgan, and Barker. This group was formed to make command decisions "on matters of major importance referred to it [which require] inter-service co-ordination or matters of joint interest."[32] Morgan later explained he had to include Barker, otherwise it would have been an all-British group, and he was keenly aware of the need to sustain the appearance of an Allied organization.

What had been the weekly staff meetings would continue but would be now considered a meeting of chiefs of staff, not necessarily attended by senior commanders. As part of the ongoing evolution of COSSAC into a supreme headquarters, the 21st Army Group and 12th U.S. Army Group were positioned outside the cabinet and were focused on tactical issues.

None of this would matter, however, if the British were able to marshal the support of the Russians in favor of immediate action in the Mediterranean at the expense of a "short" delay in the execution of OVERLORD. Despite all that had gone on, all that had been agreed, and all the brave words, from COSSAC's standpoint everything was still in doubt.

EUREKA

By the end of the Moscow foreign minister's conference on 1 November 1943, the British and Americans had presented the OVERLORD plan to their Russian ally in some detail and had emphasized the planned 1 May 1944 invasion date. The Russians were clearly well pleased by what they heard but also let it be known that they would also welcome more immediate actions if possible. When Churchill instructed Foreign Minister Anthony Eden to inform the Soviets that events in Italy might preclude or delay the transfer of seven divisions to the United Kingdom for the invasion, "Stalin did not react with anger but instead said kind things about the Italian campaign that would have warmed the hearts of Churchill and Brooke."[33]

The Americans did not share Stalin's reaction. However, the Soviet premier's comments gave the British encouragement that their views of additional operations in the Mediterranean might get agreement at the next interallied conference, setting up one final round of debates on what the Americans had thought was agreed in Washington in May and in Quebec in August, which had just been presented to the Russians in Moscow.

The British well understood what delaying the transfer of the divisions meant. They were concerned that operations in Italy were bogging down and that momentum was being lost. Brooke hoped that a winter offensive in the mountainous terrain south of Rome would restore a war of movement to the Italian peninsula. Transferring divisions to the United Kingdom would not help. His point was

> to remove a division from the Italian front, to embark it, to transfer it by sea . . . through the Mediterranean and Bay of Biscay, to unload it in England, locate it in new formations and new training areas, and finally to train it for the most difficult of operations—a combined landing against strong opposition—required a period which could only be measured in months. It will therefore be seen that every division withdrawn from Italy to England for operation OVERLORD was a division washed off the slate for a period of months.[34]

Ironically, General Marshall could make virtually the same argument in explaining why it was necessary to transfer the divisions before the end of 1943 if they were to be ready for a cross-Channel assault by May 1944. In SKYSCRAPER, Barker and Sinclair made a similar point, noting that the particular demands of a cross-Channel attack against opposition would require the military and naval forces involved to spend months together engaged in specialized training before they could achieve the required level of proficiency. The same point was made again at RATTLE.

There was another issue from the American viewpoint that perhaps the British either discounted or were unaware of. Shortly after the end of the Quebec conference, General McNarney, representing the U.S. Army, was obliged to justify in congressional testimony why a 7.7 million-man army was necessary.[35] McNarney assured Congress that this was the minimum number needed.

The case for the Army was based on strategy and the requirements that follow from that and on logistics and the timing of operations. Regarding the timing, the forces to be used for any operation needed to be inducted, trained, equipped, and moved to the theater of operations sufficiently in advance to be ready for employment on the date the operation was to start. Once strategic decisions had been made, changes and vacillation about operations would lead to delays, bottlenecks, confusion, and might not only "endanger the over-all European pattern but also jeopardize the availability of strength . . . needed to defeat Japan."[36]

At this point (early autumn 1943), a substantial majority of American ground and air units were still in the continental United States, with eight divisions in the Mediterranean, seven in the United Kingdom, and thirteen in the Pacific (not including the Marines).[37] In mid-1943, the Pentagon planners anticipated that nineteen divisions would be available for OVERLORD in May 1944, growing to over forty-five by the end of 1944.

From this point on, the growing global demands on manpower—the substantial manpower requirements for OVERLORD and the anticipated fighting in northwest Europe—the need for a strategic reserve, and the need for sufficient air and land forces to defeat Japan were a constant concern. Today we'd call the challenges they faced a sort of Rubik's Cube. As Marshall said, "It is no longer entirely a question of shipping. Basically, it is now a question of manpower."[38] It was yet another reason why the Americans were so insistent on making a plan and sticking to it.

The Cairo (SEXTANT) conferences—one held before the Tehran meeting with the Russians and with the participation of the Nationalist Chinese, and one afterward, to finish the details after Tehran—were necessary to get clear agreement on the war in the Pacific. Brooke had expected that the first Cairo conference would feature a discussion leading to a united Anglo-American front for the Tehran meeting, but the presence of Chiang Kai-Shek changed the sequence of the meeting, as the Americans had desired.

For Brooke and the British, this was unhelpful. "We should never have started our conference with Chiang; by doing so we were putting the cart before the horse. He had nothing to contribute towards the defeat of the Germans, and for the matter of that uncommonly little towards the defeat of the Japanese."[39] This was an accurate observation, but Roosevelt hoped that China would be a great power in the postwar world and was willing to give Chiang the appearance of such status. Additionally, the Americans made it clear that no discussions about the cross-Channel attack would occur without Stalin.

The first Cairo conference from 22 to 26 November 1943 was indeed primarily about the Pacific, particularly Burma, China, and Operation BUCCANEER, an intended landing on the Andaman Islands in the Bay of Bengal, roughly 880 kilometers (545 miles) west of Bangkok. Debates about operations in the Pacific are beyond the scope of this book but were important to COSSAC as the ongoing issue of landing craft figured in all of them. Some of the participants thought that canceling operations in one theater would allow for more landing craft in another while others expected to keep those craft in theater for other uses. Ultimately, the Allies would have to choose which operations would actually be launched as there were never enough landing craft for all of the proposed operations to occur.

Churchill did bring up operations in the eastern Mediterranean, particularly his current pet project, the invasion of Rhodes, Greece. General Marshall is alleged to have told him "not one American soldier is going to die on [that] God Damned beach."[40] This seemed to preclude further discussion of the issue.

The Americans also made it clear that any discussion about the transfer of the seven divisions was over. The U.S. 1st Infantry Division left Sicily on 23 October, before the start of the conference. The other U.S. divisions were out of the Mediterranean and headed toward the United Kingdom by the end of the year.[41]

The British COS were frustrated at not gaining an agreement with the Americans ahead of the Tehran conference (EUREKA) and at the rigidity with which the Americans held the OVERLORD D-day. As they wrote in their briefing paper for the CCS ahead of the meeting: "In these changed conditions [Russian successes and Italy taken out of the war], we feel that consideration of adjustments of, if not actual departures from, the decisions taken at TRIDENT and QUADRANT are not only fully justified but positively essential." They went on to state that they were still committed to OVERLORD in the spring or summer, sooner if RANKIN circumstances were obtained. "We must not, however, regard OVERLORD on a fixed date as the pivot of our whole strategy.... We should attack wherever we can do so in superior force. If we pursue the above policy, we firmly believe that OVERLORD (perhaps in the form of RANKIN) will take place next summer. We do not, however, attach vital importance to any particular date or to any particular number of divisions in the assault and follow-up."[42] Reading that statement today, it seems remarkably cavalier regarding the cross-Channel attack if taken at face value. It is understandable why the American Joint Chiefs would have questions about the commitment of British decision makers to OVERLORD after having read the British briefing.

The Americans were frustrated at British attempts to reopen topics on which they felt agreement had been reached and with the circumstances surrounding those decisions, in the American view, unchanged. In particular, they were not happy to consider that the British were going to open the Normandy/Mediterranean debate again—in front of Soviet premier Joseph Stalin—and hope for a different outcome. It was shaping up as another verse in what had become an all-too-familiar choral concert, this time to be sung without restraint.

Lt. Gen. Joseph Stillwell, USA, was at the first Cairo conference. He reported that one meeting of the CCS got so heated that "Brooke got nasty and [Ernest] King got good and sore. King almost climbed over the table at Brooke. God, he [King] was mad. I wish he [King] had socked him."[43] Brooke's diary suggests that this might have been on 23 November, when he described the afternoon meeting of the CCS as becoming "somewhat heated with King on the subject of the Andaman Islands and the possibility of landing craft being diverted from this operation to the Aegean." King, Hap Arnold, and William Leahy joined Brooke for dinner that evening, and "King was as nice as could be and quite transformed from his afternoon attitude."[44]

When the EUREKA conference opened in Tehran on 28 November 1943, FDR, who chaired the meeting, began by reviewing the war against Japan. He then presented both the British concepts for the Mediterranean and the option of the cross-Channel attack. Stalin immediately supported OVERLORD, saying that no operation in the Mediterranean could be decisive. Before doing so, he promised Soviet entry into the Pacific war once Germany had been defeated.

As one would expect, Churchill argued in favor of multiple offensives in the Mediterranean. Stalin noted that the proposed operations in the Mediterranean seemed to be unrelated to each other. The only operation in which he saw any value was the diversionary attack in Southern France that had been mentioned at Quebec, Operation ANVIL.[45] This was envisioned to be simultaneous with Normandy. That would, of course, raise the issue of landing craft yet again. The next day Stalin asked who would command OVERLORD. Roosevelt told him the decision had not yet been made. "Then nothing will come of these operations" was the response.[46]

The CCS report to the president and prime minister at the end of the conferences, dated 6 December 1943, made the following points:

A. OVERLORD and ANVIL are the supreme operations for 1944. They must be carried out during May 1944. Nothing must be undertaken in any other part of the world which hazards the success of these two operations.

B. OVERLORD as at present planned is on a narrow margin. Everything practicable should be done to increase its strength.

C. The examination of ANVIL on the basis of not less than a two-division assault should be pressed forward as fast as possible. If the examination reveals that it requires strengthening, consideration will have to be given to the provision of additional resources.

D. Operations in the Aegean, including in particular the capture of Rhodes, are desirable, provided that they can be fitted in without detriment to OVERLORD and ANVIL.[47]

The same day Eisenhower was named Supreme Allied Commander for OVERLORD. Roosevelt stopped in Algiers on his way back to Washington to personally inform the general. In the middle of December Air Marshal Arthur Tedder, who had served with Eisenhower in the Mediterranean, was appointed deputy commander. With Ramsay as naval commander, Leigh-Mallory as tactical air commander, and Bradley as commander of First U.S. Army, that left only command of the British Army unannounced. Montgomery was notified on Christmas Eve and ordered to return to London to take command of Allied ground forces for the assault.[48]

When Paget heard that Montgomery was taking over 21st Army Group, in combination with Eisenhower as Supreme Allied Commander, he wrote in his diary, "So, after a long period of speculation, we now know where we stand, and the farce of COSSAC without a commander is ended."[49] This, I think, was not a reflection on Morgan but more a reaction to the extraordinarily unconventional nature of COSSAC and the strain the absence of a commander placed on those, including Paget, who were doing all they could to be ready with the best plan possible. This was something that any conventional military officer would have found frustrating.

In the end, eight divisions were transferred from the Mediterranean to the United Kingdom. The U.S. Army transferred the 1st Infantry, 9th Infantry, 2nd Armored, and 82nd Airborne. (Initially COSSAC didn't want the 82nd Airborne, thinking more about the assault across the beach. But along with the division came additional transport aircraft.) The British Army transferred the 50th Infantry, 51st Highland Division, 7th Armored, and 1st Airborne.[50] The 1st Airborne was not employed in OVERLORD. It suffered horrific losses as part of Operation MARKET GARDEN in September 1944.

The 7th Armored, 51st Highland, and 50th Infantry did not perform well in Normandy. They were tired and war-weary. The divisional commanders of the 7th Armored and 51st Highland were relieved of duty during the fighting, as was the corps commander, General Bucknall. While performance improved with new commanders, it was clear to others who were in Normandy that fresh divisions that had been training in the United Kingdom would have performed better.[51] At minimum, some of those who had been fighting for four years should have been rotated out and replaced by fresh troops.[52]

The final item in the minutes for the COSSAC staff conference of 17 December, the last weekly meeting of the year, was a statement by Morgan, with his friend Admiral Hall at the table: "In view of the decisions reached at SEXTANT the plan for OVERLORD was no longer to be regarded as a staff study; but that all concerned should now clearly understand that there was a firm determination that the operation would take place at the agreed date."[53]

Morgan later recalled that when he learned that Eisenhower was to be the supreme commander, his "dominant sensation was one of intense relief."[54] Whether or not he went to the Cavalry Club for refreshment has gone unrecorded.

— 12 —

"MONTY DIDN'T BRING ANYTHING NEW"

At the end of the RATTLE conference in July 1943 General Paget rose to thank Mountbatten for all his efforts and for the results of the conference. The conference, he said, had "done a great deal to clear everyone's minds and show them the scope and nature of the problem." He went on to say that while he still hoped it would prove unnecessary to conduct the amphibious assault, he committed the newly formed 21st Army Group to devoting its whole attention "to the problems which had been considered at the conference."[1]

The 21st Army Group went at it with a will. By the time Eisenhower and Montgomery arrived six months later, in January 1944, the COSSAC plan and its revisions had been thoroughly examined, and many of the recommendations found their way into the final plan. For example, 1st Corps issued a report dated 16 December 1943 that served as a review of the entire plan. Their analysis agreed with the COS that the expected rate of advance was "unduly optimistic." Given the forces currently available for the assault and follow-up, the 1st Corps staff concluded that the attack was likely to be successful only under RANKIN circumstances, "thus altering the essential premises" of the plan. After a meticulous examination of the problem, the report recommended:

1. Sufficient landing craft for an assault by not less than two divisions in the CAEN-BAYEUX Sector, with two follow-up divisions on the second tide and two more on the third tide.

2. Sufficient landing craft for a simultaneous assault on the CHER-BOURG peninsula by not less than one division with one follow-up division . . .

Sufficient transport aircraft and gliders to take in one lift:
a. One Airborne Division for the CAEN sector
b. One Airborne Division for the CHERBOURG sector
c. Two parachute brigades for the CAEN sector . . .
d. Special Service Troops to delay the arrival of enemy reserves

This totals in round figures to a landing craft lift of nine divisions, and an airborne lift of three divisions, as compared with the current allotment of four and a half [divisions] and two-thirds of a division respectively.[2]

It was starting to look like Barker's and Sinclair's plan—SKYSCRAPER—hadn't been that far off the mark.[3]

Morgan, in his submission of the outline plan on 15 July, noted that "increased resources of shipping, landing craft and transport aircraft would permit the elaboration of alternative plans designed to meet more than one set of extraneous conditions, whereas the state of provision herein taken into account dictates the adoption of one course only, or none at all."[4] That plea—along with Barker's "pitch" at the Quebec conference for a landing at what was later named Utah Beach, the observations of the British Joint Service Mission in a report sent to the COS during Morgan's visit to Washington that "Assault forces for OVERLORD should be strengthened by every practicable means," and even Churchill's reaction that the attack should be strengthened by 25 percent—had no effect in changing the size of the attack. The CCS did finally acknowledge the narrow margin in their report after the Tehran conference, as seen in the last chapter.[5]

General Eisenhower first saw the outline plan on 27 October, when Brig. Gen. William Earl Chambers, USA, of the COSSAC staff arrived in Algiers to get his opinion and advice. Walter Bedell Smith was present for the meeting, and he and Eisenhower decided, "off the cuff, that a five-division attack was far more desirable."[6] Smith, of course, had gone through the plan in detail with Morgan and the OPD planners in mid-October at the Pentagon and had witnessed the questioning that had been put to Morgan by the American experts. According to Smith, "When [Morgan] mentioned the puny little assault with three divisions, I nearly fell out of my seat. After all, we had more than that for our landings [in the Mediterranean]. I told Eisenhower . . . when I got back and he said, 'My God, if I were going to do it, I would want ten or twelve divisions.'"[7] Later in the same interview, Smith makes it clear that everyone wanted a larger assault. "The addition of divisions was accepted by acclamation."

Maj. Gen. Freddie de Guingand, Montgomery's chief of staff, said much the same thing, After he and Smith looked at the plan just before Montgomery's arrival in London on 2 January 1944, they agreed that more of everything was needed. Their reactions were, in de Guingand's words, similar to those "of any trained soldier."[8] Everyone understood the limitations under which Morgan developed the plan, but there was never any question that a workable operational plan would have to look very different.

On 27 December Montgomery met with Eisenhower at the latter's headquarters in Algiers. At that meeting Eisenhower made it clear that he felt the assault force was too small and told Montgomery to convey that opinion to those in London who needed to know. He also said that he had no problem with a one-month delay if it meant getting the necessary force—and landing craft.[9] Given the fact that, after Tehran, the CCS had specified only the month of May as the target date for the invasion, this was no great change. Perhaps it was a way to refine the date range in the most advantageous way for OVERLORD and its commander.

On 31 December Montgomery was summoned by Churchill to the prime minister's temporary headquarters in Marrakesh, where he had gone after the Tehran conference to recuperate from pneumonia. Churchill shared the OVERLORD plan with Montgomery and asked for his opinion. Lord Ismay had recommended against showing the plan without Montgomery also getting a briefing from the planners so he could understand the context surrounding the decisions that had been made. The prime minister disregarded that advice. Montgomery's critical evaluation of the plan for Churchill made no reference to his meeting with Eisenhower or to Eisenhower's own views and misgivings, although the criticisms reflected the discussion in Algiers.[10]

Gen. Sir Leslie Hollis was assistant secretary to the War Cabinet and the Chiefs of Staff Committee. He was almost always within shouting distance of

Churchill during his time as prime minister. He remembered sitting alongside Churchill, Lord Beaverbrook (a friend and advisor to Churchill as well as a member of the war cabinet), and Montgomery that evening, watching the sun set "over the desert in all its glory and splendour. For a few moments, our conversation would turn to this astonishingly beautiful sight, and then back it would go to the unending topic: the impending Second Front which Churchill was convinced was the only way in which we could lose the war."[11] This may have been one of Churchill's "Black Dog" moods, but he was also too experienced and too wise a political leader not to consider all the risks and all the consequences of a particular course of action. OVERLORD was a great risk but one that, on balance, needed to be taken.

On 3 January 1944, back in London, Montgomery was briefed by McLean, Barker, and the other COSSAC planners.[12] McLean took him through the constraints with which they had worked and made it clear that they felt at least one more division was needed in the assault as well as two divisions afloat as immediate follow-up units. McLean also made a pitch for using Utah Beach and for widening the assault east of Arromanches (what was to become Sword Beach). He also brought up the desirability of employing the three airborne divisions in the initial assault. This was based on the recommendations of 1st Corps and the other ongoing studies that COSSAC had been engaged in since August.

According to Barker, Montgomery then took the floor and, "in grandiose style," said the plan was too restricted. His idea was "to attack the north side of the Brittany Peninsula, or at least as far south as Granville and St. Malo." He wanted to broaden the left flank but recognized that German shore batteries there made it challenging. Montgomery also suggested diversions in the areas of Dieppe, Le Havre, and Brest.[13] He asked the planners to study his ideas and respond the next day.[14]

At 11:00 a.m. on 4 January, the group reconvened, joined by Admiral Ramsay. The admiral, speaking for both the Royal Navy and their American counterparts, made it clear that they couldn't guarantee any landings on the west side of the Cotentin peninsula. For one thing, they would be in danger from German batteries located on the island of Alderney. For another, the prevailing winds on that side were westerly and therefore not favorable for landings.

Leigh-Mallory pointed out that there was also intense antiaircraft fire from Alderney that would jeopardize any airborne landing or close-air support. (Alderney, about three miles long, is the northernmost Channel Island, roughly twenty-five miles from Guernsey, and is the closest island to the Cherbourg Peninsula. Ships headed toward Saint-Malo or Granville would pass between the peninsula and the island.)

West and McLean presented the challenges from the army's view, and Montgomery "gave way quite readily."[15] Barker made it clear in his postwar interview that Montgomery was well within his rights as the assault force commander to raise the questions—even if it required everyone to cover ground that had been extensively examined before, notably in the annexes that were part of the outline plan.

Everyone accepted the idea of adding Utah Beach, as it had always been a desirable site if there were enough troops and craft to make it work. The planners were tasked with preparing an outline and statement of landing craft requirements for a division-sized assault. At the same time, it was also decided to expand the beachhead in the other direction and add Sword Beach in front of Caen. With the UTAH decision came the need to deploy two airborne divisions in support of that attack and to use the third airborne division not for the assault on Caen, which would now be the task of the forces landed on Sword, but on the far-left flank to hold the bridges of the Orne and Dives Rivers, including the now well-known Pegasus Bridge.

According to Barker, if a logical argument were presented, Montgomery would accept it, but he tended to be "didactic. He spoke as a god from Olympus."[16] Montgomery's evaluation of the outline plan was expressed again quite cogently at the first supreme commander's conference on 21 January 1944, at the end of Eisenhower's first week in London. Here he made it clear that he felt the present plan would not achieve the desired results. The assault force was too weak, the frontage too narrow, and it was necessary to land troops east of the marshes and streams near the town of Carentan at the neck of the Cherbourg Peninsula, restating much of what he and Eisenhower had considered in December and what had been discussed with the planners earlier in January.

Barker's reaction was that COSSAC wasn't happy with the size of the attack either. "Monty didn't bring anything new to us in that."[17] Barker felt that

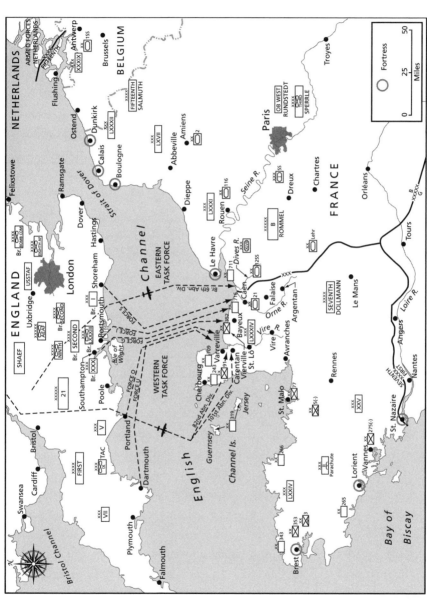

Map 2. Northwest France. Final OVERLORD plan. *Chris Robinson, based on map found from U.S. Military Academy History Department*

Montgomery's speeches weren't meant to be offensive. It was just that he had "a cocky manner and tended to imply that no one else knew his business."[18]

Lord Lovat, who attended a Montgomery briefing just before D-day, commented afterward that he felt as if he had been listening to "a headmaster taking a backward class: concise in his approach, but egotistical to a fault and, on this occasion, something of a poseur into the bargain."[19] Whatever his other considerable skills as a general, motivational speaking was apparently not high on Montgomery's list. (Although, in fairness, as Montgomery and Eisenhower worked together in the spring of 1944 and traveled to the various camps, the British general's informal speeches were well received by American soldiers as were the American general's by the British.)

The concept of broadening the assault area was a source of debate within COSSAC, with Morgan, West, and McLean, among others, favoring an approach of first having more divisions available for immediate follow-up and then, if resources permitted, broadening the assault. Montgomery and Eisenhower, with their operational experience in the Mediterranean, saw the merits of a broader frontage in the initial stage and getting more units ashore quickly. Not surprisingly, the view of the Supreme Allied Commander and the assault force commander won out.

On Sunday 23 January, eight days after Eisenhower arrived, he reported to the CCS the decisions to strengthen the assault, widen the frontage, and deploy the paratroops in support of UTAH and on the left flank. He also raised the same point with the chiefs that he brought up in his conversations with Montgomery—namely, if necessary, D-day could be delayed for a month to allow time to find the additional landing craft that would be needed. They would need that extra month. The expansion of the assault added the requirement of 47 LSTs and 216 landing craft of various types as well as another headquarters ship and attack transports. Additionally, the number of vehicles for each assault division was reduced to 2,500. SHAEF also would need more transport aircraft to lift three airborne divisions instead of two-thirds of one.[20] On 1 February the CCS signaled their approval of Eisenhower's changes.[21]

There was one more discussion to be had regarding the Mediterranean. ANVIL, the invasion of Southern France, was projected to involve two divisions in the initial assault. Almost as soon as the ink was dry on the report from the Tehran conference, the British COS started arguing for its cancelation, putting forward a series of reasons: there were not enough landing craft to mount it and OVERLORD simultaneously (which turned out to be true); the troops and craft were better used in Italy; unlike operations in Italy, ANVIL was not deemed by the COS to be necessary to the success of the cross-Channel attack; and, from Italy, the troops earmarked for ANVIL should instead move north and east through the Ljubljana Gap and then toward Vienna. That this went against what had been agreed with Stalin and how it would be explained to the Russians was not stated clearly, if at all.

Churchill and the British COS also pointed out that the increased demand for landing craft in the Mediterranean meant that BUCCANEER, the invasion of the Andaman Islands in the Indian Ocean, should be canceled. FDR agreed, shifting U.S. strategy in the Pacific even further toward the twin drives headed for the Philippines and across the central Pacific to the what was then called Formosa (Taiwan) and to the Japanese home islands.

Additional complications came from the 22 January 1944 landings at Anzio, south of Rome, which failed to break the deadlock in Italy. The forces pinned down on the bridgehead required a great deal of shipping to keep them supplied. For a while, Anzio became the fourth-largest port in the world.[22] This in turn delayed the movement of landing craft to Britain for OVERLORD. Churchill, in advocating for the Anzio landings, had hoped for a quick capture of Rome and then either a move farther north or perhaps north and then east toward the Balkans.

The idea of a drive through Italy, then through the Ljubljana Gap, and toward Vienna as an alternative to ANVIL was a short-lived but important distraction. Gen. Harold Alexander, now commander in chief of Allied armies in Italy under the new Supreme Allied Commander, British general Sir Henry Maitland Wilson, was enthusiastic about a rapid drive north to Vienna. Controversial at the time and still argued about today as an alleged means of forestalling the postwar Soviet presence in the Balkans, it was never grounded in reality.

The difficult supply lines didn't get easier as one drove north, and it was three times as far from Rome to Vienna as it was from Naples to Rome. Nor was consideration given to the challenge of crossing the Isonzo River, north of Trieste and site of twelve battles between the Italians and the Austro-Hungarians in World War I. The first eleven were just given numbers. The twelfth battle got its own name—Caporetto. The first eleven battles resulted in combined casualties of more than 750,000 men.[23] The combined Austro-Hungarian and German attack that was the twelfth battle resulted in approximately 250,000 Italian prisoners of war as well as 40,000 Italian casualties.[24] It required British and French divisions to be sent to stabilize the front. The terrain between there and Vienna was as favorable to the defense as was the Italian peninsula.

Whether the British were truly serious about this possibility is unclear. Brooke thought it unsound, but Churchill was, at least initially, intrigued. The British COS certainly believed that a better choice than ANVIL was a continued drive up the Italian peninsula north of Rome, which British military theorist and writer Maj. Gen. J. F. C. Fuller called "daft."[25] The debate as to whether or not ANVIL was necessary or a better choice than increased efforts in Italy was not settled until July, after the Normandy assault. Montgomery had argued unsuccessfully that ANVIL was a dispersion of effort and that concentrating on Normandy and Italy was the correct choice. Others, including Morgan, suggested that perhaps ANVIL would serve just as effectively as a threat and need not actually be executed to achieve its goal.

As COSSAC, Morgan also pointed out a problem from the other side of the ledger. A newly equipped and trained French army of ten divisions was now in North Africa. While it was not clear what they may or may not have been informally promised by someone, to not use them in the liberation of France would cause no end of political problems. If they weren't going to be used in Southern France, then at least some of them needed to be used for OVERLORD. That was a logistical problem that no one wanted.

In the end the Americans threatened to not transfer the landing craft previously earmarked for BUCCANEER to the Mediterranean unless ANVIL was agreed to, and in no event were there to be any Balkan adventures. This was insisted on, even though the continuing shortage of landing craft meant that ANVIL, renamed DRAGOON, was not launched until 15 August 1944. LSTs and other craft were shuttled from the Mediterranean to England and then back for the two operations.

While the two operations did not occur simultaneously, as originally envisioned, ANVIL/DRAGOON and OVERLORD complemented each other, and there were political benefits gained from French units participating in a meaningful way in the liberation of their country. Morgan made the argument after the war that ANVIL was "of vital necessity to the success" of OVERLORD, if for no other reason that it gained the port of Marseilles.[26]

With the arrival of Eisenhower, the pace of operations increased even more than with COSSAC, and the resources of the United States, particularly the U.S. Army, began to be felt much more dramatically—often, but not always, for the better. Eisenhower took over Morgan's office in Norfolk House, and the staff who were starting to come up from Algiers were squeezed into 80 Pall Mall. Smith, acting for Eisenhower, made a series of personnel changes as COSSAC became SHAEF as did Montgomery at 21st Army Group. In both instances, people who were known to the commanders replaced those who had been stationed in London and who had worked on the various iterations of the plans. There was little time for sensitive consideration of feelings or for understanding what had gone on before. Time was short, and the operational commanders needed to have people with whom they had worked successfully in key positions. This inevitably resulted in some amount of friction between those who had coped with the strictures pertaining to the creation of the outline plan, on the one hand, and those whose operational experience in the Mediterranean gave them a sense that they better understood what was needed, on the other.[27] Morgan's concept proved to be resilient enough to withstand the changes. Morgan also well understood the need for the personnel changes to be made quickly. He had faced similar situations in the creation of COSSAC, when he encountered qualified officers who simply could not adjust quickly enough to the nature of a joint and combined staff. As he said, there was no time "for the negotiation of personal reconciliations. It was necessary to resort to surgery rather than to medicine."[28]

Leigh-Mallory advocated for moving the headquarters out of London to a small town called Bushey Heath, near Stanmore, where he had his headquarters. Eisenhower knew from experience that he didn't want to be in the center of London, steps away from Whitehall and Downing Street, and agreed that his headquarters should be moved to Bushey Heath.

The U.S. Army, accustomed to communicating by teletype and telephone and moving with speed, looked at the map and then started the process of sending the engineers down "to make the path straight," as it were. Soon "dirt, trucks, bulldozers, bricks, mortar, huts, camouflage netting and so forth were flying in all directions." The headquarters quickly began to take shape, near the existing U.S. establishment known as "Widewing," the headquarters of U.S. Army Air Forces in Northwest Europe, in the village of Bushy Park, near Hampton Court in Surrey, south of London, not Bushey Heath, near Watford and Harrow, north of London. It was ready for occupancy in the middle of February 1944. When informed of the unintentional change of location for the headquarters, Smith reacted with precision, but perhaps not with strictly military phraseology: "My God, I've married the wrong woman." As Morgan pointed out, metaphorically he had, but there was no going back or undoing. There was no time.[29]

In the minutes of COSSAC's Weekly Staff Conference on 7 January 1944, RANKIN was still on the agenda, with Morgan reporting that the outline plan for RANKIN Case C was complete—the last section having to do with the repatriation of U.S. and Allied prisoners of war. Indeed, most of the meeting was taken up by issues relating to RANKIN, except for noting that General Ismay was forming a small committee to consider the issues around restricted movement and visitor bans in the South of England and other sensitive areas. General West was to be COSSAC's representative on the committee.[30] OVERLORD was awaiting the arrival of the supreme commander.

The final COSSAC weekly staff conference was held on Friday 14 January, two days before Eisenhower arrived. "COSSAC announced that General Eisenhower had signified that his designation was to be 'Supreme Commander Allied Expeditionary Force' and that his headquarters was to be known as Supreme Headquarters Allied Expeditionary Force [SHAEF]. . . . On the winding up of HQ COSSAC as such, COSSAC concluded by thanking his staff and congratulating them on the high standard of their work."[31] Monday, 17 January 1944, they all reported for work at SHAEF. As noted above, the first supreme commander's weekly staff conference was held that Friday.

EPILOGUE

By December 1943 COSSAC had reached a strength of 1,103 people; 56 percent of the 489 officers were British or from the British Empire, as were 67 percent of the 614 enlisted personnel. With SHAEF, things changed. On 12 July 1944, Eisenhower's headquarters had 4,914 officers and enlisted, with 63 percent of the 1,286 officers and 73 percent of the 3,628 enlisted being U.S. personnel. By 1 April 1945 the headquarters had greatly expanded and totaled 14,028 officers and enlisted. Of the 2,732 officers, 57 percent were American, as were 60 percent of the 11,296 enlisted.[1]

By this time the forces under SHAEF command consisted of the British 21st Army Group, which had the Second British Army of four corps plus an airborne corps and First Canadian Army of two corps. The French First Army was made up of two corps plus independent detachments. There were two U.S. Army groups, the 12th and 6th, with the First, Third, Seventh, Ninth, and Fifteenth Armies plus the First Allied Airborne Army. There were both the British Second Tactical Air Force and the U.S. Ninth Tactical Air Force.[2] The relationship between the RAF's Bomber Command, the U.S. Strategic Air Forces in Europe, and the Supreme Allied Commander was less clear. As Morgan wrote, "It will, I think, be considerable time before anybody will be able to set down in the form of an organizational diagram the channels through which General Eisenhower's orders reached his aircraft."[3] Of course, the bombers were not "Eisenhower's" even though he was Supreme Allied Commander.

On D-Day there were thirty-seven divisions available for the initial phase of the operation. (Ultimately, Eisenhower commanded ninety divisions: sixty-one American, thirteen British, ten French, five Canadian, and one Polish.[4]) By the end of 6 June 1944 there were approximately 150,000 troops ashore, supported by almost 6,500 naval vessels and landing craft as well as 11,500 aircraft of all types. In that total were almost 1,100 warships and more than 4,200 landing craft and ships (not the 8,000 that COSSAC had initially estimated). American-manned vessels represented 30 percent of the total.[5] The reconquest of Europe along the most direct route to Germany's industrial heartland had begun.

COSSAC's existence forced the debate about the cross-Channel attack to descend from the realms of theory and speculation and become a discussion of a practical nature with the demand for hard and timely decisions to be made. At Morgan's insistence, COSSAC was a truly Allied staff; therefore, its plans and recommendations could not be dismissed as the national views of one or the other of the Western Allies.

Morgan, Barker, and the COSSAC planners were under no illusion that the plan they had developed was complete in every detail, or that it employed the number of divisions they would have preferred to use. The first requirement was gaining a political agreement. As Barker pointed out, the proposal needed to be approved by the Combined Chiefs of Staff before anything else could occur. That was initially the primary objective for COSSAC. As a result of the decisions at the Quebec conference, Morgan was obliged to operate in areas and take on responsibilities uncommon to British staff officers of the time and to manage the uncertainty that came with the lack of a final political decision. It was only after the Tehran conference at the end of November 1943 that Morgan could assure his staff that OVERLORD would take place as planned. It was on the basis of the COSSAC plan that the debates on strategy occurred between August and November 1943. As a result of Morgan's work, the decision was taken to reenter the Continent not as the penultimate act of a war that had essentially already been won but with the concentration of force necessary to force the issue, dictate the terms of battle to the enemy, and gain the victory. Morgan pointed out that his job was to decide if the operation could be considered. Could it be "remitted to those who would be charged with its execution."[6] When he decided that it was "on," he expected that the shortfalls in troops, landing craft, aircraft, logistical supply, and political support would be made good by the authority vested in a supreme commander. Despite Morgan's ongoing efforts and advocacy for a commander, going as far as a face-to-face appeal to the U.S. president, it took until January 1944 for a supreme allied commander to begin to make his mark on the operation. Morgan was required to continue in his role as a "shadow supreme commander" until then.

Montgomery and Eisenhower were handed a plan that the COSSAC planners had designed to be robust enough to be adaptable, with the alternatives having been examined in detail, the reasons for not choosing them clear, and with what else was required to be done well understood by the planners who simply needed someone with the authority to obtain the extra resources. The conclusions that Smith and de Guingand reached, that more of everything was needed, came as no surprise to those at COSSAC. This is not to diminish the developments and changes to the plan made by Montgomery and Eisenhower, or to overlook it was they, as operational commanders, who accepted the risks and the responsibilities of command. It is to point out that they were not entering undiscovered country when they arrived.

COSSAC (with Mountbatten's support and assistance) ended the debate about Normandy or the Pas-de-Calais as the site for the invasion. Morgan made it clear that COSSAC, as the representative of the supreme commander, was the responsible agency for the campaign. He directed Admiral Ramsay and Air Marshal Leigh-Mallory to begin work on their operational plans, with NEPTUNE being ready in April—close to being at the last minute, given the complexity of the operation—and with the preparatory air campaign gaining momentum over the spring of 1944. His work on the contingency plan, RANKIN, led him, on his own initiative, into considering civil affairs issues and the creation of a formal method of liaison with governments-in-exile that may not have otherwise been addressed in a timely way by the British COS and American JCS.

Morgan changed the approach to planning for the reentry into the Continent, insisting that the plan be connected to a specific force level and a desired "D-day" for the operation and not just be the source of debate without resolution. The COSSAC team addressed problems arising out of the plan that had defied solution until then, developing the concept for and then overseeing the creation of the MULBERRY artificial harbors. Without the harbors, Morgan's recommendation was that the invasion should not be launched.

The failure of COSSAC's deception operation, STARKY, led to a reevaluation of deception operations in Europe that contributed substantially to the success of the XX Committee's Double-Cross agents and to the BODYGUARD deception plan that was developed for D-Day. COSSAC planners identified and solved many of the other problems related to a cross-Channel assault, often by the simple approach of trial and error. On occasion they modified or ignored directives from their superiors in order to better accomplish their mission.

Civil affairs continued to be a headache for Smith when he took over as Eisenhower's chief of staff. Without Morgan's efforts, however, the headache would have been a nightmare. Smith also had to address press relations and propaganda, another area where Morgan didn't find a completely satisfactory organizational solution but had laid the groundwork.

In a letter to Eisenhower, General Devers considered Morgan a "fine personality, the best British officer I deal with."[7] Marshall appreciated Morgan's patience and sense of humor as well as Morgan's agreement with the Americans on the importance of the cross-Channel attack. In a letter to Admiral King, Marshall gave his impression of COSSAC's time in Washington and thought it could be used as a model for future inter-Allied planning: "At the present time we are going through an illuminating experience over here with General Morgan. . . . He is present at our daily operational meetings with Arnold, Handy and me. We discuss all these matters with complete frankness and my impression is that he is so heavily on our side now as a result of such procedure that it may be embarrassing in his relation to the British Chiefs of Staff in London."[8] Indeed, it was the case that Morgan's appreciation and support for Marshall and Eisenhower created problems for him with Brooke and later with Montgomery. As Smith reported to Eisenhower in January 1944, "Morgan has hurt himself with Brooke by his square dealings with our people."[9]

At the same time that Morgan was being labeled as having "sold out to the Yanks," Ray Barker, in recognition of his time working with both the

Combined Commanders and at COSSAC, earned a reputation of having "sold out to the English." This may explain why Devers, in the same letter to Eisenhower, described Barker as "weak." Barker's record of continued service at SHAEF through the end of the war would suggest that Devers' evaluation was off the mark. Morgan's view was that he and Barker "ran well in double harness."[10]

As SHAEF was being established, Morgan was offered the opportunity to command a corps in Italy or to remain as a deputy chief of staff, working for Smith. Having some sense of ownership when it came to the OVERLORD plan and knowing little about the war in Italy, he opted to remain. He was the senior British officer at Eisenhower's headquarters. After the war, Smith called him his British alter ego, "a man I wouldn't willingly have dispensed with."[11] One could argue that rather than being a relatively minor figure in the OVERLORD story, Morgan is perhaps one of the single most-important personalities to emerge during the period.

Barker, in his first conversation with Smith, made it clear that he "wanted to get back to soldiering." He felt that he had done enough in the "planning racket" and wanted to command a division. Smith said no. Barker knew too much about too many projects and was too valuable an asset to be turned loose. He was made the G-1 for SHAEF, even though he knew nothing about managing pay and personnel matters, let alone at a supreme headquarters. Ultimately, he became a sort of special projects officer for Smith and SHAEF, getting involved in subjects like repatriation of prisoners of war, issues around fraternization with Germans after the war ended, and questions relating to the situation of inhabitants of liberated countries.[12]

Some members of COSSAC stayed on while others were replaced as Smith quickly shaped and expanded the headquarters based on his and Eisenhower's preferences and their experience with Allied Force Headquarters. Major General Bull became SHAEF's G-3, with Major General West remaining as deputy until May 1944. McLean headed up SHAEF's plans section. Major General Brownjohn became the deputy G-4 in February 1944, with U.S. major general Robert Crawford becoming G-4. Brownjohn left in August 1944, when he was transferred to become deputy quartermaster-general for British forces in the Middle East. There was a substantial flow of personnel from the Mediterranean, creating concerns that too much experience was heading to SHAEF and that the new commanders in the Mediterranean would be at a disadvantage. This reached a point where Smith and Brooke had what could be described as a shouting match over personnel issues in January, before Eisenhower arrived.[13]

The struggle to find landing craft continued. In addition to the efforts already mentioned and the addition of another month's construction, various other steps were taken. Ship types were exchanged between the Mediterranean and United Kingdom, with troop transports that carried their own landing craft on board being sent south to calmer waters and additional LSTs sent north. The loads of some LSTs were increased, in some cases to over 100 percent of capacity. Estimates of availability rates were also modified. The initial plans were based on availability rates of 85 percent overall and 90 percent for ships. This was increased to 95 percent for U.S. craft, while the British kept to the more conservative estimate. Ultimately the shipping for the assault used 99 percent of available U.S. vessels and more than 97 percent of available British vessels.[14]

The Normandy assault continues to be written about and discussed not only because its complexity provides for examination of the operation from many points of view and with new approaches to analysis but also because it was truly a turning point in the war. Everyone understood what success or failure would mean. Consequently, many senior decisionmakers tried to find a way to be there on 6 June.

As a prudent measure and understanding the importance of this D-day, the American JCS traveled to London in case it became necessary to hold a CCS meeting and make strategic decisions on 6 June in the wake of a failed assault. Churchill made plans to leave London to witness the D-day landings from a warship. Eisenhower made it abundantly clear that he would not permit the prime minister to put his life at risk at such a time or add unnecessarily to the burden of the sailors and soldiers who would have to escort him. Churchill, invoking his role as Minister of Defense, claimed he had a duty to take part. He announced that, if necessary, he would go as a member of the ship's company on board HMS *Belfast*, and it was not within Eisenhower's remit "to determine the exact composition of any ship's company in His

Majesty's Fleet."[15] He added that technically, as the *Belfast* was a British ship, he would not, in any case, be leaving British territory.

King George learned of Churchill's intentions from Pug Ismay and wrote a letter to the prime minister in which he noted that, while he would not interfere with the minister's decision, should Churchill insist on joining the invasion, he, as nominal head of all of Great Britain's armed forces, would also feel compelled to witness the invasion in a similar manner. He also reminded Churchill that as much as he would like to do so, his duty as king required him to be at his post, in London, on the crucial day. Churchill reluctantly deferred to his sovereign's wishes. Both Churchill and the CCS made it to Normandy on 12 June.

Barker, in company with Lt. Col. David Niven (the actor, who was also a Sandhurst graduate), was on board the HMS *Empire Battleaxe*, a landing ship infantry (large), off SWORD Beach on D-Day. Niven, as someone who understood both the English and Americans, went ashore late in the day to act as a liaison between the Allied forces.[16]

Members of the OPD managed to reach London in early June, including Gen. Thomas Handy, Adm. Charles Cooke (of the Joint Planners), Col. G. A. Lincoln, and Lt. Col. Paul L. Freeman Jr.[17] Handy and Cooke went ashore on D-day and spent the next week visiting various headquarters and observing the battle at first hand. According to Handy, both he and General Wedemeyer felt "a kind of paternal pride" in seeing the operation for which they had all been advocating for two years successfully begun.[18]

Jimmy Doolittle, commanding general of the Eighth Air Force, got into a P-38 and flew over the beachhead early in the morning of 6 June to see for himself. According to the notation that accompanies a painting of the event (*Doolittle's D-Day*, by Robert Taylor), he was the first to report to Eisenhower on the progress of the assault. Doolittle picked the P-38 as it was presumed to be somewhat easier than other types for nervous Allied AA gunners to recognize.

Morgan, as an assistant chief of staff, was at SHAEF headquarters. His considered view, looking back as he wrote his memoir in 1950, was that the challenges of high rank and concurrent high responsibility are not readily understood by those who don't share that responsibility. "It is one thing to be in opposition, but quite another to govern."[19] Given the lack of applicable precedent in terms of amphibious assaults, all that was being put at risk, and all that could have gone wrong at almost any stage, the most impressive aspect of OVERLORD for him was that a multinational group of politicians and generals gave the orders and took the risks.

COSSAC existed for nine months. There was no precedent to guide Morgan and Barker in the creation of the staff. What does a multinational planning staff that will evolve into a coalition's operational headquarters for the most important operation of the war look like—how does it operate without a commander? Morgan and Barker provided one answer. That it succeeded is the result of the blend of personalities, experiences, and leadership styles of a small group of men that random chance put together. As Morgan said, "It is not as though we were specially hand-picked for the Anglo-American job with meticulous care."[20] That being said, it is also clear from his writings that Morgan had a justifiable pride in COSSAC's achievements and in the people who composed the staff. Whatever arguments and disputes occurred outside Norfolk House, everyone inside worked together to get the job done. General Ismay said of Morgan, "All the spade work for the invasion fell to General Morgan, and it is no exaggeration to say that he laid the foundation for the brilliant success that was achieved."[21]

Ray Barker said of COSSAC: "There was no distinction whatever along national lines. . . . Here was a team, and whether a man wore a U.S. or a Crown made not a bit of difference, not a bit of difference. No one thought about it. You just worked together as a team and no one thought about whether a chap was British or American or Canadian . . . or South African. No one thought about that at all."[22] That was the result of leadership. Although Morgan was stationed behind a desk and not on a battlefield, he was a most effective leader at a most critical time for the Allies in the struggle against Nazi Germany.

APPENDIX A
British Chiefs of Staff (COS) and American Joint Chiefs of Staff (JCS)

Chiefs of Staff

The following served as members of the British Chiefs of Staff. It wasn't until Gen. Alan Brooke was appointed that there was continuity for the army's Chief of the Imperial General Staff.

First Sea Lord
Adm. Dudley Pound ▪ June 1939–October 1943
Adm. Sir Andrew Cunningham ▪ October 1943–May 1946

Chief of the Imperial General Staff
Lt. Gen. John Vereker, Viscount Gort ▪ December 1937–September 1939
Gen. Sir Edmund Ironside ▪ September 1939–May 1940
Gen. John Dill ▪ May 1940–December 1941
    (promoted to field marshal, December 1941)
Gen. Alan Brooke ▪ December 1941–June 1946

Chief of the Air Staff
Air Chief Marshal Sir Cyril Newall ▪ September 1937–October 1940
Air Chief Marshal Sir Charles Portal ▪ October 1940–October 1945

Chief of Combined Operations
    (became a member of the COS with the arrival of Mountbatten)
Lt. Gen. Alan Bourne ▪ June 1940–July 1940
Admiral of the Fleet Sir Roger Keyes ▪ July 1940–October 1941
Capt. (later Vice Adm.) Lord Louis Mountbatten ▪ October 1941–October 1943
Maj. Gen. Robert Laycock ▪ October 1943–October 1947

Joint Chiefs of Staff

The American Joint Chiefs of Staff had more continuity during the war.

Chief of Staff to the Commander-in-Chief of the Army and Navy
Adm. William D. Leahy ▪ July 1942–March 1949

The very well-respected Adm. William Leahy served as Chief of Naval Operations from January 1937 to August 1939. He then retired from active duty and was appointed governor of Puerto Rico, where he served from September 1939 through

October 1940. In November 1940, Leahy was appointed U.S. ambassador to Vichy France, where he had a ringside seat from which to view occupied Europe. Roosevelt summoned him home in July 1942, brought him back on active service, and appointed him as chief of staff so he could serve as the president's liaison with the newly created Joint Chiefs of Staff.

Chief of Staff, U.S. Army
Gen. George Marshall ▪ September 1939–November 1945

Commander-in-Chief, U.S. Fleet, and Chief of Naval Operations
Adm. Ernest King ▪ COMINCH, December 1941–December 1945; CNO, March 1942–December 1945

Commanding General, U.S. Army Air Forces
Gen. Henry H. "Hap" Arnold ▪ June 1941–June 1946

Sources: Holders of positions: Michael Howard, *Grand Strategy*, vol. 4, *August 1942–September 1943*, in *History of the Second World War*, edited by J. R. M. Butler (London: Her Majesty's Stationery Office, 1972), app. 11(B), p. 699; and "William Daniel Leahy," *Encyclopaedia Britannica*, https://www.britannica.com/biography/William-Daniel-Leahy. Dates of service: *Encyclopaedia Britannica*, www.britannica.com; U.S. Air Force website, www.af.mil; Naval History and Heritage Command website, https://www.history.navy .mil/; and the George C. Marshall Foundation website, www.marshallfoundation.org.

APPENDIX B
Structure of the British Army's Home Forces, 1940–44

The primary mission of the British Army after Dunkirk was home defense, and that remained so through the end of 1942, notwithstanding continuing operations in the Mediterranean and Asia. There was a desire to establish an effective offensive approach recognizing the need to employ combined arms. Whether or not doctrine and training reflected this remains a matter for debate.

The highest level of command and control for the army was the War Office and the Imperial General Staff. The War Office directed various commanders in chief, whose commands and troops were organized geographically in the United Kingdom (as opposed to functionally). There were a few exceptions, for example Anti-Aircraft Command, but those were rare.

General Headquarters Home Forces, the command of Commander-in-Chief, Home Forces, was essentially an Army Group Command. There were initially five commands under its control: Southern, Western, Eastern, Northern, and Scottish. In 1941 South Eastern Command took over responsibility for Kent, Sussex, and Surry Counties from Eastern Command. Headed by a lieutenant general as commander, each would have become an operational army if circumstances demanded it. Each command consisted of divisions and brigades, formed into corps.[1]

Bernard Montgomery, for example, took a division to France in May 1940, commanded a corps in the southwest of England after Dunkirk, and later became Commander-in-Chief, South Eastern Command. Morgan moved from a brigade command to be the commander of a division in Cornwall adjacent to Montgomery's command, then to the command of 1st Corps in Yorkshire, part of Northern Command, under Lt. Gen. Sir Thomas Ralph Eastwood.[2]

APPENDIX C
Outline OVERLORD Plan, Cover Letter, and Digest

(WO 107/154, National Archives UK)
U.S. Secret
British Most Secret

C.O.S.S.A.C. (43) 28
ANNEX B
OPERATION "OVERLORD"

The Secretary,
Chiefs of Staff Committee,
Offices of the War Cabinet   15th *July* 1943

1. In my original Directive (C. O. S. (43) 215 (O)) I was charged with the duty of preparing a plan for a full scale assault against the Continent in 1944 as early as possible.

2. This part of my Directive was subsequently amplified (see C. O. S. (43) 113th Meeting (O), Item 4), in that I was ordered to submit an outline plan for an assault, with certain specified forces, on a target date of 1st May, 1944, to secure a lodgment on the Continent from which further offensive operations can be carried out. It was indicated to me, in the course of this amplification, that the lodgment area should include ports that, suitably developed, could be used by ocean-going ships for the build-up of the initial assault forces from the United Kingdom, and for their further build-up with additional divisions and supporting units that might be shipped from the United States or elsewhere.

3. I have the honour now to report that, in my opinion, it is possible to undertake the operation described, on or about the target date named, with the sea, land and air forces specified, given a certain set of circumstances in existence at that time.

4. These governing circumstances are partly within our direct control and partly without. Those within our control relate first to the problem of beach maintenance, and secondly to the supply of shipping, naval landing craft and transport aircraft. Wherever we may attempt to land, and however many ports we capture, we cannot escape the fact that we shall be forced to maintain a high proportion of our forces over the beaches for the first two or three months while port facilities are being restored; and that, in view of the variability of the weather in the Channel, this will not be feasible unless we are able rapidly to improvise sheltered anchorages off

230

the beaches. New methods of overcoming this problem are now being examined. There is no reason to suppose that these methods will be ineffective, but I feel it is my duty to point out that this operation is not to be contemplated unless this problem of prolonged cross-beach maintenance and the provision of artificial anchorages shall have been solved.

5. As regards the supply of shipping, naval landing craft and transport aircraft, increasing resources in these would permit of the elaboration of alternative plans designed to meet more than one set of extraneous conditions, whereas the state of provision herein taken into account dictates the adoption of one course only, or none at all. In proportion as additional shipping, landing craft and transport aircraft can be made available, so the chances of success in the operation will be increased. It seems feasible to contemplate additions as a result either of stepped-up production, of strategical re-allotment or, in the last resort, of postponement of the date of assault.

6. I have come to the conclusion that, in view of the limitations in resources imposed by my directives, we may be assured of a reasonable chance of success on the 1st May, 1944, only if we concentrate our efforts on an assault across the Norman beaches about Bayeux.

7. As regards circumstances that we can control only indirectly, it is, in my opinion, necessary to stipulate that the state of affairs existing at the time, both on land in France and in the air above it, shall be such as to render the assault as little hazardous as may be so far as it is humanly possible to calculate. The essential discrepancy in value between the enemy's troops, highly organized, armed and battle-trained, who await us in their much vaunted impregnable defences, and our troops, who must of necessity launch their assault at the end of a cross-Channel voyage with all its attendant risks, must be reduced to the narrowest possible margin. Though much can be done to this end by the means available and likely to become available to us in the United Kingdom to influence these factors, we are largely dependent upon events that will take place on other war fronts, principally on the Russian front, between now and the date of the assault.

8. I therefore suggest to the Chiefs of Staff that it is necessary, if my plan be approved, to adopt the outlook that Operation "Overlord" is even now in progress, and to take all possible steps to see that all agencies that can be brought to bear are, from now on, co-ordinated in their action as herein below described, so as to bring about the state of affairs that we would have exist on the chosen day of assault.

9. Finally, I venture to draw attention to the danger of making direct comparisons between operation "Husky" and operation "Overlord." No doubt the experience now being gained in the Mediterranean will prove invaluable when the detailed planning stage of "Overlord" is reached, but viewed as a whole the two

operations could hardly be more dissimilar. In "Husky," the bases of an extended continental coastline were used for a converging assault against an island, whereas in "Overlord" it is necessary to launch an assault from an island against an extended continental mainland coastline. Furthermore, while in the Mediterranean the tidal range is negligible and the weather reasonably reliable, in the English Channel the tidal range is considerable and the weather capricious.

10. Attached hereto are papers setting forth the plan that I recommend for adoption.

F. E. Morgan, Lieutenant-General,
Chief of Staff to the Supreme Allied Commander (Designate)
H.Q. C.O.S.S.A.C.,
Norfolk House,
St. James's Square, S. W. 1

Digest of Operation "Overlord"
Object.

1. The object of Operation "Overlord" is to mount and carry out an operation, with forces and equipment established in the United Kingdom, and with target date the 1st May, 1944, to secure a lodgement on the Continent from which further offensive operations can be developed. The lodgement area must contain sufficient port facilities to maintain a force of some twenty-six to thirty divisions, and enable that force to be augmented by follow-up shipments from the United States or elsewhere of additional divisions and supporting units at the rate of three to five divisions per month.

Selection of a Lodgement Area

2. In order to provide sufficient port facilities to maintain these large forces, it will be necessary to select a lodgement area which includes a group of major ports. We must plan on the assumption that ports, on capture, will be seriously damaged and probably blocked. It will take some time to restore normal facilities. We shall thus be forced to rely on maintenance over beaches for an extended period.

3. A study of the beaches on the Belgian and Channel coasts show that the beaches with the highest capacity for passing vehicles and stores inland are those in the Pas de Calais [assumed here to be the area between Gravelines and the River Somme] and Caen-Cotentin area. ["Caen area" is taken as that between the River Orne and the base of the Cotentin Peninsula; "Cotentin" area is the peninsula in which Cherbourg is situated.] Of these, the Caen beaches are the most favourable, as they are, unlike the others, sheltered from the prevailing winds. Naval and air considerations point to the area between the Pas de Calais and the Cotentin as the most suitable for the initial landing, air factors of optimum air support and

rapid provision of airfields indicating the Pas de Calais as the best choice, with Caen as an acceptable alternative.

4. Thus, taking beach capacity and air and naval considerations together, it appears that either the Pas de Calais area or the Caen-Cotentin area is the most suitable for the initial main landing.

5. As the area for the initial landing, the Pas de Calais has many obvious advantages such that good air support and quick turn around for our shipping can be achieved. On the other hand, it is a focal point of the enemy fighters disposed for defense, and maximum enemy air activity can be brought to bear over this area with the minimum movement of his air forces. Moreover, the Pas de Calais is the most strongly defended area on the whole French coast. The defenses would require very heavy and sustained bombardment from sea and air: penetration would be slow, and the result of the bombardment of beach exits would severely limit the rate of build-up. Further, this area does not offer good opportunities for expansion. It would be necessary to develop the bridgehead to include either Belgian ports as far as Antwerp or the Channel ports Westwards to include Havre and Rouen. But an advance to Antwerp across numerous water obstacles, and a long flank march of some 120 miles to the Seine ports must be considered unsound operations of war unless the German forces are in a state not far short of final collapse.

6. In the Caen-Cotentin area it would be possible to make our initial landing either partly on the Cotentin Peninsula and partly on the Caen beaches, wholly in the Cotentin or wholly on the Caen beaches. An attack with part of our forces in the Cotentin and part on the Caen beaches, is, however, considered to be unsound. It would entail dividing our limited forces by the low-lying marshy ground and intricate river system at the neck of the Cotentin Peninsula; thus exposing them to defeat in detail.

7. An attack against the Cotentin Peninsula, on the other hand, has a reasonable chance of success, and would ensure the early capture of the port of Cherbourg. Unfortunately, very few airfields exist in the Cotentin, and that area is not suitable for rapid airfield development. Furthermore, the narrow neck of the Peninsula would give the Germans an easy task in preventing us from breaking out and expanding our initial bridgehead. Moreover, during the period of our consolidation in the Cotentin the Germans would have time to reinforce their coastal troops in the Caen area, rendering a subsequent amphibious assault in that area much more difficult.

8. There remains the attack on the Caen beaches. The Caen sector is weakly held; the defenses are relatively light and the beaches are of high capacity and sheltered from the prevailing winds. Inland the terrain is suitable for airfield development and for the consolidation of the initial bridgehead; and much of it is unfavourable

for counter-attacks by panzer divisions. Maximum enemy air opposition can only be brought to bear at the expense of the enemy air defense screen covering the approaches to Germany; and the limited number of enemy airfields within range of the Caen area facilitates local neutralization of the German fighter force. The sector suffers from the disadvantage that considerable effort will be required to provide adequate air support to our assault forces and some time must elapse before the capture of a major port.

After a landing in the Caen sector it would be necessary to seize either the Seine group of ports or the Brittany group of ports. To seize the Seine ports would entail forcing a crossing of the Seine, which is likely to require greater forces than we can build up through the Caen beaches and the port of Cherbourg. It should, however, be possible to seize the Brittany ports between Cherbourg and Nantes and on them build up sufficient forces for our final advance Eastwards.

Provided that the necessary air situation can first be achieved, the chances of a successful attack and of rapid subsequent development are so much greater in this sector than in any other that it is considered that the advantages far outweigh the disadvantages.

The Lodgement Area Selected

9. In the light of these factors, it is considered that our initial landing on the Continent should be effected in the Caen area, with a view to the eventual seizure of a lodgement area comprising the Cherbourg-Brittany group of ports (from Cherbourg to Nantes.)

Opening Phase up to the Capture of Cherbourg

10. The opening phase in the seizing of this lodgement would be the effecting of a landing in the Caen sector with a view to the early capture and development of airfield sites in the Caen area, and of the port of Cherbourg.

11. The main limiting factors affecting such an operation are the possibility of attaining the necessary air situation; the number of offensive divisions which the enemy can make available for counter attack in the Caen area; the availability of landing ships and craft and of transport aircraft; and the capacity of the beaches and ports in the sector.

12. Although the strength of the G.A.F. [German Air Force, or Luftwaffe] available in 1944 on the Western front cannot be forecast at this stage, we can confidently expect that we shall have a vast numerical superiority in bomber forces. The first-line strength of the German fighter force is, however, showing a steady increase and although it is unlikely to equal the size of the force at our disposal, there is no doubt that our fighters will have a very large commitment entailing

dispersal and operations at maximum intensity. Our fighters will also be operating under serious tactical disadvantages in the early stages, which will largely offset their numerical superiority. Before the assault takes place, therefore, it will be necessary to reduce the effectiveness of the G.A.F., particularly that part which can be brought to bear against the Caen area.

13. The necessary air situation to ensure a reasonable chance of success will therefore require that the maximum number of German fighter forces are contained in the Low Countries and North-West Germany, that the effectiveness of the fighter defense in the Caen area is reduced and that air reinforcements are prevented from arriving in the early stages from the Mediterranean. Above all, it will be necessary to reduce the overall strength of the German fighter force between now and the date of the operation by destruction of the sources of supply, by the infliction of casualties by bringing on air battles, and, immediately prior to the assault, by disorganization of G.A.F. installations and control system in the Caen area.

14. As it is impossible to forecast with any accuracy the number and location of German formations in reserve in 1944, while, on the other hand, the forces available to us have been laid down, an attempt has been made in this paper to determine the wisest employment of our own forces and then to determine the maximum number of German formations which they can reasonably overcome. Apart from the air situation, which is an over-riding factor, the practicability of this plan will depend principally on the number, effectiveness, and availability of German divisions present in France and the Low Countries in relation to our own capabilities. This consideration is discussed below (paragraph 35).

15. A maximum of thirty and a minimum of twenty-six equivalent divisions are likely to be available in the United Kingdom for cross-Channel operations on the 1st May 1944. Further build-up can be at the rate of three to five divisions per month.

16. Landing ships and craft have been provided to lift the equivalent of three assault divisions and two follow-up divisions, without "overheads," and it has been assumed that the equivalent of an additional two divisions can be afloat in ships.

17. Airborne forces amounting to two airborne divisions and some five or six parachute regiments will be available, but largely owing to shortage of transport aircraft, it is only possible to lift the equivalent of two-thirds of one airborne division simultaneously, on the basis of present forecasts.

18. Even if additional landing ships and craft could be made available, the beaches in the Caen area would preclude the landing of forces greater than the equivalent of the three assault and two follow-up divisions, for which craft have already been provided. Nevertheless, an all-around increase of at least 10 percent in

landing ships and craft is highly desirable in order to provide a greater margin for contingencies within the framework of the existing plan. Furthermore, sufficient lift for a further assault division could most usefully be employed in an additional landing on other beaches.

19. There is no port of any capacity within the sector although there are a number of small ports of limited value. Maintenance will, therefore, of necessity be largely over the beaches until it is possible to capture and open up the port of Cherbourg. In view of the possibilities of interruption by bad weather it will be essential to provide early some form of improvised sheltered waters.

20. Assuming optimum weather conditions, it should be possible to build up the force over the beaches to a total by D plus 6 of the equivalent of some eleven divisions and five tank brigades and thereafter to land one division a day until about D plus 24.

Proposed Plan

Preliminary Phase.

21. During the preliminary phase, which must start forthwith, all possible means including air and sea action, propaganda, political and economic pressure, and sabotage, must be integrated into a combined offensive aimed at softening the German resistance. In particular, air action should be directed towards the reduction of the German air forces on the Western front, the progressive destruction of the German economic system and the undermining of German morale.

22. In order to contain the maximum German forces away from the Caen area diversionary operations should be staged against other areas such as the Pas de Calais and the Mediterranean Coast of France.

Preparatory Phase

23. During this phase air action will be intensified against the G.A.F., particularly in North-West France, with a view to reducing the effectiveness of the G.A.F. in that area, and will be extended to include attacks against communications more directly associated with movement of German reserves which might affect the Caen area. Three naval assault forces will be assembled with the naval escorts and loaded up at ports along the South Coast of England. Two naval assault forces carrying the follow-up forces will also be assembled and loaded, one in the Thames Estuary and one on the West Coast.

The Assault

24. After a very short air bombardment of the beach defenses three assault divisions will be landed simultaneously on the Caen beaches, followed up on D Day by the equivalent of two tank brigades (United States regiments) and a brigade group

(United States regimental combat team). At the same time, airborne forces will be used to seize the town of Caen; and subsidiary operations by commandos and possibly by airborne forces will be undertaken to neutralize certain coast defenses and seize certain important river crossings. The object of the assault force will be to seize the general line Grandcamp-Bayeux-Caen.

Follow-up and Build-up Phase

25. Subsequent action will take the form of a strong thrust Southwards and South-Westwards with a view to destroying enemy forces, acquiring sites for airfields, and gaining depth for a turning movement into the Cotentin Peninsula directed on Cherbourg. When sufficient depth has been gained a force will advance into the Cotentin and seize Cherbourg. At the same time a thrust will be made to deepen the bridgehead South-Eastwards in order to cover the construction and operation of additional airfields in the area South-East of Caen.

26. It is considered that, within fourteen days of the initial assault, Cherbourg should be captured and the bridgehead extended to include the general line Trouville-Alençon-Mont St. Michel. By this date, moreover, it should have been possible to land some eighteen divisions and to have in operation about fourteen airfields from which twenty-eight to thirty-three fighter-type squadrons should be operating.

Further Developments after Capture of Cherbourg

27. After the capture of Cherbourg the Supreme Allied Commander will have to decide whether to initiate operations to seize the Seine ports or whether he must content himself with first occupying the Brittany ports. In this decision he will have to be guided largely by the situation of the enemy forces. If the German resistance is sufficiently weak, an immediate advance could be made to seize Havre and Rouen. On the other hand, the more probable situation is that the Germans will have retired with the bulk of their forces to hold Paris and the line of the Seine, where they can best be covered by their air forces from North-East France and where they may possibly be reinforced by formations from Russia. Elsewhere they may move a few divisions from Southern France to hold the crossings of the Loire and will leave the existing defensive divisions in Brittany.

It will therefore most probably be necessary for us to seize the Brittany ports first, in order to build up sufficient forces with which we can eventually force the passage of the Seine.

28. Under these circumstances, the most suitable plan would appear to be to secure first the left flank and to gain sufficient airfields for subsequent operations. This would be done by extending the bridgehead to the line of the River Eure from Dreux to Rouen and thence along the line of the Seine to the sea, seizing at the same time Chartres, Orleans and Tours.

29. Under cover of these operations a force would be employed in capturing the Brittany ports; the first step being a thrust Southwards to seize Nantes and St. Nazaire, followed by subsidiary operations to capture Brest and the various small ports of the Brittany Peninsula.

30. This action would complete the occupation of our initial lodgement area and would secure sufficient major ports for the maintenance of at least thirty divisions. As soon as the organization of the L. of C. in this lodgement area allowed, and sufficient air forces had been established, operations would then begin to force the line of the Seine, and to capture Paris and the Seine ports. As opportunity offered, subsidiary action would also be taken to clear the Germans from the Biscay ports to facilitate the entry of additional American troops and the feeding of the French population.

Command and Control

31. In carrying out Operation "Overlord" administrative control would be greatly simplified if the principle were adopted that the United States forces were normally on the right of the line and the British and Canadian forces on the left.

Major Conditions Affecting Success of the Operation

32. It will be seen that the plan for the initial landing is based on two main principles—concentration of force and tactical surprise. Concentration of the assault forces is considered essential if we are to ensure adequate air support and if our limited assault forces are to avoid defeat in detail. An attempt has been made to obtain tactical surprise by landing in a lightly defended area—presumably lightly defended as, due to its distance from a major port, the Germans consider a landing there unlikely to be successful. This action, of course, presupposes that we can offset the absence of a port in the initial stages by the provision of improvised sheltered waters. It is believed that this can be accomplished.

33. The operation calls for a much higher standard of performance on the part of the naval assault forces than any previous operation. This will depend upon their being formed in sufficient time to permit of adequate training.

34. Above all, it is essential that there should be an over-all reduction in the German fighter force between now and the time of the surface assault. From now onwards every practical method of achieving this end must be employed. This condition, above all others, will dictate the date by which the amphibious assault can be launched.

35. The next condition is that the number of German offensive divisions in reserve must not exceed a certain figure on the target date if the operation is to have a reasonable chance of success. The German reserves in France and the Low

Countries as a whole, excluding divisions holding the coast, G.A.F. divisions and training divisions, should not exceed on the day of the assault twelve full-strength first quality divisions. In addition, the Germans should not be able to transfer more than fifteen first-quality divisions from Russia during the first two months. Moreover, on the target date the divisions in reserve should be so located that the number of first-quality divisions which the Germans could deploy in the Caen area to support the divisions holding the coast should not exceed three divisions on D Day, five divisions on D plus 2, or nine divisions by D plus 8.

During the preliminary period, therefore, every effort must be made to dissipate and divert German formations, lower their fighting efficiency and disrupt communications.

36. Finally, there is the question of maintenance. Maintenance will have to be carried out over beaches for a period of some three months for a number of formations, varying from a maximum of eighteen divisions in the first month to twelve divisions in the second month, rapidly diminishing to nil in the third month. Unless adequate measures are taken to provide sheltered waters by artificial means, the operation will be at the mercy of the weather. Moreover, special facilities and equipment will be required to prevent undue damage to craft during this extended period. Immediate action for the provision of the necessary requirements is essential.

37. Given these conditions—a reduced G.A.F., a limitation in the number or effectiveness of German offensive formations in France, and adequate arrangements to provide improvised sheltered waters—it is considered that Operation "Overlord" has a reasonable prospect of success. To ensure these conditions being attained by the 1st May, 1944, action must start now and every possible effort made by all means in our power to soften German resistance and to speed up our own preparations.

Offices of the War Cabinet, S.W. 1
30th July, 1943

———

NB: The complete outline plan contains far more detail than can be reasonably included in this volume. It included ten maps, twenty-four appendices, ranging from appendix A, "Port Capacities," to appendix X, "Methods of Improving Discharge Facilities on the French Coast."[1] Bernard Fergusson described it as being half the length of his four-hundred page book, *The Watery Maze*, perhaps a slight exaggeration. The attention to detail and thoroughness of the plan is a primary reason it was accepted by the planners who evaluated it.

APPENDIX D
Organizational Charts of COSSAC,
Initial Formation and as of January 1944

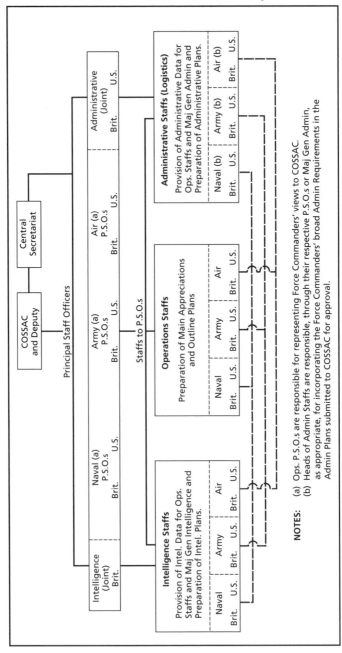

NOTES: (a) Ops. P.S.O.s are responsible for representing Force Commanders' views to COSSAC.

(b) Heads of Admin Staffs are responsible, through their respective P.S.O.s or Maj Gen Admin, as appropriate, for incorporating the Force Commanders' broad Admin Requirements in the Admin Plans submitted to COSSAC for approval.

History of COSSAC, www.history.army.mil/documents/cossac/COSSAC.htm.

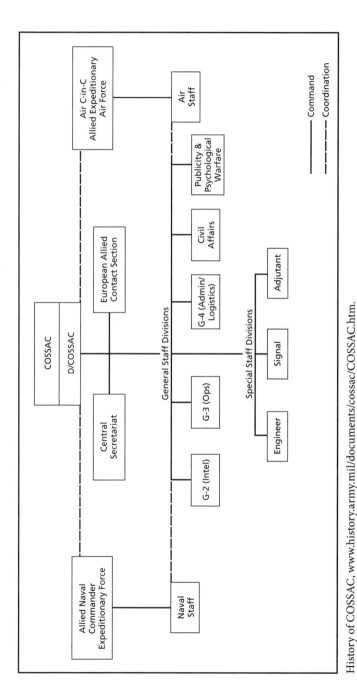

	COSSAC	
	D/COSSAC	

Air C-in-C
Allied Expeditionary
Air Force

Air
Staff

Publicity &
Psychological
Warfare

Civil
Affairs

European Allied
Contact Section

General Staff Divisions

G-4 (Admin/
Logistics)

G-3 (Ops)

Central
Secretariat

Special Staff Divisions

Adjutant

Signal

Engineer

G-2 (Intel)

Allied Naval
Commander
Expeditionary Force

Naval
Staff

——— Command
– – – – Coordination

History of COSSAC, www.history.army.mil/documents/cossac/COSSAC.htm.

APPENDIX E

Organizational Chart of Western Allies Command Structure

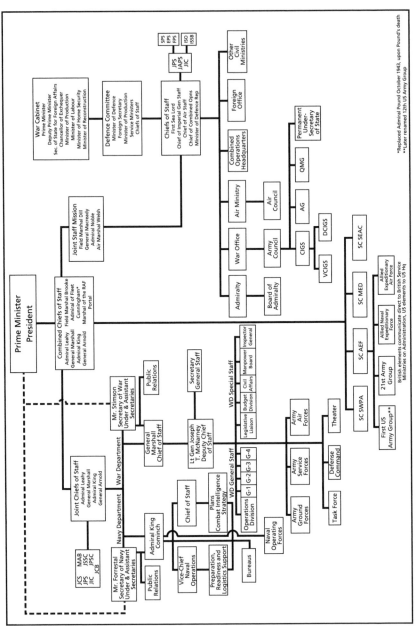

Forrest C. Pogue, *U.S. Army in World War II: The Supreme Command* (Washington, D.C.: Center of Military History, 1996), 38.

APPENDIX F

Organization Chart of the Chain of Command from the Combined Chiefs of Staff to the Supreme Allied Commander for OVERLORD

This represents the final evolution of the COSSAC structure into SHAEF. Prior to the arrival of Eisenhower and Air Chief Marshal Arthur Tedder as deputy commander, Morgan, as COSSAC, reported directly to the Combined Chiefs of Staff. The various force commanders were added during the COSSAC period.

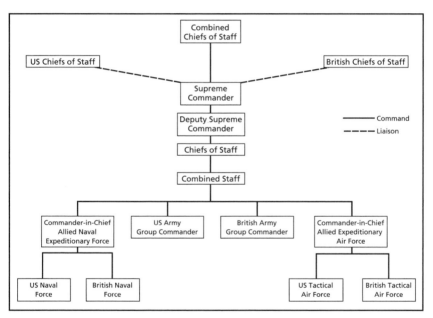

Forest C. Pogue, *U.S. Army in World War II: The Supreme Command* (Washington, D.C.: Center of Military History, 1996), 54.

243

GLOSSARY OF SELECTED CODE NAMES AND ABBREVIATIONS

Interallied Conferences (Chronological Order)

Code Name	Date	Location
ARCADIA	December 1941–January 1942	Washington, D.C.
SYMBOL	January 1943	Casablanca
TRIDENT	May 1943	Washington, D.C.
QUADRANT	August 1943	Quebec City
SEXTANT	November 1943 and December 1943	Cairo
EUREKA	November 1943	Tehran
OCTAGON	September 1944	Quebec City
ARGONAUT	February 1945	Yalta
TERMINAL	July 1945	Potsdam

Operations

ANVIL Invasion of Southern France, August 1944; later renamed DRAGOON

AVALANCHE Allied landings at Salerno, Italy, September 1943

BODYGUARD Allied deception plan approved in December 1943 with the goal of inducing the Germans to make faulty strategic dispositions in northwest Europe; led to SHAEF creating the FORTITUDE plans in February 1944

BOLERO Buildup of American forces in the United Kingdom starting in 1942

COCKADE   Name for a group of deception operations in 1943 that had the intent of pinning down German forces in northwest Europe and luring the German Air Force into battle over the Channel

DRAGOON   Final name for invasion of Southern France

FORTITUDE   Allied deception plans in support of OVERLORD: FORTITUDE North suggested an invasion of Norway; FORTITUDE South posed the threat to the Pas-de-Calais

HUSKY   Allied invasion of Sicily

JAEL   Tentative deception plan created by COSSAC and the London Controlling Station after the Quebec conference in September 1943; ultimately superseded by FORTITUDE

JUBILEE   The Dieppe raid, August 1942

JUPITER   A possible invasion of Norway, favored by Winston Churchill

MARKET GARDEN   British operation in September 1944 intended to use three airborne divisions to capture a series of bridges leading to the upper Rhine in the Netherlands, with units from 21st Army Group driving from the Dutch frontier toward the Rhine and linking up with the paratroops; it was not successful

NEPTUNE   The naval operations that opened OVERLORD, including loading out the troops in the United Kingdom, crossing the Channel on 6 June 1944, and initial landings; commanded by Adm. Sir Bertram Ramsay, RN

OVERLORD   The plan for the Normandy assault and creation of the lodgment in Normandy, up to D+90

POINTBLANK   The Combined Bomber Offensive, 1943–44

RANKIN   Plan for the reentry into the Continent against weakened opposition or upon the collapse of Nazi Germany

RATTLE   Conference held at Largs, Scotland, July 1943; resolved issues related to the cross-Channel assault

ROUNDUP   Concept in 1942 for a cross-Channel assault in 1943

SHINGLE   Allied landings at Anzio, Italy, January 1944

SKYSCRAPER   Concept for a cross-Channel assault, written in March 1943, the first serious attempt to estimate what forces would be necessary to successfully reenter the Continent against determined German resistance; used by COSSAC planners as a primary source for the outline OVERLORD plan, which was approved at the Quebec Conference

SLEDGEHAMMER   Concept for a limited-objective assault across the Channel in 1942, intended as a "sacrificial" attempt to attract German forces and take pressure off the Soviets

STARKY   Operation designed as an amphibious feint against the Pas-de-Calais in September 1943, intended to draw the German Air Force into battle under favorable circumstances; part of COCKADE

TORCH   Allied invasion of North Africa, November 1942

Abbreviations

AFHQ   Allied Force Headquarters, Eisenhower's headquarters for the invasion of North Africa, November 1942, and for subsequent operations in the Mediterranean

CCS   Combined Chiefs of Staff (British and American heads of military, naval, and air forces). They reported directly to the President and Prime Minister

CNO   Chief of Naval Operations (U.S. Navy)

COHQ   Combined Operations Headquarters (British)

COMINCH   Commander in Chief, U.S. Fleet

COS   Chiefs of Staff (British)

COSSAC   Chief of Staff, Supreme Allied Commander, also his headquarters

ETOUSA   European Theater of Operations United States Army

FCNL   French Committee of National Liberation

JCS   Joint Chiefs of Staff (U.S.)

LCA   landing craft, assault

LCC   landing craft, control

LCH   landing craft, headquarters

LCI   landing craft, infantry

LCI(L)   landing craft, infantry, large

LCM   landing craft, mechanized

LCT   landing craft, tank

LCVP   landing craft, vehicle and personnel

LSI(L)   landing ship, infantry, large

LSM   landing ship, medium

LST   landing ship, tank

OKH   German Army High Command

OKW   German Armed Forces High Command

OPD   Operations Division of the Office of the Chief of Staff (U.S. Army); successor to the War Plans Division

RAF   Royal Air Force

RN   Royal Navy

SHAEF   Supreme Headquarters Allied Expeditionary Force

USA   U.S. Army

USN   U.S. Navy

NOTES

Preface

1. Mollie Panter-Downes, "Letter from London," June 11, 1944, in *The New Yorker Book of War Pieces* (New York: Schocken, 1988), 310–11.
2. Just a few of the better-known books would include Stephen Ambrose, *D-Day: The Climatic Battle of World War II* (New York: Simon and Schuster, 1994); Eversley Belfield and H. Essame, *The Battle for Normandy* (London: Severn House, 1975); Arthur Bryant, *Triumph in the West, 1943–1946: Based on the Diaries and Autobiographical Notes of the Viscount Alanbrooke* (London: Collins, 1959); Carlo D'Este, *Decision in Normandy* (New York: Harper Perennial, 1994); Gordon Harrison, *Cross-Channel Attack* (Washington, D.C.: Office of the Chief of Military History, 1951); Max Hastings, *OVERLORD, D-Day and the Battle for Normandy, 1944* (London: Michael Joseph, 1984); John Keegan, *Six Armies in Normandy: From D-Day to the Liberation of Paris, June 6th–August 25th, 1944* (New York: Viking, 1982); Adrian Lewis, *Omaha Beach: A Flawed Victory* (Chapel Hill: University of North Carolina Press, 2001); Cornelius Ryan, *The Longest Day* (London: Gollancz, 1961); Craig Symonds, *Neptune: The Allied Invasion of Europe and the D-Day Landings* (Oxford: Oxford University Press, 2014); Chester Wilmot, *The Struggle for Europe* (London: Collins, 1952); and Theodore A. Wilson, ed., *D-Day 1944* (Lawrence: University Press of Kansas, 1994).
3. Morgan was assigned three tasks by the Combined Chiefs of Staff: in addition to the outline plan for the creation of a lodgment somewhere in France, he was to plan for a return to the Continent with whatever forces could be scraped together in case of a German collapse, and he was to design and conduct a feint

across the Channel as a deception operation in September of 1943 in the hope that the German Air Force could be lured into battle over the Pas-de-Calais.

4. The American-British-Dutch-Australian Command that was formed to defend the Dutch East Indies (Indonesia) in 1942 was a failure.

5. By January 1944 COSSAC totaled 489 officers and 614 enlisted. There were perhaps a dozen officers or so in key leadership positions. For the "rank and file," the work week was five and a half days. The senior planners, Morgan and Barker, would work a full Saturday as well as Sunday morning.

6. Admiral Pound died in September 1943. He was replaced by Adm. Andrew Cunningham.

Prologue

1. Winston Churchill, quoted in Eliot A. Cohen, "Churchill and Coalition Strategy in World War II," in *Grand Strategies in War and Peace*, edited by Paul Kennedy, 43–70 (New Haven, Conn.: Yale University Press, 1991), 46.

2. Maurice Matloff and Edwin M. Snell, *Strategic Planning for Coalition Warfare, 1941–1942*, in *United States Army and World War II* (Washington, D.C.: Government Printing Office, 1953), 42, 43.

Chapter 1. "A Common Bond of Danger"

1. The Americans' prewar Rainbow Plans were five rough outlines based on various theoretical sets of circumstances (the United States with Britain and France as allies, the United States without allies, etc.). They were not the basis for the development of a practical strategy based on the changed circumstances of late 1941, although some basic concepts (e.g., stay on the defensive in the Pacific, launch an early offensive in Europe) found their way into the approach developed after American entry into the war. See Mark Skinner Watson, *Chief of Staff: Prewar Plans and Preparations*, in *US Army in World War II* (Washington, D.C.: Center of Military History, 1991), 103–22.

2. Washington War Conference, American and British Strategy, "Memorandum by the United States and British Chiefs of Staff (WW1)," Appendix I, in *Grand Strategy*, vol. 4, *August 1942–September 1943*, ed. Michael Howard, in *History of the Second World War*, edited by J. R. M. Butler, 597–99 (London: Her Majesty's Stationery Office, 1972), 597.

3. Washington War Conference, American and British Strategy, 597.

4. Washington War Conference, American and British Strategy, 599.

5. Annex 1 to ABC-4, JCCSs-1, W.W.-1. (U.S. rev.), Washington War Conference, 24 December 1941, in *World War II Inter-Allied Conferences* (Washington, D.C.: Joint History Office, 2003), Ike Skelton Combined Arms Research Library, World

War II Operational Documents, CD R000226 2003 c 2, http://cgsc.contentdm
.oclc.org/utils/getdownloaditem/collection/p4013coll8/id/3686/filename/3696
.pdf/mapsto/pdf/type/singleitem, pp. 28–33.

6. The meeting in Cairo (SEXTANT) in November 1943 also included the Nationalist
Chinese government. The Tehran (EUREKA) conference in November–December
1943, the Yalta (ARGONAUT) conference in February 1945, and the Potsdam
(TERMINAL) conference in July of 1945 included the Soviet Union.

7. Ray S. Cline, *Washington Command Post: The Operations Division* (Washington,
D.C.: Center of Military History, 1991), 149. The other two objectives were the
"maintenance of the United Kingdom" and the "maintenance of a position in the
India-Middle East area which will prevent physical junction of the two principal
enemies." Memo, WPD for CofS, 28 February 42, quoted in Cline, 149.

8. Prime Minister's Personal Minute, Serial no. D 116/2, 8th June 1942, WO 205/886,
National Archives, Kew. It is important to note that Churchill, even at this early
stage, was keenly aware of both the political environment that would surround
a cross-Channel assault and the need for Russian successes before an invasion
could be launched.

9. John Hughes-Hallett, *Before I Forget*, unpublished manuscript, Hartley Library,
University of Southampton, UK, Mountbatten Papers, MB1/B46, p. 139.

10. Quoted in Richard M. Leighton and Robert W. Coakley, *Global Logistics and
Strategy: 1940–1943*, in *The U.S. Army and World War II* (Washington, D.C.:
Center of Military History, 1955), 387.

11. Leighton and Coakley, 387.

12. Quoted in Matloff and Snell, *Strategic Planning for Coalition Warfare, 1941–1942*,
325.

13. Personal letter, Eisenhower to Marshall, 21 September 1942, quoted in Matloff
and Snell, 325.

14. Quoted in Carlo D'Este, *Eisenhower: Allied Supreme Commander* (London:
Cassell, 2004), 306.

15. Among the many books on the subject, see Simon Ball, *The Bitter Sea* (London:
Harper, 2010); Carlo D'Este, *World War II in the Mediterranean, 1942–1945*
(Chapel Hill, N.C.: Algonquin Books of Chapel Hill, 1990); Matloff and Snell,
Strategic Planning for Coalition Warfare, 1941–1942; Matloff, *Strategic Planning
for Coalition Warfare, 1943–1944*; Douglas Porch, *The Path to Victory: The
Mediterranean Theater in World War II* (New York: Farrar, Straus and Giroux,
2004); Mark A. Stoler, *Allies and Adversaries: The Joint Chiefs of Staff, the Grand
Alliance, and U.S. Strategy in World War II* (Chapel Hill: University of North
Carolina Press, 2000); and Mark A. Stoler, *Allies in War: Britain and America
Against the Axis Powers, 1940–1945* (London: Hodder Arnold, 2005).

16. COS (42) 392 (O), COS (42) 397 (O), COS (42) 181st Mtg. (O), quoted in Howard, *Grand Strategy*, vol. 4, 228.

17. Lord Alanbrooke, *War Diaries, 1939-1945*, edited by Alex Danchev and Daniel Todman (Berkeley: University of California Press, 2001), comments after entry for 31 January 1943, p. 376.

18. Alex Danchev, "Waltzing with Winston: Civil-Military Relations in Britain in the Second World War," in *Government and the Armed Forces in Britain, 1856-1990*, edited by Paul Smith (London: Hambledon, 1996), 208 (for both quotes regarding Brooke and Churchill).

19. Joint Chiefs of Staff, Minutes of Conference 16 January 1943, "Wartime Conferences of the Combined Chiefs of Staff," 59, microfilm, King's College London, Liddell Hart Centre for Military Archives.

20. Combined Chiefs of Staff 58th Meeting, 16 January 1943, "Wartime Conferences of the Combined Chiefs of Staff," microfilm, King's College London, Liddell Hart Centre for Military Archives.

21. Combined Chiefs of Staff 58th Meeting, 16 January 1943.

22. Alanbrooke, *War Diaries, 1939-1945*, notes to 1 February 1943, p. 377.

23. J.S. (Q) 4 (Final), 8th August 1943, Policy towards Turkey, National Archives, Kew.

24. Alan Wilt, "The Significance of the Casablanca Decisions, January 1943," *Journal of Military History* 55, no. 4 (October 1991): 518-19; emphasis added.

25. Leighton and Coakley, *Global Logistics*, 487.

26. COS (42) 97th Meeting, 22 August 1942, Mountbatten Papers, Southampton, MB1/B27, emphasis added.

27. Quoted in Mountbatten Papers, MB1/B27, p. 198, Southampton.

28. Harrison, *Cross-Channel Attack*, 44.

29. Harrison, 44.

Chapter 2. "No Substantial Landing in France Unless We Are Going to Stay"

1. Sir Frederick Morgan, *Peace and War: A Soldier's Life* (London: Hodder and Stoughton, 1961), 147.

2. Morgan, 148.

3. See, among others, John M. P. McErlean, "Corsica 1794: Combined Operations," in *New Interpretations in Naval History: Selected Papers from the Tenth Naval History Symposium*, edited by Jack Sweetman, 105-28 (Annapolis, Md.: Naval Institute Press, 1993); and Randolf G. S. Cooper, "Amphibious Options in Colonial India: Anglo-Portuguese Intrigue in Goa, 1799," in *New Interpretations in Naval*

History: Selected Papers from the Twelfth Naval History Symposium, edited by William B. Cogar, 95–113 (Annapolis, Md.: Naval Institute Press, 1997).

4. L. E. H. Maund, *Assault from the Sea* (London: Methuen, 1949), 3.

5. Bernard Fergusson, *Watery Maze: The Story of Combined Operations* (New York: Holt, Reinhart, Winston, 1961), 109–10; and Maund, *Assault from the Sea*, 63.

6. Lewis, *Omaha Beach*, 55.

7. Lewis, 67.

8. Lewis, 74.

9. Quoted in Fergusson, *Watery Maze*, 47.

10. Fergusson, 47.

11. Fergusson, 32.

12. Fergusson, 55.

13. Maund, *Assault from the Sea*, 74.

14. Maund, 64.

15. "Operation Corkscrew: Pantelleria 11th June 1943," http://www.combinedops .com/pantellaria.htm, accessed 12 February 2019.

16. Fergusson, *Watery Maze*, 85.

17. Fergusson, 83.

18. Brian Loring Villa, *Unauthorized Action: Mountbatten and the Dieppe Raid* (Oxford: Oxford University Press, 1994), 165.

19. Albert Norman, *Operation Overlord: The Allied Invasion of Western Europe* (Harrisburg, Pa.: Military Service Publishing, 1952; reprint Uncommon Valor Reprint Series, Createspace, 2016), app. 2, pp. 212–14.

20. There was simultaneous appreciation for and development of close-in fire support in both the Atlantic and Pacific theaters of operation. For example, Samuel Eliot Morison tells the story of an officer on Adm. William Halsey's staff who came up with the idea of converting two landing craft infantry to light gunboats, called LCI(G), for the invasion of the Treasury Islands in October 1943. It doesn't appear that the ideas or lessons learned in the Pacific were of interest to their European counterparts. Samuel Eliot Morison, *History of United States Naval Operations in World War II*, vol. 6, *Breaking the Bismarcks Barrier: 22 July 1942–1 May 1944* (Boston: Little, Brown, 1968), 294.

21. Two entertaining novels that are centered in amphibious operations in World War II, albeit in the Pacific, are Kenneth Dodson, *Away All Boats* (New York: Little, Brown, 1954), and Herman Wouk, *The Caine Mutiny* (New York: Doubleday, 1951). In my opinion, both were better books than films.

22. Villa, *Unauthorized Action*, 160.

23. Morgan, *Peace and War*, 149.

24. Morgan, 149–50.

25. Sir Frederick Morgan, *Overture to Overlord* (Garden City, N.Y.: Doubleday, 1950), 9.

26. Ferdinand Foch was a distinguished French officer who, at the end of World War I, was marshal of France and supreme commander of the Allied armies on the Western Front. Many officers of Morgan's generation, particularly those who had served in France, held him in great esteem.

27. Commodore Parry had been commanding officer of the Royal New Zealand Navy cruiser *Achilles* and participated in the Battle of the River Plate, which resulted in the scuttling of the German cruiser *Graf Spee*. See S. D. Waters, "Organisation of Naval Staff," in *The Royal New Zealand Navy* (Wellington, N.Z.: Historical Publications Branch, 1956), http://nzetc.victoria.ac.nz/tm/scholarly /tei-WH2Navy-c27.html. Information about General Candee is from the U.S. Air Force website, https://www.af.mil/About-Us/Biographies/Display/Article/107488 /brigadier-general-robert-c-candee/.

28. Morgan, *Overture to Overlord*, 14.

29. Morgan, 12.

30. Morgan, 6.

31. Morgan, 3.

32. Morgan, 18.

33. Lieutenant General Sir Frederick Morgan, Interview (Pogue), 8 February 1947, Morgan, OCHM Coll., The Supreme Command, Pogue, Temp Box 24, USAHEC (4921), accessed 15 August 2017.

34. Morgan, *Overture to Overlord*, 20.

35. Morgan, 24.

Chapter 3. "For What Are We to Plan?"

1. Mountbatten Papers, MB1/B27, University of Southampton, citing (J.P. [41] 1028) and Meeting of the COS (COS [42] 2nd Meeting, 3 January 1942).

2. COS Meeting of February 13, 1942, cited in Mountbatten Papers, MB/B27, University of Southampton.

3. Hughes-Hallett, *Before I Forget*, 106.

4. Hughes-Hallett, 106.

5. Howard, *Grand Strategy*, vol. 4, *August 1942–September 1943*, 20.

6. Alanbrooke, *War Diaries, 1939–1945*, 237–38, 10 March 1942.

7. Fergusson, *Watery Maze*, 146–47; see also Mountbatten Papers, MB1/B27, p. 203.

8. Hughes-Hallett, *Before I Forget*, 108.

9. Morgan, *Overture to Overlord*, 60.

10. Morgan, 21.

11. General Ray W. Barker Oral History (OH 331, interview 2), by Dr. Maclyn Burg, 16 July 1972, Eisenhower Presidential Library, accessed on 8 May 2018, https://www.eisenhowerlibrary.gov/sites/default/files/research/oral-histories/oral-history-transcripts/barker-general-ray.pdf, p. 26. Hereafter, Barker Oral History.

12. Mollie Panter-Downes, "Letter from London," in *The New Yorker Book of War Pieces* (New York: Shocken, 1988), September 14, 1940, p. 63.

13. Panter-Downes, September 21, 1940, p. 65.

14. Panter-Downes, October 5, 1940, p. 69. It should be noted that 43,000 civilians died in the London Blitz between September 1940 and May 1941, while another 139,000 were injured.

15. Barker Oral History, 30.

16. Barker Oral History, 34.

17. Barker Oral History, 36.

18. Quoted in D'Este, *Eisenhower*, 335.

19. COS (42) 97th Meeting, 22 August 1942, Mountbatten Papers, MB1/B78/f2.

20. COS (42) 97th Meeting, 22 August 1942, Mountbatten Papers, MB1/B27; emphasis added.

21. COS (42) 97th Meeting, 22 August 1942, Mountbatten Papers, MB1/B78/f2?, CCS 94 dated 24 July 1942, quoted by Portal in 22 August meeting and in those minutes.

22. C.C. (42) 78, 28 September 1942, Subject: Exercise "CAVENDISH," Ray Barker Papers, Box 1, Combined Commanders Meetings, September 1942, Eisenhower Library.

23. C.C. (42) 75 (sixth draft), 28 September 1942, Combined Commanders, Future Planning for Operation "Round-UP," Memorandum to the Chiefs of Staff, Barker Papers, Box 1, Combined Commanders Meetings, September 1942, Eisenhower Library.

24. C.C. (42) 74 (third draft), 28 September 1942, Combined Commanders, Planning for Offensive Combined Operations, Barker Papers, Box 1, Combined Commanders Meetings, September 1942, Eisenhower Library.

25. C.C. (42) 74 (third draft).

26. Prime Minister's Personal Minute, Serial No. D. 116/2, 8 June 1942, attached to COS (42) 157 (0) Final, Operation Imperator, WO 205/886, National Archives, Kew.

27. David Reynolds, *In Command of History* (London: Penguin, 2004), 315.

28. Barker Oral History, 76.

29. Hughes-Hallett, *Before I Forget*, 145.

30. COS (42) 345 (O) (Final) of 30.10.42, quoted in Michael Howard, *Grand Strategy*, vol. 4, *August 1942–September 1943*, 205; emphasis added.

31. Barker Oral History, 47.

32. Barker Oral History, 48.

33. Review of Certain Factors Affecting Preparations for a Return to the Continent, HF/00/570/G (Plans), 18th March 1943, AIR 37/223, National Archives, Kew.

34. Review of Certain Factors Affecting Preparations; emphasis in the original.

35. Review of Certain Factors Affecting Preparations.

36. General Bernard Paget, Letter to Liddell Hart, 10 August 1960, Liddell Hart Correspondence, 1/562, King's College London, Liddell Hart Centre for Military Affairs.

37. Morgan, *Peace and War*, 157.

38. Morgan, 157.

39. Alanbrooke, *War Diaries*, 391, 1 April.

40. *History of COSSAC 1943–1944*, Supreme Headquarters, Allied Expeditionary Force, May 1944, pp. 6–7, accessed 1 December 2009, http://www.history.army.mil/documents/cossac/Cossac.htm.

41. CCS 242/6 (Final Revision) Trident, "Report to the President and Prime Minister of the Final Agreed Summary of Conclusions Reached by the Combined Chiefs of Staff," microfilm, King's College London, Liddell Hart Centre for Military Archives.

42. Morgan, *Overture to Overlord*, 23.

43. Morgan, 23.

Chapter 4. To Plan the Reconquest of Europe

1. Morgan, *Overture to Overlord*, 23.

2. Morgan, 70.

3. Morgan, 31.

4. Barker Oral History (OH 331, interview 2), 75.

5. Morgan interview (Pogue); and Morgan, *Overture to Overlord*, 60.

6. Major General Kenneth R. McLean interview (Pogue), 11–13 March 1947, McLean, OCHM Coll., The Supreme Command, Pogue, Temp Box 24, USAHEC (4920), accessed 15 August 2017.

7. Barker Oral History, 76, 80.

8. Alanbrooke, *War Diaries*, 389.

9. Barker Oral History, 55.

10. "Norfolk House: The Lost London Palace That Was Razed to the Ground, Recreated 80 Years On," 10 June 2018, accessed 22 February 2019, www.countrylife.co.uk/architecture/norfolk-house-londons-missing-palace-178996.

NOTES TO PAGES 45-53

11. At least I have it on good authority that the Free French HQ was located there. While researching my master's dissertation, I stayed at the Naval and Military Club, also on St. James's Square. The very capable bartender there affirmed that we were standing in the former Free French HQ. I never dispute able barmen.

12. Barker Oral History, 69.

13. Morgan, *Peace and War*, 154; emphasis added.

14. Morgan, *Overture to Overlord*, 72.

15. Morgan, 71–72.

16. Morgan, 77.

17. *History of COSSAC 1943–1944*, Supreme Headquarters, Allied Expeditionary Force, May 1944, p. 13, accessed 1 December 2009, http://www.history.army .mil/documents/cossac/Cossac.htm; and McLean interview (Pogue).

18. Quoted in *History of COSSAC*, 14.

19. Forrest C. Pogue, *US Army in World War II: The Supreme Command* (Washington, D.C.: Center of Military History, 1996), 67.

20. Barker Oral History, 76.

21. McLean interview (Pogue).

22. Fergusson, *Watery Maze*, 273.

23. Hughes-Hallett, *Before I Forget*, 245, 248.

24. Morgan, *Overture to Overlord*, 52–53.

25. Opening Address by Lt. Gen. F. E. Morgan, 17 April 1943, attachment to COSSAC (43) 2nd Meeting, 27 April 1943, COSSAC Staff Meeting, Saturday, 24 April 1943, Barker Papers.

26. While no such map exists, Morgan did put three maps together, albeit of different projections, that showed North America, the Atlantic, and Europe. Morgan, *Overture to Overlord*, 81.

27. Morgan, Opening Address, COSSAC Staff Meeting Minutes, 1943–1944, Eisenhower Library, Barker Papers; and Morgan, *Overture to Overlord*, 62.

28. Morgan, *Overture to Overlord*, 31.

29. Minutes of Weekly Staff Conferences, COSSAC (43) 7th meeting, 1 June 1943, Eisenhower Library, Barker Papers.

30. Barker Oral History, 62.

31. Barker Oral History, 63.

32. Morgan, *Overture to Overlord*, 47.

33. Morgan, 48.

34. Morgan, 48.

35. Food rationing in Great Britain evolved into a complex system of foods that were rationed, foods that could be purchased with "points" assigned by the

government and that could increase or decrease in cost depending on availability, and unregulated foods like bread, flour, fish, and fresh vegetables. Canteens were also established where workers could eat energy-heavy meals at subsidized prices without using their ration cards; "British Restaurants" also provided similar meals to the general public. While lower-income families suffered more, "by the beginning of 1942 the British Ministry of Food had succeeded in creating a stable system which distributed food relatively evenly across the civilian population. . . . Despite the U-boats, the shipping shortage and wrangling with US officials, the British were able to maintain a satisfactory level of food supply throughout the war." Lizzie Collingham, *The Taste of War* (New York: Penguin, 2011), 361–66.

36. Roger Hesketh, *Fortitude: The D-Day Deception Campaign* (London: St. Ermin's Press, 1999).

37. Thaddeus Holt, *The Deceivers: Allied Military Deception in the Second World War* (New York: Lisa Drew Books/Scribner, 2004), 54–55.

38. Morgan, *Overture to Overlord*, 99.

39. Holt, *The Deceivers*, 487.

40. Holt, 486.

41. *History of COSSAC*, 32.

42. Holt, *The Deceivers*, 486.

43. Michael Howard, *Strategic Deception in the Second World War* (New York: Norton, 1995), 80.

44. Hesketh, *Fortitude*, 2.

45. Hesketh, 492.

46. Hesketh, 3.

47. Barker Oral History, 38.

48. Daniel W. B. Lomas, " '. . . the Defense of the Realm and Nothing Else': Sir Findlater Stewart, Labour Ministers and the Security Service," *Intelligence and National Security* 30, no. 6 (2014): 793–816. doi:10.1080/02684527.2014.900268.

49. Organizational Chart and notes, HyperWar Foundation website, accessed 11 June 2018, http://www.ibiblio.org/hyperwar/USA/USA-E-Logistics1/charts /USA-E-Logistics1-2.jpg; and Morgan, *Overture to Overlord*, 95.

50. Morgan, 96.

51. Lomas, " . . . the Defense of the Realm," 6.

52. Lomas, 7.

53. Lomas, 8.

54. Holt, *The Deceivers*, 493.

55. Morgan, *Overture to Overlord*, 101.

56. COS (43)779 (O) (Revise), dated 25 December 1943, quoted in Hesketh, *Fortitude*, 17.

57. Howard, *Strategic Deception*, 105.

Chapter 5. The Indian Army and Chasing Pancho Villa

1. Morgan, *Peace and War*, 13.

2. Morgan, 23.

3. Morgan, 28.

4. Morgan, 31.

5. Morgan, 41.

6. Brian Bond, "Biography of Lieutenant General Sir Frederick Morgan," in *Oxford Dictionary of National Biography* (Oxford: Oxford University Press), accessed 5 February 2007, http://www.oxforddnb.com/view/printable/35103.

7. A typical British infantry division in World War I consisted of a divisional headquarters, three brigades of infantry, a headquarters field artillery that commanded a brigade of field artillery—up to four battalions—as well as engineers, signals, medical, and cavalry (reconnaissance) units. "Structure of the British Army in WW1," Research the Lives and Service Records of World War One Soldiers, accessed 2 July 2018, www.researchingww1.co.uk /structure-of-the-british-army-in-ww1.

8. Brooke, also a field artillery officer, would have probably known Morgan from their shared experience in World War I. At the end of World War II, as various honors were awarded, Brooke became Field Marshal Lord Alanbrooke, thus sowing confusion upon generations of rookie historians.

9. Morgan, *Peace and War*, 55.

10. Morgan, 59.

11. See, among other examinations of the massacre, Kim A. Wagner, "'Calculated to Strike Terror': The Amritsar Massacre and the Spectacle of Colonial Violence," *Past and Present* 233, no. 1 (November 2016): 185–225, https://doi.org/10.1093 /pastj/gtw037.

12. Morgan, *Peace and War*, 62, 73.

13. Morgan, 74.

14. Spencer C. Tucker and Priscilla Roberts, eds., *World War I*, vol. 4: *S–Z* (Santa Barbara, Calif.: ABC-Clio Information Services, 2005), 1196.

15. Morgan, *Peace and War*, 80.

16. Morgan, 82–83.

17. Field Marshal Sir Claude Auchinleck said of Slim: "One of [his] chief characteristics was his quite outstanding determination and inability to admit defeat or the

possibility of it: also, his exceptional ability to gain and retain the confidence of those under him and with him, without any resort to panache. Success did not inflate him, or misfortune depress him." "William Slim: The Soldiers' Soldier," National Army Museum website, accessed 2 July 2018, https://www.nam.ac.uk /explore/william-slim.

18. Morgan, *Peace and War*, 85.

19. Morgan, 88.

20. Morgan, 88.

21. Field Marshal Sir Claude Auchinleck, "The Staff College as I Saw It," in Pakistan Army, Staff College, *First Fifty Years of the Staff College 1905-1955* (Quetta: Staff College, 1962).

22. David French, *Raising Churchill's Army* (Oxford: Oxford University Press, 2000), 164.

23. Morgan, *Peace and War*, 89; and Robert M. Citino, *The Wehrmacht Retreats: Fighting a Lost War, 1943* (Lawrence: University Press of Kansas, 2012), 19.

24. Morgan, *Peace and War*, 97.

25. Morgan, 101.

26. Morgan, 111.

27. G. C. Peden, *British Rearmament and the Treasury, 1932-1939* (Edinburgh: Scottish Academic Press, 1979), 179. In 1919 Great Britain adopted the "Ten Year Rule," which assumed that for budgetary planning purposes, there would be no major war during the next ten years. Each budget year thereafter, the "Rule" was extended. While understandable at the end of the Great War, by the time of Japan's aggression in Manchuria in early 1932, it was no longer viable and was dropped by the British government in March 1932. See also G.A.H Gordon, *British Seapower and Procurement between the Wars* (Annapolis, MD: Naval Institute Press, 1988); Phillips Payson O'Brien, *British and American Naval Power, Politics and Policy, 1900-1936* (Westport, CT: Praeger, 1998); and Carolyn J. Kitching, *Britain and the Geneva Disarmament Conference* (New York: Palgrave Macmillan, 2003).

28. B. C. Denning, *The Future of the British Army: The Problem of its Duties, Cost and Composition* (London: H. F. & G. Witherby, 1928), 12.

29. Zara Steiner, *The Triumph of the Dark: European International History 1933-1939* (Oxford: Oxford University Press, 2011), 296.

30. Bond, "Biography of Morgan."

31. Fergusson, *Watery Maze*, 39-40; Maund, *Assault from the Sea*, 6-7; and Morgan, *Peace and War*, 129-31. The story is taken from all three sources.

32. Morgan, Pogue interview.

33. Morgan, Pogue interview.

34. Ginge Thomas, "Voices of D-Day" transcript, *BBC History*, accessed 3 July 2018, www.bbc.co.uk/history/worldwars/wwtwo/dday_audio.shtml. Thomas was a stenographer assigned to Morgan.

35. Barker Oral History (OH 331, interview 2), 56.

36. "Ray Wehnes Barker, Major General, United States Army," Arlington National Cemetery website, accessed 24 April 2018, http://www.arlingtoncemetery.net /rwbarker.htm; and Papers of Ray W. Barker, Biographical note, Eisenhower Library.

37. Edward M. Coffman, *The Regulars: The American Army, 1898–1941* (Cambridge, Mass.: Belknap Press of Harvard University Press, 2004), 177.

38. Coffman, 178.

39. Coffman, 179.

40. Coffman, 281.

41. Coffman, 197.

42. Division Historical Association, *Lightning: The History of the 78th Infantry Division* (Washington, D.C.: Infantry Journal Press, 1947), accessed 4 July 2018, https://archive.org/details/Lightning78thInfantry.

43. Chronology from Papers of Ray W. Barker, Biographical note, Eisenhower Library. See also Barker Oral History, 26–27; and Steen Ammentorp, "Generals.dk" website, www.generals.dk/general/barker/ray_Wehnes/usa.html.

44. Gen. J. Lawton Collins, quoted in Coffman, *The Regulars*, 289.

45. Morgan, Pogue interview.

46. Morgan, Pogue interview.

47. Barker Oral History, 57–58.

48. Memo, Gen. R. W. Barker to COSSAC, "Comment on Commodore Hughes-Hallett's Paper Regarding Outline Plan," 18 June 1943, WO 219/614, National Archives, Kew.

Chapter 6. "For the First Time I Really Believe in This Operation"

1. Minutes of COSSAC Weekly Staff Conference, Saturday 8 May 1943, COSSAC (43) 4 meeting, Barker Papers, Eisenhower Library.

2. French, *Raising Churchill's Army*, 205.

3. Julian Paget, *The Crusading General: The Life of Gen. Sir Bernard Paget GCB, DSO, MC* (Barnsley, UK: Pen & Sword Military, 2008), chaps. 1, 2, 4, and 5.

4. Morgan, *Overture to Overlord*, 130.

5. Morgan, 131.

6. Memo, Gen. R. W. Barker to COSSAC, "Comment on Commodore Hughes-Hallett's Paper," 18 June 1943, WO 219/614, National Archives, Kew.

7. Morgan, *Overture to Overlord*, 136, 137; emphasis added.

8. Letter, Morgan to Basil Liddell Hart, 5 July 1959, Liddell Hart Correspondence, 1/526-25, King's College London, Liddell Hart Centre for Military Archives.

9. Hughes-Hallett, *Before I Forget*, 161.

10. Evan Mawdsley, *World War II: A New History* (Cambridge: Cambridge University Press, 2009), 307.

11. Morgan, *Overture to Overlord*, 64.

12. Lord Louis Mountbatten, transcript of audio tape interview with Michael Harrison, June 1965, Mountbatten Papers, Hartley Library.

13. Morgan, Pogue interview.

14. Hughes-Hallett, *Before I Forget*, 260.

15. Papers of Wing Commander the Marquis de Casa Maury, "Strategy in 1943," p. 231, Mountbatten Papers, Hartley Library.

16. Hughes-Hallett, *Before I Forget*, 260.

17. Hughes-Hallett, 261.

18. Hughes-Hallett, 261.

19. COS (43) 123 (O), quoted in Maury, Mountbatten Papers, 214.

20. Letter, Morgan to Mountbatten, COSSAC/3140/Sec., 16 June 1943, Mountbatten Papers; emphasis added.

21. Letter Morgan to Mountbatten, 22 June 1943, WO 219/615, National Archives, Kew.

22. Morgan, *Overture to Overlord*, 137–38.

23. Morgan, 138.

24. Morgan, 138.

25. Fergusson, *Watery Maze*, 272–73. Fergusson lists five Canadians, fifteen Americans (including two from COHQ), two from the Admiralty, three from the Air Ministry, nine each from COSSAC, War Office, and 21st Army Group, thirteen from ETOUSA, and seven from Fighter Command. Fergusson, 273.

26. CO (R) 25 July 1943, RATTLE, Record of a Conference held at HMS Warren from 28 June to 2 July to Study the Combined Operations Problems of OVERLORD WO 106/4261, National Archives, Kew.

27. CO (R) 25 July 1943, RATTLE.

28. Fergusson, *Watery Maze*, 275.

29. Fergusson, *Watery Maze*, 276.

30. Hughes-Hallett, *Before I Forget*, 265.

31. Morgan, *Overture to Overlord*, 139.

32. Fergusson, *Watery Maze*, 278.

33. Morgan, *Overture to Overlord*, 261.

34. A. T. Murchie, *The Mulberry Harbour Project in Wigtownshire, 1942–1944*, 2nd ed. (Wigtown, UK: G. C. Book Publishers, 1999), 5–41.

35. Fergusson, *Watery Maze*, 280.

36. Royal Navy (RN) Officers, 1939–1945, https://www.unithistories.com/officers/RN_OfficersL2.html.

37. Hughes-Hallett, *Before I Forget*, 263.

38. D'Este, *Decision in Normandy*, 61.

39. Hughes-Hallett, *Before I Forget*, 268.

40. Peter R. Mansoor, *The GI Offensive in Europe: The Triumph of American Infantry Divisions, 1941–1945* (Lawrence: University Press of Kansas, 1999), 52.

41. Hughes-Hallett, *Before I Forget*, 269–70.

42. Correlli Barnett, *Engage the Enemy More Closely: The Royal Navy in the Second World War* (London: Hodder & Stoughton, 1991), 814–15.

43. Samuel Eliot Morison, *History of United States Naval Operations in World War II*. Vol. 11, *The Invasion of France and Germany, 1944–1945* (Boston: Little, Brown, 1957), app. 1, pp. 334–36.

44. Fergusson, *Watery Maze*, 278.

45. Enclosure to COO's No. C.R. 7127/43 *Annex*, Points arising from RATTLE Conference, Mountbatten Papers, MB1/B27.

46. CCO Report to COS (CR 7137/43), 7 July 1943. Mountbatten Papers.

47. CCO Report to COS.

48. Quoted in C.O. (R)35, July 1943, RATTLE, Record of a Conference held at HMS Warren, WO 219/616, National Archives, Kew.

49. Fergusson, *Watery Maze*, 281.

Chapter 7. The Primary U.S.-British Ground and Air Effort in Europe

1. Matloff, *Strategic Planning for Coalition Warfare*, 391. There were 768,200 troops deployed to the British Isles versus a target of 1,026,000.

2. Horst Boog, Werner Rahn, Reinhard Stumpf, and Bernd Wegner, *Germany and the Second World War*, vol. 6, *The Global War*, edited by Ewald Osers, John Brownjohn, Patricia Crampton, and Louise Willmot; translation edited by Ewald Osers (Oxford: Clarendon, 2015), 1162.

3. Gerhard L. Weinberg, *A World at Arms: A Global History of World War II* (Cambridge: Cambridge University Press, 1994), 446.

4. Barnett, *Engage the Enemy More Closely*, 612.

5. Citino, *The Wehrmacht Retreats*, 113.

6. Phillips Payson O'Brien, *How the War Was Won* (Cambridge: Cambridge University Press, 2015), 279–80.

7. Harrison, *Cross-Channel Attack*, 64.

8. Howard, *Grand Strategy*, vol. 4, *August 1942–September 1943*, 419–21.

9. Morgan, *Overture to Overlord*, 126.

10. Alanbrooke, *War Diaries*, 11 December 1942, 348.

11. Matloff, *Strategic Planning for Coalition Warfare*, 266–67.

12. "All these [German] forces were handled centrally and served by the most perfect East and West railway system in existence. . . . . The North and South communications were, however, nothing like as efficient, comprising only one double line of railway through the leg of Italy and one through the Balkans to Greece." Alanbrooke, *War Diaries*, comments after entry for 20 November 1943, p. 476.

13. Reynolds, *In Command of History*, 373–84.

14. Howard, *Grand Strategy*, vol. 4, *August 1942–September 1943*, 426.

15. Matloff, *Strategic Planning for Coalition Warfare*, 132.

16. Combined Chiefs of Staff (final revision), Trident Conference Final Report to the President and Prime Minister, CCS 242/6, *World War II Interallied Conferences* (Washington, D.C.: Joint History Office, 2003), Ike Skelton Combined Arms Research Library, World War II Operational Documents, CD R000226 2003 c 2, http://cgsc.contentdm.oclc.org/cdm/singleitem/collection/p4013coll8/id/3693/rec/3, pp. 169–82.

17. McLean interview (Pogue).

18. McLean interview (Pogue).

19. Other divisions had arrived in the United Kingdom, notably the 1st Infantry and 1st Armored divisions. They had redeployed to North Africa as part of TORCH. Matloff, *Strategic Planning for Coalition Warfare*, Appendix D-1, 551.

20. Matloff, *Strategic Planning for Coalition Warfare*, 391.

21. J. Rickard, "J. Lawton Collins, 1986–1987 (Lighting Joe)," 28 May 2009, *History of War* website, http://www.historyofwar.org/articles/people_collins_j_lawton.html.

22. A base command would be responsible for the permanent infrastructure of the base as well as permanent facilities, a hospital, the barracks and other housing, permanent security, and so forth. The operational command would control the combat and combat support units that were stationed at the base and would deploy from there for an operation. The planning for the operation would normally rest with the operational command as they would be expected to train for and execute the assigned mission. ETOUSA provided generally the same sort of support as a base command but at the theater level. The Service of Supply, for example, was part of ETOUSA. When Eisenhower became the Supreme Allied Commander, he was also appointed as Commander of ETOUSA, and he made Maj. Gen. John C. H. Lee of the Service of Supply ETOUSA's G-4 and deputy theater commander. Barry J. Dysart, "Materialschlact: The "'Materiel Battle'" in the European Theater," in *The Big L: American Logistics in World War II*, edited by Alan Gropman (Washington, D.C.: National Defense University Press, 1997), 369.

23. Morgan, *Overture to Overlord*, 50–51.

24. McLean interview (Pogue).

25. *Operation "OVERLORD"*: *Appendices*, Ike Skelton Combined Arms Research Library, http://cgsc.contentdm.oclc.org/cdm/singleitem/collection/p4013coll8 /id/4543/rec/1, appendices to COSSAC (43)28.

26. McLean interview (Pogue).

27. Morgan, *Peace and War*, 165.

28. OVERLORD—Digest of Plan. War Cabinet, Chiefs of Staff Committee, 30 July 1943, COS (43) 415 (0), National Archives, Kew; and Minutes of COSSAC Staff Conference, 9 July 1943, COSSAC (43) 14 Meeting, Barker Papers.

29. OVERLORD—Digest of Plan.

30. Lewis, *Omaha Beach*, 104.

31. Barker Oral History (OH 331, interview 2), 91.

32. Morgan, *Overture to Overlord*, 152; and OVERLORD, Digest of Plan.

33. WO 107/154, COSSAC (43) 28, 15 July 1943, National Archives, Kew.

34. OVERLORD, Digest of Plan.

35. Morgan, *Overture to Overlord*, 156.

36. Morgan, *Overture to Overlord*, 156.

37. Harrison, *Cross-Channel Attack*, 77.

38. Alanbrooke, *War Diaries*, 4 August 1943, p. 435.

39. Morgan, *Overture to Overlord*, 158.

40. Morgan, 80.

41. Alanbrooke, *War Diaries*, 4 August 1943, p. 436.

42. Morgan, *Overture to Overlord*, 161.

43. Morgan, 162.

44. Morgan, 163.

45. Cline, *The Operations Division*, 300.

46. Matloff, *Strategic Planning for Coalition Warfare*, 164–67.

47. Matloff, 168n17.

48. Matloff, 173.

49. Matloff, 173.

50. CCS 303, Combined Chiefs of Staff, Strategic Concept for the Defeat of the Axis in Europe, Memorandum by the U.S. Joint Chiefs of Staff, 9 August 1943, microfilm, Liddell Hart Centre for Military Archives, King's College London; all emphasis in the original.

51. Alanbrooke, *War Diaries*, 6 August 1943, p. 437.

52. COS (Q) 3 (Revise) 6 August 1943, National Archives, Kew.

53. COS (Q) 3 (Revise).

54. COS (Q) 3 (Revise).

55. Minutes of COSSAC Staff Conference, 30 August 1943, Report on QUADRANT, Barker Papers, Eisenhower Library.

56. CAB 80/74, QUADRANT Conference, Minutes of Meeting, Sunday, 15 August, CCS 108th Meeting, National Archives, Kew.

57. CAB 80/74, QUADRANT Conference.

58. CAB 80/74, QUADRANT Conference.

59. CAB 80/74, CCS 303/1, 16 August 1943, Strategic Concept for the Defeat of the Axis in Europe, National Archives, Kew.

60. CAB 80/74, CCS 303/1.

61. Barker Oral History, 91.

62. CAB 80/74, QUADRANT Conference, Minutes of Meeting, Monday, 16 August, CCS 109th Meeting, National Archives, Kew.

63. CCS 319/5, 24 August 1943, Final Report to the President and Prime Minister, cited in Howard, *Grand Strategy*, vol. 4, *August 1942–September 1943*, app. 7, p. 684.

64. Alanbrooke, *War Diaries*, 17 August 1943, p. 443.

65. Alanbrooke, 15 August 1943, p. 441.

Chapter 8. "A Passing Phase"

1. David French, "British Military Strategy," in *The Cambridge History of the Second World War*, vol. 1, *Fighting the War*, ed. by John Ferris and Evan Mawdsley (Cambridge: Cambridge University Press, 2015), 35.

2. See Collingham, *The Taste of War*, for a full discussion of the food policies of the major combatants.

3. Morgan, *Overture to Overlord*, 104–5.

4. *History of COSSAC 1943-1944*, Supreme Headquarters, Allied Expeditionary Force, May 1944, accessed 1 December 2009, http://www.history.army.mil/documents /cossac/Cossac.htm, pp. 30–34.

5. *History of COSSAC 1943–1944*, 31.

6. Earl F. Ziemke, *The U.S. Army in the Occupation of Germany, 1944–1946* (Washington, D.C.: Center of Military History, 2003), 26.

7. At the Quebec conference, it was noted that the British and U.S. governments would take responsibility for civil affairs activities in those countries that each of them liberated. Also in August of 1943 the Combined Civil Affairs Committee decreed that Supreme Allied Commanders should take responsibility for Civil Affairs at the military level. This gave Morgan some cover as he formed COSSAC's Civil Affairs group. It wasn't until January 1944 that the London Sub-Committee of the Combined Civil Affairs Committee was formed. Even after this, there were disagreements between the British and Americans regarding process and jurisdiction. Pogue, *U.S. Army in World War II*, 78–80.

8. *History of COSSAC*, 31.

9. Morgan, *Overture to Overlord*, 57.

10. Conversation with the M. R. D. Foot, 2002. Foot's book is *SOE: An Outline History of the Special Operations Executive, 1940–46* (London: BBC, 1984).

11. Minutes of COSSAC Staff Conference, 23 July 1943, Barker Papers, Eisenhower Library.

12. Operation RANKIN, Memorandum by COSSAC to Principal Staff Officers, 27 July 1943, COSSAC (43) 33, WO 219/106/4245, National Archives, Kew.

13. Operation RANKIN . . . National Archives, Kew.

14. Minutes of COSSAC Staff Conference, 30 July 1943, Barker Papers, Eisenhower Library.

15. "Morgenthau Plan (Sept. 1944)," Oxford Reference, accessed 26 August 2018, https://www.oxfordreference.com/view/10.1093/acref/9780191870903.001.0001 /acref-9780191870903-e-1558?rskey=AbO6KH&result=1.

16. Morgan, *Overture to Overlord*, 115.

17. COSSAC (43) 26th Meeting, Minutes of Staff Conference, 17 September 1943, Barker Papers, Eisenhower Library.

18. Norman, *Operation Overlord*, 88.

19. Declaration on German Atrocities, October 30, 1943, VI Documents on American Foreign Relations 231, 232 (1945), quoted in Matthew Lippman, "Prosecutions of Nazi War Criminals Before Post-World War II Domestic Tribunals," *University of Miami International and Comparative Law Review* 8, no. 1 (2015), http://repository.law.miami.edu/umiclr/vol8/iss1/2. The agreement was that "major war criminals . . . will be punished by the joint decision of the Governments of the Allies." Unless the crimes were committed in specific territories, in which case they would be sent back to those places where "their abominable deeds were done in order that they may be judged and punished according to the laws of the liberated countries and of the free governments which will be created therein."

20. Morgan, *Overture to Overlord*, 116.

21. In the end, the French were also awarded a sector in Berlin, carved out of the original British and American sectors.

22. COSSAC (43) 20th Meeting Minutes of Staff Conference, Friday 13 August 1943, Barker Papers, Eisenhower Library.

23. Morgan, *Overture to Overlord*, 117.

24. Ziemke, *U.S. Army in the Occupation of Germany*, 27.

25. Ziemke, 28.

26. Adm. Jean-François Darlan was the commander of Vichy's armed forces in North Africa. He had been thought of as Marshal Philippe Pétain's favorite but was passed over for prime minister in favor of Pierre Laval, largely at German insistence. He ordered a modest degree of resistance to TORCH while at the

same time entering prolonged negotiations with the Americans. To obtain a cease-fire, the Americans had to agree to keep Darlan in power. No one liked the deal, crafted in mid-November 1942, which seemed to confer legitimacy on the Vichy regime. The best Eisenhower could do was claim military expediency. "Darlan made no move to honor Roosevelt's requests to lift anti-Jewish laws and degrees," nor did he release the nine thousand Jews and pro-Allied prisoners of war under his control. He was assassinated on Christmas Eve 1942. Douglas Porch, *The Path to Victory: The Mediterranean Theater in World War II* (New York: Farrar, Straus and Giroux, 2004), 358–66. Mark Clark called it "an act of providence [that] lanced . . . a troublesome boil." Porch, 366.

27. Morgan, *Overture to Overlord*, 216.
28. Morgan interview (Pogue).
29. An excellent description of this system in operation can be found in A. J. Liebling, "A Letter from France," July 14, 1944, pp. 348–52, in *The New Yorker Book of War Pieces* (New York: Schocken, 1988).
30. Morgan interview (Pogue).
31. Thomas R. Fisher, "Allied Military Government in Italy," *Annals of the American Academy of Political and Social Science* 267, Military Government (January 1950): 115, https://www.jstor.org/stable/1026733.
32. Morgan, *Overture to Overlord*, 235.
33. Harry L. Coles and Albert K. Weinberg, *Civil Affairs: Soldiers Become Governors* (Washington, D.C.: Center of Military History, 1986), 654.
34. Morgan, *Overture to Overlord*, 232.
35. D'Este, *Eisenhower*, 535.
36. Morgan, *Overture to Overlord*, 217.
37. Morgan, 233–34; and Gilbert Laithwaite, Olaf Caroe, and Stewart Perowne, "Obituary, Sir Roger Lumley," *Journal of the Royal Central Asian Society* 56, no. 3 (1969): 285–88, doi:10.1080/03068376908732086.
38. Morgan interview (Pogue).
39. Ziemke, *U.S. Army in the Occupation of Germany*, 32.
40. Ziemke, 33.
41. Pogue, *U.S. Army in World War II*, 82.
42. COSSAC (43) 21st Meeting, Minutes of Staff Conference, Friday, 20 August 1943, Barker Papers, Eisenhower Library.
43. COSSAC (43) 21st Meeting.
44. COSSAC (43) 29th Meeting, Minutes of Staff Conference, Friday, 8 October 1943, Barker Papers, Eisenhower Library.
45. COSSAC (43) 28th Meeting, Minutes of Staff Conference, Friday, 1 October 1943, Barker Papers, Eisenhower Library.

46. Quoted in Mark Stoler, *Allies and Adversaries: The Joint Chiefs of Staff, The Grand Alliance and U.S. Strategy in World War II* (Chapel Hill: University of North Carolina Press, 2000), 129.

47. Walter Lippmann, *US Foreign Policy: Shield of the Republic* (Boston: Little, Brown, 1943), quoted in Stoler, *Allies and Adversaries*, 131.

48. Mark Stoler, "The 'Second Front' and American Fear of Soviet Expansion, 1941–1943," *Military Affairs* 39, no. 3 (October 1975): 136–41.

49. Stoler, 140.

50. Stoler, *Allies and Adversaries*, 163.

51. COS (43) 607 (O), CAB 122/1238, National Archives, Kew.

52. Pogue, *U.S. Army in World War II*, 105.

53. F. H. Hinsley, E. E. Thomas, C. A. G. Simkins, and C. F. G. Ranson, *British Intelligence in the Second World War: Its Influence on Strategy and Operations*, vol. 3, part 2 (London: Her Majesty's Stationery Office, 1988), 19–39.

54. McLean interview (Pogue).

55. Directive to Supreme Commander, Allied Expeditionary Force, Appendix B, in Harrison, *Cross-Channel Attack*, 456.

56. Harrison, 458.

Chapter 9. The Far Shore

1. Horst Boog, Gerhard Krebs, and Detlef Vogel, *Germany and the Second World War*, vol. 7, *The Strategic Air War in Europe and the War in the West and East Asia, 1943–1944/5*, Potsdam, Research Institute for Military History, translated by Derry Cook-Radmore, Francisca Garvie, Ewald Osers, Barry Smerlin, and Barbara Wilson (Oxford: Clarendon, 2006), 465.

2. Boog et al., 7:465.

3. Weinberg, *A World at Arms*, 515.

4. Peter Lieb, "The Germans in Normandy, 1944," Second World War Research Group Podcast, King's College London, 27 March 2017, accessed 12 October 2018, https://www.swwresearch.com/single-post/2017/03/27/The-Germans-in-Normandy-1944.

5. As the *Service du travail obligatoire*, or compulsory work service, started to take more young Frenchmen for work in German factories, a growing percentage became "evaders" and hid in the mountains or forests. Generally, however, few actually joined a resistance movement. See Jean Guéhenno, *Diary of the Dark Years, 1940–1944: Collaboration, Resistance and Daily Life in Occupied Paris*, translated and annotated by David Ball (Oxford: Oxford University Press, 2014), 208–10, and 241–43.

6. As a comparison, 1.75 percent of the French prewar population was killed between 1939 and 1945. For Yugoslavia, the total military and civilian dead was 10.6 percent. Tony Judt, *A Grand Illusion? An Essay on Europe* (New York: New York University Press, 2011), 61. Among the many books on occupied France, see Ronald C. Rosbottom, *When Paris Went Dark: The City of Light under German Occupation, 1940–1944* (New York: Back Bay, 2014); Guéhenno, *Diary of the Dark Years*; Robert Gildea, *Fighters in the Shadows: A New History of the French Resistance* (Cambridge: Belknap Press of Harvard University Press, 2015); and Charles Kaiser, *The Cost of Courage* (New York: Other Press, 2015).

7. Fuehrer Headquarters, 23 March 1942, Directive No. 40, appendix C in Harrison, *Cross-Channel Attack*, 459.

8. Harrison, 461.

9. Harrison, 135.

10. Harrison, 137.

11. Boog et al., *Germany and the Second World War*, 7:470.

12. Boog et al., 7:471.

13. Boog et al., 7:473.

14. Harrison, *Cross-Channel Attack*, 142.

15. French, *Raising Churchill's Army*, 274.

16. Boog et al., *Germany and the Second World War*, 7:469–70.

17. Harrison, *Cross-Channel Attack*, 142–51.

18. Fuehrer Headquarters, 3 November 1943, Directive No. 51, appendix D in Harrison, *Cross-Channel Attack*, 464–65.

19. Williamson Murray and Allan R. Millett, *A War to Be Won: Fighting the Second World War, 1937–1945* (Cambridge, Mass.: Belknap Press of Harvard University Press, 2000), 212.

20. Directive No. 51, appendix D in Harrison, *Cross-Channel Attack*, 466.

21. Boog et al., *Germany and the Second World War*, 7:14.

22. Boog et al., 7:14; all data on the results of the British attacks and British bomber losses are from this source.

23. Boog et al., 7:50.

24. Quoted in F. H. Hinsley, E. E. Thomas, C. F. G. Ranson, and R. C. Knight, eds., *British Intelligence in World War II: Its Influence on Strategy and Operations*, vol. 3, part 1 (London: Her Majesty's Stationery Office, 1984), 297.

25. Hinsley et al., 299.

26. Hinsley et al., 301.

27. Williamson Murray, *Strategy for Defeat: The Luftwaffe, 1933–1945* (Montgomery, Ala.: Maxwell Air Force Base, Air University Press, 1983), 220.

28. Murray, 212.

29. Quoted in Boog et al., *Germany and the Second World War*, 7:100.
30. Quoted in Murray, *Strategy for Defeat*, 170.
31. Murray, 222–23.
32. Tami Davis Biddle, "Anglo-American Strategic Bombing, 1940–1945," in *The Cambridge History of the Second World War*, vol. 1, *Fighting the War*, edited by John Ferris and Evan Mawdsley (Cambridge: Cambridge University Press, 2015), 506.
33. Boog et al., *Germany and the Second World War*, 7:79.
34. Weinberg, *A World at Arms*, 617.
35. Boog et al., *Germany and the Second World War*, 7:417.
36. Boog et al., chart, 7:419.
37. Boog et al., 7:498.
38. Roberta Wohlstetter, *Pearl Harbor: Warning and Decision* (Stanford, Calif.: Stanford University Press, 1962).
39. Boog et al., *Germany and the Second World War*, 6:498–507, map II.III.3, 7:505.
40. Hinsley et al., *British Intelligence in the Second World War*, vol. 3, part 2, 74n.
41. Hinsley et al., appendix 10 (iv) COS Minute to the Prime Minister, 23 May 1944, pp. 807–9.

Chapter 10. "Your Army, Your General Marshall and Your Ambassador Biddle"

1. Letter, Roosevelt to Pershing, 30 September 1943, quoted in Matloff, *Strategic Planning for Coalition Warfare*, 275.
2. Marshall did not keep a "little black book," as is often believed, but he did note and remember those officers who had qualities that impressed him. See the Jeffrey Kozak, "Marshall Myths: Marshall's 'Little Black Book'," George C. Marshall Foundation website, December 11, 2015, https://www.marshallfoundation.org/blog/marshall-myths-marshalls-little-black-book.
3. Barker Oral History (OH 331, interview 2), 91–93; and Morgan, *Peace and War*, 168.
4. Forrest Pogue, *George C. Marshall: Organizer of Victory, 1943–1945* (New York: Viking, 1973), 276.
5. Barker Oral History, 91–93.
6. Carlo D'Este, *World War II in the Mediterranean, 1942–1945* (Chapel Hill, N.C.: Algonquin Books of Chapel Hill, 1990), 40.
7. Douglas Porch, *The Path to Victory: The Mediterranean Theater in World War II* (New York: Farrar, Straus and Giroux, 2004), 419.
8. D'Este, *World War II in the Mediterranean*, 42–46; and Porch, *Path to Victory*, 418–20.

9. D'Este, *World War II in the Mediterranean*, 78–85; and Porch, *Path to Victory*, 456–68, 485–87.

10. Armies were from the United States, Great Britain, Canada, and France plus a Polish division and smaller units from Belgium and the Netherlands.

11. Morgan, *Overture to Overlord*, 190.

12. Morgan, 192.

13. Lt. Gen. Sir Frederick Morgan, *Diary of a Visit to U.S.A.—October 1943*, Morgan Papers, Imperial War Museum, London.

14. Morgan.

15. "Gen. Joseph McNarriey [*sic*], 78, Dies; Succeeded Eisenhower in 1945," *New York Times*, 3 February 1972, accessed 5 January 2019, https://www.nytimes.com/1972/02/03/archives/gen-joseph-mcnarriey-78-dies-succeeded-eisenhower-in-1945.html.

16. Possibly Lt. Col. J. B. Morgan of the OPD, but he isn't identified further.

17. Morgan, *Overture to Overlord*, 193.

18. For the evolution of these briefings and other means the COS used to stay in touch with conditions and operations around the world, see Cline, *Washington Command Post*, 135–42.

19. Morgan, *Overture to Overlord*, 195.

20. Alex Danchev, *Very Special Relationship* (London: Brassey's, 1986), 145–46, quoted in Alex Danchev, "The Strange Case of Field Marshal John Dill," *Medical History* 35, no. 3 (July 1991): 353–57, https://www.ncbi.nlm.nih.gov/pmc/articles/PMC1036485/pdf/medhist00050-0077.pdf.

21. Morgan, *Diary of a Visit*, 4.

22. Morgan, 5.

23. Julian Kimble, "10 Exclusive Places in Washington D.C. You'll Never Get Into," *Complex*, 22 August 2013, https://www.complex.com/pop-culture/2013/08/exclusive-places-in-washington-dc-youll-never-get-into/.

24. Morgan, *Diary of a Visit*, 40.

25. Symonds, *Neptune*, 163.

26. Joint Chiefs of Staff, Minutes of Conference January 16, 1943, "Wartime Conferences of the Combined Chiefs of Staff," p. 59, microfilm, King's College London, Liddell Hart Centre for Military Archives.

27. Robert Lovett was brought into the War Department by Secretary of War Stimson as assistant secretary of war for air, overseeing the expansion of the Army Air Forces. As he told the story, one method he used to get production moving was to issue a manufacturer a letter of intent before contracts had been written or the funds appropriated. "If it weren't for the fact that a war was going on, I'd have ended up in Leavenworth." He did end up as the fourth U.S. secretary of

defense. Walter Isaacson and Evan Thomas, *The Wise Men: Six Friends and the World They Made* (New York: Simon and Schuster, 1986), 202–4.

28. Leighton and Coakley, *Global Logistics and Strategy: 1940–1943*, 378–79.

29. Leighton and Coakley, 380.

30. Leighton and Coakley, 380.

31. Barnett, *Engage the Enemy More Closely*, 771.

32. COSSAC (43) 23rd Meeting, Minutes of COSSAC Staff Conference, 28 August 1943, Barker Papers, Eisenhower Library.

33. "Streets of Washington," Troika Menu, 1940, posted December 19, 2014, accessed 17 October 2018, www.flickr.com.

34. Morgan, *Diary of a Visit*, 9.

35. Morgan, 7.

36. Morgan, *Overture to Overlord*, 196.

37. Morgan, 197.

38. "General Carl A. Spaatz," U.S. Air Force website, accessed 21 October 2018, https://www.af.mil/About-Us/Biographies/Display/Article/105528/general -carl-a-spaatz/.

39. Cline, *Washington Command Post*, 173.

40. Ronald Schaffer, "General Stanley D. Embick, Military Dissenter," *Military Affairs* 37, no. 3 (October 1973): 89–93, www.jstor.org/stable/1984244; "General Muir S. Fairchild," U.S. Air Force website, accessed 16 August 2018, https://www.af.mil /About-Us/Biographies/Display/Article/107112/general-muir-s-fairchild/; and Raymond P. Schmidt, *From Code-Making to Policy Making: Four Decades in the Memorable Career of Russell Willson*, Summer 2016, accessed 21 October 2018, https://www.archives.gov/files/publications/prologue/2016/summer/willson .pdf. The Dumbarton Oaks conference, held in Washington, D.C., in October of 1944, was the first step in defining a new postwar international organization to replace the League of Nations.

41. Morgan, *Overture to Overlord*, 201–3.

42. Morgan, *Peace and War*, 171. Adm. Philip Vian, RN, observed of Admiral King, "Admiral King's attitude has sometimes been ascribed to anglo-phobia. This is not altogether true. Certainly, the Admiral's loyalty was given whole-heartedly to the Navy he served. It was a feeling which led him to look upon even the United States Army and Air Force as little better than doubtful allies." Sir Philip Vian, *Action This Day: War Memoirs of Admiral of the Fleet Sir Philip Vian* (London: Frederick Muller Ltd., 1960), 155.

43. Matloff, *Strategic Planning for Coalition Warfare*, 264.

44. David F. Schmitz, *Henry L. Stimson: The First Wise Man* (Wilmington, Del.: SR Books, 2001), 38.

45. Quoted in Schmitz, *Stimson*, 115.

46. Schmitz, 124.

47. Morgan, *Overture to Overlord*, 199.

48. COS (43) 639 (O), 19 October 1943, CAB 80/75, National Archives, Kew, emphasis added.

49. Morgan, *Diary of a Visit*, 28.

50. Morgan, 30.

51. Weinberg, *A World at Arms*, 620–22.

52. Matloff, *Strategic Planning for Coalition Warfare*, 302.

53. Matloff, 304–6.

54. Morgan, *Diary of a Visit*, 34.

55. D. K. R. Crosswell, *Beetle: The Life and Times of General Walter Bedell Smith* (Lexington: University Press of Kentucky, 2012), 545.

56. Crosswell, 35.

57. Crosswell, 37.

58. Crosswell, 39–40.

59. Morgan, *Diary of a Visit*, 40.

60. Harrison, *Cross-Channel Attack*, 115.

61. Harrison, 116, quoting COSSAC, to CinC 21 A Gp, Operation Overlord, 29 November 1943, COSSAC (43) 76.

62. Alanbrooke, *War Diaries*, note following 20 January 1943, p. 365.

63. Alanbrooke, 19 October 1943, p. 461; and 1 November 1943, p. 465. In a note following the entry for 1 November 1943, Brooke comments that "reading between some of the lines I wrote I am inclined to think that I cannot have been very far off from a nervous breakdown at that time. Nevertheless there is a great deal in what I wrote on the evening of November 1st." The strain on all the senior decision-makers by this point in the war must have been tremendous. Both Roosevelt's and Churchill's health problems are well known, but clearly there was immense pressure on all of them.

64. Alanbrooke, note after 20 November 1943, p. 476.

65. Morgan, *Overture to Overlord*, 224.

66. Matloff, *Strategic Planning for Coalition Warfare*, 306.

Chapter 11. "The Supreme Operations for 1944"

1. Morgan, *Peace and War*, 165.

2. Morgan, *Overture to Overlord*, 169.

3. Quoted in Morgan, 169.

4. Quoted in Harrison, *Cross-Channel Attack*, 106.

5. Minutes of Weekly Staff Conference, 30 August 1943, COSSAC (43) 23rd Meeting; and 3 September 1943, COSSAC (43) 24th Meeting, Barker Papers.

6. Morgan, *Overture to Overlord*, 52.

7. Morgan, 44.

8. Just after being given command for TORCH, Eisenhower asked Barker for his recommendations of British officers for his headquarters (Eisenhower had been in the United Kingdom for less than two months at that point). Barker recommended Gen. Sir Richard Gale as his chief supply officer and Kenneth Strong as his intelligence officer. Both stayed with Eisenhower for the rest of the war. Barker Oral History (OH 331, interview 2), 44–45.

9. F. H. Hinsley et al., *British Intelligence in World War II*, vol. 3, part 2, appendix 1, The Intelligence Branch at Cossac and Shaef, 750–51.

10. Morgan, *Overture to Overlord*, 175.

11. Morgan, Letter to Lord Mountbatten, 3 September 1943, Mountbatten Papers, MB1/B19, Southampton, United Kingdom.

12. D'Este, *Decision in Normandy*, 112n.

13. Quoted in the Pegasus Archive: The British Airborne Forces, 1940–1945, by Mark Hickman, www.pegasusarchive.org/normandy/lord_lovat.htm.

14. Lee was an experienced engineer with a reputation of being an empire builder. When Eisenhower became the Supreme Allied Commander and commanding general of ETOUSA and made Lee the deputy theater commander, Lee became, in reality, the de facto commander. Barker felt that Lee "got away with murder." Major General Ray W. Barker, Interview (Pogue and Ruppenthal), 16 October 1946, Barker, OCHM Coll., The Supreme Command, Pogue, Temp Box 24, USAHEC (4919), accessed 15 August 2017. The U.S. logistics structure and supply system created in support of OVERLORD was a fragile one, "ill-suited to the inconvenient realities of the battlefield and one that would require constant attention to run at all." Dysart, "Materialschlact," 368.

15. Morgan, *Overture to Overlord*, 270–71. This was, of course, long before anyone knew of the health risks caused by exposure to asbestos.

16. McLean, Pogue interview.

17. Morgan, Pogue interview; and COSSAC Staff Conference 17 September 1943, COSSAC (43) 26th Meeting, Barker Papers, Eisenhower Library.

18. The 6th U.S. Army Group, commanded by General Devers, was formed out of the 7th U.S. Army and 1st French Army, which landed in Southern France during Operation DRAGOON (formerly ANVIL).

19. Alanbrooke, *War Diaries*, notes for 21 September 1943, p. 454.

20. Morgan, Pogue interview.

21. Holt, *The Deceivers*, 495–96.

22. Minutes of COSSAC Staff Conference, 29 October 1943, COSSAC (43) 31st Meeting, Barker Papers, Eisenhower Library.

23. Holt, *The Deceivers*, 497–98.

24. Hesketh, *Fortitude*, 52–55.

25. F. H. Hinsley et al., *British Intelligence in the Second World War*, vol. 3, part 1, 385–86.

26. Hinsley et al., 402–3, and map GSGS 4042, sheets 1, 2, 4, and 5, between pages 402 and 403.

27. Morgan, *Peace and War*, 176.

28. Minutes of COSSAC Staff Conference, 27 November 1943, COSSAC, (43) 35th Meeting, 27 November 1943, Barker Papers, Eisenhower Library.

29. See "Rotundas," *Subterranea Britannica*, https://www.subbrit.org.uk/sites /rotundas/.

30. The shelters were put to good use. S. N. Behrman, writing in the 27 January 1945 issue of the *New Yorker* magazine, describes the deep shelters like the Rotundas as "amazing." They were "cities hundreds of feet underground. A companion and I timed the decent to one in the lift; it took several minutes." They met a father and son there who got up each morning and left for work and school before 6:30, as that was when the elevator stopped. They had been bombed out and had been living in the shelter for eight months. S. N. Behrman, "The Suspended Drawing Room," in *The New Yorker Book of War Pieces* (New York: Schocken, 1988), 430–31.

31. Minutes of COSSAC Staff Conference, 20 November 1943, COSSAC (43) 34th Meeting, 22 November 1943, Barker Papers, Eisenhower Library.

32. Minutes of COSSAC Staff Conference, 20 November 1943, COSSAC (43) 34th Meeting, 22 November 1943, Barker Papers, Eisenhower Library.

33. Weinberg, *World at Arms*, 622.

34. Alanbrooke, *War Diaries*, note after 30 November 1943, pp. 487–88.

35. This number did include 320,000 women in the U.S. Army at the time. Matloff, *Strategic Planning for Coalition Warfare*, 266.

36. Matloff, 266.

37. Matloff, 267.

38. Matloff, 265.

39. Alanbrooke, *War Diaries*, note after 21 November 1943, p. 477.

40. Quoted in Stoler, *Allies in War*, 139.

41. Weinberg, *World at Arms*, 625.

42. CCS 409, 25 November 1943, "OVERLORD" and the Mediterranean, note by the British Chiefs of Staff, CAB 88, National Archives, Kew.

43. Quoted in Stoler, *Allies in War*, 139.

44. Alanbrooke, *War Diaries*, 23 November 1943, p. 478.

45. Stoler, *Allies in War*, 140–41.

46. U.S. Department of State, *Foreign Relations of the United States: The Conferences at Cairo and Tehran, 1943* (Washington, D.C., 1961), 541, quoted in Stoler, *Allies in War*, 143.

47. CCS 426/1, Report to the President and Prime Minister of the Agreed Summary of Conclusions Reached at the "SEXTANT" Conferences, 6 December 1943, in *World War II Inter-Allied Conferences* (Washington, D.C.: Joint History Office, 2003), Ike Skelton Combined Arms Research Library, World War II Operational Documents, CD R000226 2003 c 2, http://cgsc.contentdm.oclc .org/utils/getdownloaditem/collection/p4013coll8/id/3691/filename/3701.pdf /mapsto/pdf/type/singleitem, 297–306.

48. D'Este, *Decision in Normandy*, 53.

49. Paget, *The Crusading General*, 98.

50. See Hesketh, *Fortitude*, 61, for list of divisions.

51. Maj. Gen. G. L. Verney, new commander of the 7th Armored; Maj. Gen. T. G. Rennie, new commander of the 51st Highland; Lt. Gen. Brian Horrocks, new XXX Corps commander, all quoted in D'Este, *Decision in Normandy*, 271–77.

52. D'Este, *Decision in Normandy*, 271–76.

53. Minutes of COSSAC Staff Conferences, Meeting of 17 December 1943, COSSAC (43) 38th Meeting, Barker Papers, Eisenhower Library.

54. Morgan, *Peace and War*, 177.

Chapter 12. "Monty Didn't Bring Anything New"

1. Quoted in CO (R) 35, July 1943, RATTLE, Record of a Conference held at HMS Warren from 28 June to 2 July to study the Combined Operations Problems of OVERLORD, WO 219/616, SHAEF, National Archives, Kew.

2. 21 A Group/00/65/Ops., Part Two, Commander 1st Corps Letter dated 14 December 1943. WO 205/37, 21st Army Group: Military HQ Papers, National Archives, Kew.

3. On 6 June, elements of six divisions went across the beach, along with three airborne divisions, commandos, rangers, engineer units, independent tank units, and other specialist units, not counting follow-up formations.

4. COSSAC (43) 28, Annex B, Operation Overlord, 15 July 1943, para. 5, WO 107/154, Office of the Commander in Chief and War Office, National Archives, Kew.

5. The British Staff Mission message from BRITMAN can be found at CAB 120/420, Minister of Defense Secretariat, National Archives, Kew. They also supported

Morgan's desire to strengthen the assault by exploiting the air lift capacity that should be available by D-day, echoing Morgan's conversations with General Arnold.

6. Eisenhower, letter to Ismay, 3 December 1960, Eisenhower Library, quoted in D'Este, *Decision in Normandy*, 55.

7. Smith, interview with Dr. Forrest C. Pogue, 9 May 1947. Quoted in D'Este, *Decision in Normandy*, 56. Eisenhower's comment was a reference to the size of the beachhead—that it should accommodate that many divisions, and not a suggestion that he wanted that many divisions in the initial assault.

8. Pogue, *U.S. Army in World War II*, 107.

9. D'Este, *Decision in Normandy*, 56.

10. D'Este, 57. D'Este quotes from Montgomery's written analysis of the plan submitted to Churchill at the time: "Today, 1st January 1944 is the first time I have seen the Appreciation and proposed plan or considered it in any way."

11. James Leasor, *War at the Top, Based on the Experiences of General Sir Leslie Hollis K.C.B. K.B.E.* (London: Michael Joseph, 1959), 269.

12. Morgan had spent Christmas and the following week in hospital. It may have been that he was simply not available for these early meetings. Morgan, *Overture to Overlord*, 256.

13. Pogue, *U.S. Army in World War II*, 109.

14. Barker, Pogue interview.

15. Barker.

16. Barker.

17. Barker Oral History (OH 331, interview 2), 91.

18. Barker, Pogue interview.

19. Brigadier Lord Lovat, www.pegasusarchive.org/normandy/lord_lovat.htm, accessed 3 February 2019.

20. Harrison, *Cross-Channel Attack*, 166 and 166n.

21. Dwight D. Eisenhower, *Report by the Supreme Commander to the Combined Chiefs of Staff on the Operations in Europe of the Allied Expeditionary Force, 6 June 1944 to 8 May 1945* (London: Her Majesty's Stationery Office, 1946), 6–7.

22. Stoler, *Allies and Adversaries*, 171.

23. Alessandro Salvador, "Isonzo, Battles of," in *1914–1918 Online: International Encyclopedia of the First World War*, ed. Ute Daniel, Peter Gatrell, Oliver Janz, Heather Jones, Jennifer Keene, Alan Kramer, and Bill Nasson (Berlin: Freie Universität Berlin, last updated March 9, 2016), doi:10.15463/ie1418.10855, accessed 15 May 2019.

24. Elizabeth Greenhalgh, *Foch in Command: The Forging of a First World War General* (Cambridge: Cambridge University Press, 2011), 248.

25. For the Fuller quote, see Stoler, *Allies in War*, 149.

26. Morgan, *Peace and War*, 189. While DRAGOON occurred roughly two weeks after the start of the COBRA breakout in Normandy, and thus did not contribute to the success of the initial landings, having the ports of Marseille and Toulon were significant additions for the drive across France and for operations in 1945.

27. See D'Este, *Decision in Normandy*, 58; and Crosswell, *Beetle*, 569–70.

28. Morgan, *Overture to Overlord*, 41.

29. Morgan, *Overture to Overlord*, 256–58; Morgan, *Peace and War*, 181–82; and Eisenhower, *Report by the Supreme Commander*, 4. There is an additional small detail to note. In the fall of 1943 General Marshall had, in anticipation of his assuming command of OVERLORD, sent over to Norfolk House a set of flags and a desk set that he intended to use. With the arrival of General Eisenhower, the rather nice desk set found its way into Ray Barker's office. Barker oral history.

30. Minutes of COSSAC Staff Conference, Friday 7 January 1944, COSSAC (44) 1 Meeting, Barker Papers, Eisenhower Library.

31. Minutes of COSSAC Staff Conference, Friday 14 January 1944, COSSAC (44) 2 Meeting, Barker Papers, Eisenhower Library.

Epilogue

1. Pogue, *The Supreme Command*, app. B.

2. Pogue, app. D.

3. Morgan, *Overture to Overlord*, 41.

4. Pogue, *The Supreme Command*, app. D.

5. For ship totals, see Eric Grove, "The West and the War at Sea" in *The Oxford Illustrated History of World War II*, edited by Richard Overy, 135–67 (Oxford: Oxford University Press, 2015), 158. For troop totals, see Murray and Millett, *A War to be Won*, 420. There were ships and craft from the United States, Great Britain, Canada, France, the Netherlands, Poland, Norway, and Greece. Vincent P. O'Hara, "A Tale of Two Invasions," *Naval History* 33, no. 3 (June 2019), https://www.usni.org/magazines/naval-history-magazine/2019/june/tale-two-invasions.

6. Morgan, *War and Peace*, 165.

7. Crosswell, *Beetle*, 545.

8. Quoted in Pogue, *George C. Marshall*, 276.

9. Quoted in Crosswell, *Beetle*, 553.

10. Morgan, *Peace and War*, 158.

11. Pogue, *U.S. Army in World War II*, 64.

12. Barker Oral History (OH 331, interview 2), 96; and Barker, Pogue interview.

13. Crosswell, *Beetle*, 552.

14. Harrison, *Cross-Channel Attack*, 171 and 171n44.

15. D'Este, *Eisenhower*, 524.
16. Michael Munn, *David Niven: The Man behind the Balloon* (London: JR Books, 2009).
17. Cline, *Washington Command Post*, 232.
18. Cline, 299–300.
19. Morgan, *Overture to Overlord*, 279.
20. Morgan, 287.
21. Letter of Reference, Ismay to Morgan, 1945, Ismay Correspondence, 4/23/6, King's College London, Liddell Hart Center for Military Archives.
22. Barker Oral History, 64.

Appendix B. Structure of the British Army's Home Forces, 1940-44

1. Timothy Harrison Place, *Military Training in the British Army, 1940-1944: From Dunkirk to D-Day* (London: Frank Cass, 2000), 6.
2. Morgan, *Peace and War*, 147.

Appendix C. Outline OVERLORD Plan, Cover Letter, and Digest

1. Fergusson, *Watery Maze*, 282.

BIBLIOGRAPHY

Archival Material

National Archives, Kew, United Kingdom
AIR 37/223 (Operation SKYSCRAPER)
CAB 79 COS Minutes
CAB 80 COS Memoranda
CAB 88 CCS Minutes
CAB 120 Minister of Defense Secretariat
DEFE 2 Combined Operations HQ Reports
WO 106 COS Committee
WO 107 Office of the Commander in Chief and War Office
WO 199 Home Forces
WO 205 21st Army Group: Military HQ Papers
WO 219 SHAEF (including COSSAC)

Imperial War Museum, London
Papers of Lieutenant General Sir Frederick Morgan

Hartley Library, University of Southampton, United Kingdom
Mountbatten Papers; Includes unpublished manuscript of John Hughes-Hallett,
Before I Forget, MB1/B19, MB1/B27, MB1/B46, MB1/B47, MB1/B78

Liddell Hart Centre for Military Archives, King's College London
General Lord Ismay Correspondence
Liddell Hart Papers, Correspondence with Lieutenant General Sir Frederick Morgan, General Sir Bernard Paget
Microfilm, Combined Chiefs of Staffs, Minutes and Reports of Conferences

Dwight D. Eisenhower Presidential Library, Abilene, Kansas
General Ray Barker Oral History (OH 331, interview 2), by Dr. Maclyn Burg, 16 July 1972, https://www.eisenhowerlibrary.gov/sites/default/files/research/oral-histories/oral-history-transcripts/barker-general-ray.pdf.
General Thomas T. Handy Oral History (OH 486 Interview 3), https://eisenhower.archives.gov/research/oral_histories/oral_history_transcripts/handy_thomas_486.pdf.
Major General Ray S. Barker Papers
SHAEF, Office of the Secretary, General Staff Records, 1943–1945 (Microfilm) Box 3, Reel 21 (Operation RATTLE).

U.S. Army Heritage and Education Center at Carlisle Barracks, Pennsylvania
Lieutenant General Sir Frederick Morgan, Interview (Pogue), 8 February 1947, Morgan, OCHM Coll., The Supreme Command, Pogue, Temp Box 24, USAHEC (4921), accessed 15 August 2017.
Major General Kenneth R. McLean, Interview (Pogue), 11–13 March 1947, McLean, OCHM Coll., The Supreme Command, Pogue, Temp Box 24, USAHEC (4920), accessed 15 August 2017.
Major General Ray W. Barker, Interview (Pogue and Ruppenthal), 16 October 1946, Barker, OCHM Coll., The Supreme Command, Pogue, Temp Box 24, USAHEC (4919), accessed 15 August 2017. Cited as Barker, Pogue interview.

Ike Skelton Combined Arms Research Library Digital Library
Annex 1 to ABC-4, JCCSs-1, W.W.-1. (U.S. rev.), Washington War Conference, 24 December 1941, in World War II Inter-Allied Conferences (Washington, D.C.: Joint History Office, 2003).
CCCS 426/1, Report to the President and Prime Minister of the Agreed Summary of Conclusions Reached at the "SEXTANT" Conferences, 6 December 1943, in World War II Inter-Allied Conferences (Washington, D.C.: Joint History Office, 2003). Combined Chiefs of Staff (final revision), Trident Conference Final Report to the President and Prime Minister, CCS 242/6, World War II Interallied Conferences (Washington, D.C.: Joint History Office, 2003).
Operation "OVERLORD": Appendices, appendices to COSSAC (43)28.

Published Works

Alanbrooke, Lord. *War Diaries, 1939–1945: Field Marshal Lord Alanbrooke.* Edited by Alex Danchev and Daniel Todman. Berkeley: University of California Press, 2001.

Ambrose, Stephen. *D-Day: The Climatic Battle of World War II.* New York: Simon and Schuster, 1994.

Auchinleck, Claude. "The Staff College as I Saw It." In Pakistan Army, Staff College, First Fifty Years of the Staff College, 1905–1955 (Quetta: Staff College, 1962).

Ball, Simon. *The Bitter Sea: The Brutal World War II Fight for the Mediterranean.* London: Harper, 2010.

Barnett, Correlli. *Engage the Enemy More Closely: The Royal Navy in the Second World War.* London: Hodder & Stoughton, 1991.

Barr, Niall. *Eisenhower's Armies: The American–British Alliance during World War II.* New York: Pegasus, 2015.

Behrman, S. N. "The Suspended Drawing Room." In *The New Yorker Book of War Pieces.* New York: Schocken Books, 1988.

Belfield, Eversley, and H. Essame. *The Battle for Normandy.* London: Severn House, 1975.

Biddle, Tami Davis. "Anglo-American Strategic Bombing, 1940–1945." In *The Cambridge History of the Second World War.* Vol. 1, *Fighting the War,* edited by John Ferris and Evan Mawdsley, chap. 17. Cambridge: Cambridge University Press, 2015.

Boog, Horst, Gerhard Krebs, and Detlef Vogel. *Germany and the Second World War.* Vol. 7, *The Strategic Air War in Europe and the War in the West and East Asia, 1943–1944/5.* Potsdam, Research Institute for Military History, translated by Derry Cook-Radmore, Francisca Garvie, Ewald Osers, Barry Smerlin, and Barbara Wilson. Oxford: Clarendon, 2006.

Boog, Horst, Werner Rahn, Reinhard Stumpf, and Bernd Wegner. *Germany and the Second World War.* Vol. 6, *The Global War.* Potsdam, Research Institute for Military History, translated by Ewald Osers, John Brownjohn, Patricia Crampton, and Louise Willmot; translation edited by Ewald Osers. Oxford: Clarendon, 2001.

Bryant, Arthur. *Triumph in the West, 1943–1946: Based on the Diaries and Autobiographical Notes of the Viscount Alanbrooke.* London: Collins, 1959.

Budiansky, Stephen. *Blackett's War: The Men Who Defeated the Nazi U-Boats and Brought Science to the Art of Warfare.* New York: Alfred A. Knopf, 2013.

Citino, Robert M. *The Wehrmacht Retreats: Fighting a Lost War, 1943.* Lawrence: University Press of Kanas, 2012.

Cline, Ray S. *Washington Command Post: The Operations Division.* Washington, D.C.: Center of Military History, 1990.

Coffman, Edward M. *The Regulars: The American Army, 1898–1941.* Cambridge, MA: Belknap Press of Harvard University Press, 2004.

Coles, Harry L., and Albert K. Weinberg. *Civil Affairs: Soldiers Become Governors.* Washington, D.C.: Center of Military History, 1986.

Collingham, Lizzie. *The Taste of War: World War II and the Battle for Food.* New York: Penguin, 2013.

Cooper, Randolf G. S. "Amphibious Options in Colonial India: Anglo-Portuguese Intrigue in Goa, 1799." In *New Interpretations in Naval History: Selected Papers from the Twelfth Naval History Symposium,* edited by William B. Cogar, 95–113. Annapolis, Md.: Naval Institute Press, 1997.

Crosswell, D. K. R. *Beetle: The Life of General Walter Bedell Smith.* Lexington: University Press of Kentucky, 2012.

Danchev, Alex. "The Strange Case of Field Marshal John Dill." *Medical History* 35, no. 3 (July 1991): 353–57, https://www.ncbi.nlm.nih.gov/pmc/articles/PMC1036485/pdf/medhist00050-0077.pdf.

———. "Waltzing with Winston: Civil-Military Relations in Britain in the Second World War." In *Government and the Armed Forces in Britain, 1856–1990,* edited by Paul Smith, 191–216. London: Hambledon, 1996.

Denning, B. C. *The Future of the British Army.* London: H. F. & G. Witherby, 1928.

D'Este, Carlo, *Decision in Normandy.* New York: Harper Perennial, 1994.

———. *Eisenhower: Allied Supreme Commander.* London: Cassell, 2004.

———. *World War II in the Mediterranean, 1942–1945.* Chapel Hill, N.C.: Algonquin Books of Chapel Hill, 1990.

Dodson, Kenneth. *Away All Boats.* New York: Little, Brown, 1954.

Dysart, Barry J. "Materialschlact: The 'Materiel Battle' in the European Theater." In *The Big "L": American Logistics in World War II: An Industrial College of the Armed Forces Study,* edited by Alan Gropman. Washington, D.C.: National Defense University Press, 1997.

Eisenhower, Dwight D. *Report by The Supreme Commander to the Combined Chiefs of Staff on the Operations in Europe of the Allied Expeditionary Force, 6 June 1944 to 8 May 1945.* London: Her Majesty's Stationery Office, 1946.

Fergusson, Bernard. *The Watery Maze: The Story of Combined Operations.* New York: Holt, Rinehart, and Winston, 1961.

Ferris, John, and Evan Mawdsley, eds. *The Cambridge History of the Second World War.* Vol. 1, *Fighting the War.* Cambridge: Cambridge University Press, 2015.

Fisher, Thomas R. "Allied Military Government in Italy." *Annals of the American Academy of Political and Social Science* 267, Military Government (January 1950): 114–22, https://www.jstor.org/stable/1026733.

French, David. "British Military Strategy." In *The Cambridge History of the Second World War.* Vol. 1, *Fighting the War,* edited by John Ferris and Evan Mawdsley. Cambridge: Cambridge University Press, 2015.

———. *Raising Churchill's Army: The British Army and the War against Germany 1919–1945*. Oxford: Oxford University Press, 2000.

Gabel, Christopher R. *The U.S. Army GHQ Maneuvers of 1941*. Washington, D.C.: Center of Military History, U.S. Army, 1992.

Gildea, Robert. *Fighters in the Shadows: A New History of the French Resistance*. Cambridge: Belknap Press of Harvard University Press, 2015.

Greenhalgh, Elizabeth. *Foch in Command: The Forging of a First World War General*. Cambridge: Cambridge University Press, 2011.

Grove, Eric. "The West and the War at Sea." In *The Oxford Illustrated History of World War II*, edited by Richard Overy, 135–67. Oxford: Oxford University Press, 2015.

Guéhenno, Jean. *Diary of the Dark Years, 1940–1944: Collaboration, Resistance and Daily Life in Occupied Paris*, translated and annotated by David Ball. Oxford: Oxford University Press, 2014.

Harrison, Gordon A. *Cross-Channel Attack*. Washington, D.C.: Office of the Chief of Military History, 1951.

Hastings, Max. *OVERLORD, D-Day and the Battle for Normandy, 1944*. London: Michael Joseph, 1984.

Hesketh, Roger. *Fortitude: The D-Day Deception Plan*. London: St. Ermin's, 1999.

Hinsley, F. H., and C. A. G. Simkins. *British Intelligence in the Second World War: Its Influence on Strategy and Operations*, vol. 4, *Security and Counter-Intelligence*. London: Her Majesty's Stationery Office, 1990.

Hinsley, F. H., E. E. Thomas, C. A. G. Simkins, and C. F. G. Ranson. *British Intelligence in the Second World War: Its Influence on Strategy and Operations*, vol. 3, part 2. London: Her Majesty's Stationery Office, 1988.

Hinsley, F. H., E. E. Thomas, C. F. G. Ranson, and R. C. Knight, eds. *British Intelligence in the Second World War: Its Influence on Strategy and Operations*, vol. 3, part 1. London: Her Majesty's Stationery Office, 1984.

Holt, Thaddeus. *The Deceivers: Allied Military Deception in the Second World War*. New York: Lisa Drew Books/Scribner, 2004.

Howard, Michael. *The Continental Commitment: The Dilemma of British Defence Policy in the Era of the Two World Wars*. London: Ashfield, 1989.

———. *Grand Strategy*. Vol. 4, *August 1942–September 1943*. In *History of the Second World War*, edited by J. R. M. Butler. London: Her Majesty's Stationery Office, 1972.

———. *The Mediterranean Strategy in the Second World War: The Lees-Knowles Lectures at Trinity College, Cambridge, 1966*. London: Weidenfeld and Nicolson, 1968.

———. *Strategic Deception in the Second World War: British Intelligence Operations against the German High Command*. New York: Norton, 1995.

Huston, James A. "Normandy to the German Border: Third Army Logistics." In *The U.S. Army and World War II: Selected Papers from the Army's Commemorative*

Conferences, edited by Judith L. Bellafaire. Washington, D.C.: Center of Military History, 1998.

Isaacson, Walter, and Evan Thomas. *The Wise Men: Six Friends and the World They Made*. New York: Simon and Schuster, 1986.

Judt, Tony. *A Grand Illusion? An Essay on Europe*. New York: New York University Press, 2011.

Kaiser, Charles. *The Cost of Courage*. New York: Other Press, 2015.

Keegan, John. *Six Armies in Normandy: From D-Day to the Liberation of Paris, June 6th–August 25th, 1944*. New York: Viking, 1982.

Kennedy, Paul, ed. *Grand Strategies in War and Peace*. New Haven, Conn.: Yale University Press, 1991.

Laithwaite, Gilbert, Olaf Caroe, and Stewart Perowne. "Obituary, Sir Roger Lumley." *Journal of the Royal Central Asian Society* 56, no. 3 (1969): 285–88, doi:10.1080/03068376908732086.

Leasor, James. *War at the Top: Based on the Experiences of General Sir Leslie Hollis K.C.B., K.B.E.* London: Michael Joseph, 1959.

Leighton, Richard M., and Robert W. Coakley. *Global Logistics and Strategy: 1941–1943*. In *The U.S. Army and World War II*. Washington, D.C.: Office of the Chief of Military History, 1955.

Lewis, Adrian R. *Omaha Beach: A Flawed Victory*. Chapel Hill: University of North Carolina Press, 2001.

Liebling, A. J. "Letter from France, July 14, 1944." In *The New Yorker Book of War Pieces*. New York: Schocken, 1988.

Lippman, Matthew. "Prosecutions of Nazi War Criminals Before Post-World War II Domestic Tribunals." *University of Miami International and Comparative Law Review* 8, no. 1 (2015), http://repository.law.miami.edu/umiclr/vol8/iss1/2.

Lomas, Daniel W. B. "'. . . the Defense of the Realm and Nothing Else': Sir Finlater Stewart, Labour Ministers and the Security Service." *Intelligence and National Security* 30, no. 6 (2014): 793–816. doi:10.1080/02684527.2014.900268.

Lukacs, John. *The Last European War: September 1939–December 1941*. New York: Anchor/Doubleday, 1976.

Mansoor, Peter R. *The GI Offensive in Europe: The Triumph of American Infantry Divisions, 1941–1945*. Lawrence: University Press of Kansas, 1999.

Marshall, George C. *Biennial Reports of the Chief of Staff of the United States Army to the Secretary of War, 1 July 1939–30 June 1945*. Reproduced in one volume. Washington, D.C.: Center of Military History, 1996.

Masterman, J. C. *The Double-Cross System in the War of 1939–1945*. New Haven, Conn.: Yale University Press, 1972.

Matloff, Maurice. *Strategic Planning for Coalition Warfare, 1943–1944*. In *U.S. Army and World War II*. Washington, D.C.: Center of Military History, 1959.

Matloff, Maurice, and Edwin M. Snell. *Strategic Planning for Coalition Warfare, 1941–1942*. In *U.S. Army and World War II: The Collected Works*. Washington, D.C.: Government Printing Office, 1953.

Maund, L. E. H. *Assault from the Sea*. London: Methuen, 1949.

Mawdsley, Evan. *World War II: A New History*. Cambridge: Cambridge University Press, 2009.

McErlean, John M. P. "Corsica 1794: Combined Operations." In *New Interpretations in Naval History: Selected Papers from the Tenth Naval History Symposium*, edited by Jack Sweetman, 105–28. Annapolis, Md.: Naval Institute Press, 1993.

Morgan, Sir Frederick. *Overture to Overlord*. Garden City, N.Y.: Doubleday, 1951.

———. *Peace and War: A Soldier's Life*. London: Hodder and Stoughton, 1961.

Morison, Samuel Eliot. *History of United States Naval Operations in World War II*. Vol. 6, *Breaking the Bismarcks Barrier, 22 July 1942–1 May 1944*. Boston: Little, Brown, 1968.

———. *History of United States Naval Operations in World War II*. Vol. 11, *The Invasion of France and Germany 1944–1945*. Boston: Little, Brown, 1957.

Mosely, Philip E. "The Occupation of Germany." *Foreign Affairs*, July 1950, https://www.foreignaffairs.com/articles/united-states/1950-07-01/occupation-germany.

Munn, Michael. *David Niven: The Man behind the Balloon*. London: JR Books, 2009.

Murchie, A. T. *The Mulberry Harbour Project in Wigtownshire, 1942–1944*, 2nd ed. Wigtown, UK: G. C. Book Publishers, 1999.

Murray, Williamson. *Strategy for Defeat: The Luftwaffe, 1933–1945*. Montgomery, Ala.: Maxwell Air Force Base, Air University Press, 1983.

Murray, Williamson, and Allan R. Millett. *A War to Be Won: Fighting the Second World War, 1937–1945*. Cambridge, Mass.: Belknap Press of Harvard University Press, 2000.

Newland, Samuel J. and Clayton K. S. Chun. *The European Campaign: Its Origins and Conduct*. Carlisle, PA: Strategic Studies Institute, 2011.

Norman, Albert. *Operation Overlord: The Allied Invasion of Western Europe*. Harrisburg, Pa.: Military Service Publishing, 1952. Reprint, Uncommon Valor Reprint Series, Createspace, 2016.

O'Brien, Phillips Payson. *How the War Was Won*. Cambridge: Cambridge University Press, 2015.

O'Hara, Vincent P. "A Tale of Two Invasions," *Naval History* 33, no. 3 (June 2019). https://www.usni.org/magazines/naval-history-magazine/2019/june/tale-two-invasions.

Paget, Julian. *The Crusading General: The Life of General Sir Bernard Paget GCB DSO MC*. Barnsley, UK: Pen & Sword Military, 2008.

Panter-Downes, Mollie. "Letter from London, September 14, 1940"; "Letter from London, September 21, 1940"; "Letter from London, October 5, 1940"; "Letter from London, June 11, 1944." In *The New Yorker Book of War Pieces*. New York: Schocken, 1988.

Peden, G. C. *British Rearmament and the Treasury, 1932–1939*. Edinburgh: Scottish Academic Press, 1979.

Place, Timothy Harrison. *Military Training in the British Army, 1940–1944: From Dunkirk to D-Day*. London: Frank Cass, 2000.

Pogue, Forrest C. *George C. Marshall: Organizer of Victory, 1943–1945*. New York: Viking, 1973.

———. *U.S. Army in World War II: The Supreme Command*. Washington, D.C.: Center of Military History, 1996.

Porch, Douglas. *The Path to Victory: The Mediterranean Theater in World War II*. New York: Farrar, Straus and Giroux, 2004.

Reynolds, David. *From Munich to Pearl Harbor: Roosevelt's America and the Origins of the Second World War*. Chicago: Ivan R. Dee, 2001.

———. *In Command of History: Churchill Fighting and Writing the Second World War*. London: Penguin, 2004.

Rolf, David. *The Bloody Road to Tunis: Destruction of the Axis Forces in North Africa, November 1942–May 1943*. London: Greenhill, 2001.

Rosbottom, Ronald C. *When Paris Went Dark: The City of Light under German Occupation, 1940–1944*. New York: Back Bay, 2014.

Rottman, Gordon L. *US World War II Amphibious Tactics: Mediterranean and European Theaters*. Oxford: Osprey, 2006.

Ryan, Cornelius. *The Longest Day*. London: Gollancz, 1961.

Salvador, Alessandro. "Isonzo, Battles of." In *1914–1918 Online: International Encyclopedia of the First World War*, ed. Ute Daniel, Peter Gatrell, Oliver Janz, Heather Jones, Jennifer Keene, Alan Kramer, and Bill Nasson. Berlin: Freie Universität Berlin, last updated March 9, 2016. doi:10.15463/ie1418.10855, accessed 15 May 2019.

Schaffer, Ronald. "General Stanley D. Embick: Military Dissenter." *Military Affairs* 37, no. 3 (October 1973): 89–95. www.jstor.org/stable/1984244.

Schmitz, David F. *Henry L. Stimson: The First Wise Man*. Wilmington, Del.: SR Books, 2001.

Steiner, Zara. *The Triumph of the Dark: European International History 1933–1939*. Oxford: Oxford University Press, 2011.

Stoler, Mark A. *Allies and Adversaries: The Joint Chiefs of Staff, The Grand Alliance, and U.S. Strategy in World War II*. Chapel Hill: University of North Carolina Press, 2000.

———. *Allies in War: Britain and America against the Axis Powers, 1940–1945*. London: Hodder Arnold, 2005.

———. "The 'Second Front' and American Fear of Soviet Expansion, 1941–1943." *Military Affairs* 39, no. 3 (October 1975): 136–41.

Symonds, Craig. *Neptune: The Allied Invasion of Europe and the D-Day Landings.* Oxford: Oxford University Press, 2014.

Tucker, Spencer C., and Priscilla Roberts, eds. *World War I.* Vol. 4: *S–Z.* Santa Barbara, Calif.: ABC-Clio Information Services, 2005.

Van Creveld, Martin. *Supplying War: Logistics from Wallenstein to Patton.* Cambridge: Cambridge University Press, 1977.

Vian, Sir Philip. *Action This Day: War Memoirs of Admiral of the Fleet Sir Philip Vian.* London: Frederick Muller Ltd., 1960.

Villa, Brian Loring. *Unauthorized Action: Mountbatten and the Dieppe Raid.* Oxford: Oxford University Press, 1994.

Wagner, Kim A. "'Calculated to Strike Terror': The Amritsar Massacre and the Spectacle of Colonial Violence." *Past and Present* 233, no. 1 (November 2016): 185–225, https://doi.org/10.1093/pastj/gtw037.

Watson, Mark Skinner. *Chief of Staff: Prewar Plans and Preparations.* In *US Army and World War II.* Washington, D.C.: Center of Military History, 1991.

Weinberg, Gerhard L. *A World at Arms: A Global History of World War II.* Cambridge: Cambridge University Press, 1994.

Wieviorka, Olivier. *Normandy: The Landings to the Liberation of Paris.* Translated by M. B. DeBevoise. Cambridge, Mass.: Belknap Press of Harvard University Press, 2008.

Wilmot, Chester. *The Struggle for Europe.* London: Collins, 1952.

Wilson, Theodore A., ed. *D-Day 1944.* Lawrence: University Press of Kansas, 1994.

Wilt, Alan. "The Significance of the Casablanca Decisions, January 1943." *Journal of Military History* 55, no. 4 (October 1991): 517–29.

Wohlstetter, Roberta. *Pearl Harbor: Warning and Decision.* Stanford, Calif.: Stanford University Press, 1962.

Wouk, Herman. *The Caine Mutiny.* New York: Doubleday, 1951.

Ziemke, Earl F. *The U.S. Army in the Occupation of Germany, 1944–1946.* Washington, D.C.: Center of Military History, 2003.

INDEX

by, 211; Morgan's return to England
and, 183–84; organizational structure
and, 46–47, 164; outline plan and, 78,
118–19; personality of, 74; Quebec
conference and, 118; Sicily invasion
and, 96; on size of the attack, 212, 214;
SKYSCRAPER and, 36–37; Spaatz and,
175; Special Observers Group, London
and, 30, 31; unresolved conflicts sent
to, 102; on U.S. Army and Navy and
planning, 43; weekly schedule, office
culture and, 49–51
Berlin, 49, 130, 141, 154–55, 267n21
Bevan, John, 53, 54, 59, 195–96
Biddle, Anthony J., Jr., 141, 176, 177
Birdwood, William, 64, 65
BODYGUARD, 59, 197–98, 222
BOLERO, 3, 4, 31, 57, 94, 100
Bomber Command, RAF, 27, 32–33, 54,
219–20; Combined Bomber Offensive
and, 153, 154–55, 270n22
Bradley, Omar, 104, 188, 193–94, 206
Brooke, Alan: British Chiefs of Staff and,
xiv; on Churchill and planning, 7–8;
COSSAC staff and, 44; on fighting in
Italy and cross-Channel assault, 99; on
landing in France, 28; on Montgomery
replacing Paget, 194; Morgan and, 222,
259n8; on Morgan and cross-Channel
invasion plans, 111; on opening the
Mediterranean, 98; on OVERLORD
outcome, 185, 274n63; proposed U.S./
British planning staff and, 11; Quebec
conference and, 117; reading outline
plan, 115; Supreme Allied Commander
position and, 119, 120; tensions at Cairo
and, 204
Brownjohn, Nevil, 43, 88–89, 166, 179, 223
Bucknall, Gerard Corfield, 90, 206
Bull, H. R., 189, 223

Cairo conferences (Nov. and Dec. 1943),
202–3, 204, 251n6
Camberly, Staff College at, 65, 66
Canadian I Corps, 55
Canadian staff and officers, 45

Casablanca conference (Jan. 1943), 7–9,
10–11, 19, 94
Channel: invasion season for, 32. *See also*
amphibious warfare
Cherbourg Peninsula, 27, 28, 34, 77–78. *See
also* ROUNDUP
Chiang Kai-Shek, 203
Chief of Staff, Supreme Allied Commander.
See COSSAC
Chiefs of Staff (COS), British: British
Joint Service Mission in DC and, xviii;
Combined Chiefs and, xiv; division
and landing craft estimates and, 100;
estimating OVERLORD success,
159–60; Keyes on strategy and, 18;
members of, 227; Morgan's Washington
visit and, 166; Mountbatten and, 18–19,
28, 92–93; "Operations in the European
Theatre of War," 115–16; outline plan
review, 111; planning customs, 29; on
rigidity of OVERLORD date, 203–4;
unresolved conflicts sent to, 102; on war
planning, 9
Churchill, Winston: on coalitions of
allies, xvii; COSSAC as Allied staff
and, 45–46; D-Day plans, 224–25;
on IMPERATOR, 4–5; on landing in
France, 5, 20–22, 34, 251n8; Morgan
approved by, 40–41; on offensive war,
15; on OVERLORD, 116–17, 160,
210–11; on OVERLORD and fighting
in Italy, 99; on OVERLORD and
Mediterranean campaign, 114, 179–80,
203; postwar French government and,
136; on Supreme Allied Commander,
119–20; Tehran conference and, 205
civil affairs: COSSAC discussions in
Washington on, 170; headquarters,
Morgan's call for, 124; Morgan hiring
administrator for, 137–38; Morgan on
occupation forces managing, 131–34,
221; Smith's headaches with, 222; U.S.
General Lee joins conferences on, 192;
Vichy, Nazi occupation troops and, 146,
270n5, 271n6
Clark, Mark, 22, 164, 165

ABOUT THE AUTHOR

Stephen C. Kepher, a former U.S. Marine Corps officer and an independent scholar, received his MLitt (with distinction) in war studies from the University of Glasgow and holds a BA in international relations from the University of Southern California. He has presented papers on COSSAC at the Society for Military History's annual conference and at Normandy 75 at the University of Portsmouth, UK.